Political Readings of Descartes in Continental Thought

Bloomsbury Studies in Continental Philosophy

Presents cutting edge scholarship in the field of modern European thought. The wholly original arguments, perspectives and research findings in titles in this series make it an important and stimulating resource for students and academics from across the discipline.

Political Readings of Descartes in Continental Thought

Alon Segev

BLOOMSBURY ACADEMIC
LONDON • NEW YORK • OXFORD • NEW DELHI • SYDNEY

BLOOMSBURY ACADEMIC
Bloomsbury Publishing Plc
50 Bedford Square, London, WC1B 3DP, UK
1385 Broadway, New York, NY 10018, USA

First published in Great Britain 2019

A catalogue record for this book is available from the British Library.

A catalog record for this book is available from the Library of Congress.

ISBN: HB: 978-1-3500-6971-8
ePDF: 978-1-3500-6972-5
eBook: 978-1-3500-6973-2

Series: Bloomsbury Studies in Continental Philosophy

Typeset by Newgen KnowledgeWorks Pvt. Ltd., Chennai, India
Printed and bound in Great Britain

To find out more about our authors and books visit www.bloomsbury.com
and sign up for our newsletters.

To Ada and Immanuel with love

Contents

Preface

I began working on the *Political Readings of Descartes in Continental Thought* over five years ago. The book does not deal with the philosophy of Descartes, but rather discusses the political stance of other people towards Descartes's philosophy and the use they make of it in promoting their own political views. I started working on the current book while preparing the publication of my book *Thinking and Killing: Philosophical Discourse in the Shadow of the Third Reich*. I am currently working on a book on the German theologian Gerhard Kittel. These studies treat entirely different subjects in different historical contexts and from different perspectives. Yet, they are linked through my interest in the relationship between philosophy, theology, history, and politics. Both philosophers and theologians profess to convey the truth to us. Their view is, however, limited by the historical context and, knowingly or unknowingly, they are often motivated by political agendas which determine their theories.

My purpose is not to judge, not to wreak havoc by exposing piquant stories from the biography of this or that person, but rather to try to understand their views. People rushed to judge Heidegger as a rabid Nazi and an anti-Semite following the publication of the 'notorious' *Black Notebooks*, without trying or even willing to deal with the complex context of those texts, which contain, inter alia, sharp critiques of Nazi ideology, Alfred Rosenberg, unrestrained technological expansion, the world wars and the arms race, the overuse of power, and the outbreak of barbarism in the twentieth century. Likewise, Husserl is commonly seen as the poor rational victim of his irrational, *völkisch* disciple; the former is always mentioned in connection with his Jewish origin and the latter has been branded as an evil Nazi. Led by these false prejudices, people overlook Husserl's chauvinistic political worldview and overt aversion to non-European people as he voiced in his lectures in 1935. Franz Xaver von Baader has been regarded as an ecstatic irrational Catholic enemy of the Enlightenment. Careful study of his complicated writings and the context in which he wrote reveals his close intellectual friendship with Ignaz von Döllinger and his influence on the foundation of the Old Catholic

Church (*Altkatholische Kirche*) which emerged out of the tension with and the separation from the Vatican as well as the attempt to overcome the schism between the Catholic and the Eastern Orthodox Church. Baader's critique was directed against the rational Enlightenment and nihilism no less than against the irrational pietism of his time. Franz Borkenau has been regarded as a supporter of Stalinism and thus his connection with the Frankfurt School has been cut. Careful reading of his work along with the critique delivered by Henryk Grossmann, who was commissioned by the Frankfurt School to attack Borkenau, reveals his reliance on Karl Marx and an attempted Marxist reading of Descartes.

Since the work on the current book lasted for a long time, during which I was exposed to new material that led me to examine and revise my views very often, the last stage of writing the book consisted mainly of adapting old drafts to my current views. Exchanges with friends, colleagues, and students enriched my perspectives and improved my understanding. I owe them all my gratitude. They are many, and within the limited space of this preface, I can express my gratitude only to those people whose help and support are more closely related to the 'end product'. I would have continued my research on political readings of Descartes ad infinitum without ever reaching the point at which I could stop to write down my ideas and turn them into a printed book had Andreas Oberprantacher not invited me to give a seminar at Innsbruck University on the political readings of Descartes and encouraged me throughout my time at Innsbruck. Richard Wolin and Jerrold Seigel invited me to present my chapter on Husserl at their seminar on intellectual history at the Graduate Center of City University of New York. Their feedback on my text was helpful and led to a fruitful exchange with David Carr, with whom I discussed earlier drafts of my chapters on Husserl and Baader. Andrew Cutroffelo, David Ingram, and Gregory Fried read part of the manuscript and encouraged me to complete it with their insightful comments and suggestions. Rebecca Toueg read the whole manuscript, the earlier and later drafts, and made helpful suggestions on the style and content. I am blessed to have Liza Thompson, Lucy Russell, Frankie Mace, and Daisy Edwards as wonderful editors.

Introduction: Home and exile

What brought me to write the present book is the realization that the statement *cogito ergo sum*, which is supposed to convey the highest point of intimacy that we can ever achieve, that is, the identity of the human subject with itself, the home to which the subject is called back from its dispersion in the world, turns out instead to be the highest point of alienation.[1] In this home, released from false and misleading prejudices and assessments, the subject is supposed to be wholly by itself. Its perceptions are now supposed to be evident and trustworthy. It can now legitimately embark on the path of true philosophy, which should lead from then onwards to the secure foundation of science. Some philosophers, as we shall later see, thought that at this point the subject has indeed found its home. Other philosophers felt that detaching man from his culture and tradition and reducing him to pure thought condemns him to an exile in which he is alienated from everything that makes up his existence. Giambattista Vico (1668–1744) was apparently the first philosopher to voice his uneasiness with this exile, which he equated with the Cartesian philosophy and spirit. Truth, according to Vico, is that which is made (*factum*). Vico says, 'The true is precisely what is being made' (*verum esse ipsum factum*). Thus, Vico concludes, 'The first truth is in God, because God is the first Maker' (Vico, 1988, p. 46). If producing or making, *facere*, is the criterion of truth, the subject can never fully know itself in truth, because it did not create itself (ibid., p. 52). It does not, however, say that the subject cannot *evidently* intuit its existence, as in the *cogito* statement. In other words, truth and clear evidence are not identical in Vico's eyes.[2] Furthermore, *cogitatio* (thought), according to Vico, refers to discursive thinking, thinking which does not perceive its object at once, as God's *intelligentia* does, but rather gradually (ibid., p. 46). This means that only God can properly be said to be at home, whereas humans can never be so, since they are always dispersed due to the discursive mode of their thinking. Furthermore, human existence is much broader and richer than what man can encompass by means of the geometrical method. In other words, Descartes denies the status of knowledge and truth of important faculties of the human mind such as imagination, passions, prudence, opinion, politics, and rhetoric, without which human existence would become unthinkable, Vico says. Following this, various facets of human existence are absent in the Cartesian philosophy. And without these capabilities and facets, man can never be at home. Vico writes:

> But the greatest drawback of our educational methods is that we pay an excessive amount of attention to the natural sciences and not enough to ethics. Our chief fault is that we disregard that part of ethics which treats of human character, of its dispositions, its passions and of the manner of adjusting these factors to public life and eloquence. We neglect that discipline which deals with the differential features of the virtues and vices, with good and bad behavior-patterns, with the typical characteristics of the various ages of man, of the two sexes, of social and economic class, race and nation, and with the art of seemly conduct in life, the most difficult of all arts. As a consequence of this neglect, a noble and important branch of studies, i.e., the science of politics, lies almost abandoned and untended. (Vico, 1965, p. 33)

In a poem, the German poet Friedrich Schiller (1759–1805) writes:

One of the crowd:

Cogito ergo sum. I think and therefore I am. If the one is just true, then the other is certain.

I:

I think, therefore I am. Indeed! But who can always be thinking? I have often existed and have actually thought of nothing.[3] (Schiller, 1893, p. 100)

It turns out, *cogito* does not render the meaning and fact of my existence as a whole, but only very partially, namely, only as long as I think. It does not convey the highest point of intimacy which we expected from it. Similarly, Friedrich Wilhelm Joseph Schelling (1775–1854) claims that the *sum* which is implied by the *cogito* refers only to *sum qua cogitans*. 'I exist as a thinking substance, that is, in this given way of existence which is called thinking, and it is only a different mode of existence than, for example, that of the body whose kind of existence is to occupy space' (Schelling, 1861, p. 10).[4] Schelling discerns the source of the *ego* in God. In other words, the subject can never be at home, it is not by itself, but rather outside itself, in God. Likewise, Ludwig Feuerbach (1804–1872) views the ego as emerging out of the historical process (Feuerbach, 1833, p. 187). The ego, in Feuerbach's eyes, is a historical product; it can find its home only in history, outside itself. Georg Christoph Lichtenberg (1742–1799) sees in the statement *cogito ergo sum* nothing but a grammatical means to distinguish between internal experience and external events (Lichtenberg, 1994, p. 412). It does not refer to any real existing and thinking substance. Nietzsche claims that the statement *cogito ergo sum* stems from a grammatical habit (i.e. of using substance and predicates in sentence) and does not refer to any I (Nietzsche, 1906, §484). Since madness ceased to be seen as a holy phenomenon following the Reformation and the Renaissance and consequently mentally ill people were put into confinement, Descartes, according to Michel Foucault (1926–1984), did not take madness seriously in his attempt to capture the essence of a human being (Foucault, 2006, pp. 44–77). Madness as a possible component of human existence is discarded in Descartes's *Meditations* and *Discourse* due to the emergence of a new historical era in which madness is no longer related to holiness, according to Foucault.

My interest in home and exile led me to study various readings of Descartes's philosophy. In these readings, Descartes's philosophy is almost never considered and studied as such. It is rather conceived as representative of a given sociopolitical worldview. It is epitomized either as bearing the sense of home, of a return to the roots, from which philosophy and science can safely develop, or as bearing a sense of alienation from one's own existence, society, and history. Descartes's philosophy either represents the progress of society and its advance to a better future or its falling apart and decay. The fascination of people with Descartes, either their praise or loathing of him, is what piqued my interest and brought me to write this book.

The following account is an illustrative example for such fascination with Descartes. In 1666, Descartes's remains, which were originally buried in

Sweden, were disinterred and returned to France for an official ceremonial burial. The French ambassador to Sweden, Hughues de Terlon, was in charge of the exhumation and transport of the remains to France. In his book *Descartes's Bones*, Russell Shorto relates the following story:

> Terlon arranged for the body to travel with him as far as Copenhagen. He had a special copper coffin made that was only two and a half feet long. The improbable reason for this – besides the fact that the original wooden box in which the body had been laid had rotted – was that his superiors in France were concerned that if it became known that he was transporting the remains of René Descartes his party might be attacked and robbed. The cult of Cartesianism had grown strong in the years since Descartes's death, and others had developed an interest in the remains. (Shorto, 2008, p. 48)

At some point, Terlon halted the process in which the remains were exhumed and put in a copper coffin to be sent to France in order to make the following request to the assembled Catholic clergy:

> He asked the assembled Catholic clergy if he might 'religiously' be allowed to take one of the bones for himself. In particular, he had his eye on the right index finger – a bone 'which had served as an instrument in the immortal writings of the deceased'. (Ibid., p. 49)

> The priests granted the request; the chevalier was allowed to take the finger. He must have kept it until his death in 1690. (Ibid., p. 51)

The French historian Paul Hazard also reports on the cult around Descartes at the end of the seventeenth century: '*Nulla nunc celebrior, clamorosiorque secta quam Cartesianorum* [There is today no sect more famous and great than Cartesianism], loudly asserts a contemporary writer in a work bearing the significant title *Historia rationis* [history of reason].[5] And it is a fact that, by the end of the century, Descartes had become King' (Hazard, 2013, p. 130). Then Hazard touches upon another important point which will occupy us later:

> But his sway was not unlimited, for there is not, and never has been, such a thing as an absolute monarchy in the realms of the intellect. There is a certain national or racial element that persists in clinging to every philosophy no matter how impersonal and abstract, an abiding and inalienable note, or characteristic. Descartes never succeeded in ousting that stubborn *residuum*

which gives to the Englishman or to the Italian his unmistakable national character. (Ibid., italics in original)

Race and nationality will turn out to be main factors in both the praising and loathing evaluations of Descartes by other philosophers. As Hazard claims, Vico's critique of Descartes also contains national and racial factors. 'When, a little later on, Vico sought to endow his country with a philosophy that should be essentially Italian, the adversary with whom he had to measure swords was not Aristotle, now dethroned, but Descartes, who reigned in his stead' (ibid.). The title of a recent publication *Née Cartésienne* (Born Cartesian) refers explicitly to that anthropological factor in evaluating Descartes (Koops, Dorsman, and Verbeek, 2005).

Among the first examples that attracted my attention was the German art historian and philosopher, anti-Semite and advocate of the *völkisch* movement, Julius Langbehn (1851–1907). In 1890, he published his book *Rembrandt als Erzieher* (Rembrandt as Educator), that was very popular at the time of its publication – thirty-nine editions were printed within two years! Langbehn saw in rationality, scientism (*Wissenschaftlichkeit*), materialism, liberalism, cosmopolitanism, and cultural–spiritual uniformity nothing but decadence which the Enlightenment, along with the process of urbanization, had brought about. As an antithesis to that hated modernity, he proposed the Low German (*Niederdeutsch*) type of man and a way of life which he saw embodied in the painter Rembrandt. Langbehn expected a *völkisch* rebirth through the experience of art. *Rembrandt as Educator* had a strong influence on the Youth Movement (*Jugendbewegung*), the Low Germany Movement (*Niederdeutsche Bewegung*), and Nazi art education. The title *Rembrandt as Educator* alludes to Nietzsche's third *Untimely Meditation*, that is, *Schopenhauer als Erzieher* (Schopenhauer as Educator). Langbehn adopted ideas from the young Nietzsche and integrated them in his nationalistic worldview. In *Rembrandt as Educator* he writes:

In so far as self-expression is the foundation of any work of art and inference is the foundation of all science, one should therefore by necessity acknowledge what we have already said [namely,] that philosophy is not science but rather art. One should now turn Descartes's statement *cogito, ergo sum* into *sum, ergo cogito*; that is: I am – in a totally definite form which is given only to me once and for all time, in my individuality! With Descartes, the critical period of philosophy starts; with his successors, who continue to work until this day, it ceases; now, the artistic period of it [of philosophy] commences. Philosophy must be [German] nationalistic (*volksthümlich*). It can be nationalistic only in so far that it is individualistic; German philosophy has so far failed to be that. Nobody will claim that there is any living philosophical system today in Germany. It does not fulfill artistic demands, not even to some limited extent. The national spirit denied philosophy, because philosophy denied the national spirit.[6] (Langbehn, 1890, pp. 54–5)

The idea that existence (*esse*) precedes thinking (*cogitare*) is not new. We know this from Kierkegaard, Heidegger, and Sartre. However, the reason why Langbehn gives precedence to existence over thinking differs from theirs: existence is individual, according to Langbehn, and it is different in every nation. Langbehn wants to found philosophy on the particular existence of the German nation. Therefore, he rejects Cartesianism in which *reason* or *thinking* is identical in all humans and admits of no race or nationality.

Franz Xaver von Baader (1765–1841) was a Catholic thinker, physician, mining engineer, and philosopher. He was the first to talk about the distress of the proletariat, long before Marx and Engels did. Today, he is almost completely forgotten. Back in his time, he was a renowned figure and maintained contact with Hegel, Schelling, and other philosophers. He had a strong influence on Ignaz von Döllinger and Søren Kierkegaard. According to Baader, the ego can never conceive itself as an independent thinking thing (*res cogitans*). It is rather *conceived* as a dependent thinking thing (*res cogitans*) from an *external point of view*, and not of the ego but rather of God. Therefore, instead of *cogito ergo sum*, 'I think, therefore I exist', we should say '*cogitor (a deo) ergo sum*', 'I am thought (by God), therefore I exist' (Baader, 1860, p. 238).[7] Long before Baader, Pierre-Daniel Huet (1630–1721) delivered a similar critique against Descartes in his important work *Censura Philosophiae Cartesianae*, 1723 (*Against Cartesian Philosophy*, Huet). In the same vein, the Austrian philosopher Alois Riehl (1844–1921) concludes his discussion of Descartes with the following revision of the *cogito* statement: '*cogito, ergo sum et est*', that is, 'I think, therefore I am and it is.' Similarly, Arthur Schopenhauer says: '*cogito, ergo est*', that is, 'I think, therefore it is' (cited in Funke, 1960, pp. 169–70). For Baader, however, the main issue with Descartes is not philosophical but rather social, political, and religious. Descartes's statement *cogito ergo sum* sets the human subject at the centre of the cosmos and drives God out to the periphery. Baader is deeply troubled by that social deterioration and secularization. Shortly before his death, he stated: 'It is my mission to put an end to Cartesianism in philosophy' (cited in Geldhof, 2005, p. 249).

In his work *Der Übergang vom feudalen zum bürgerlichen Weltbild* (The Transition from the Feudal to the Bourgeois Worldview), Franz Borkenau (1900–1957), a forgotten scholar primarily related to the Frankfurt School, shows how Descartes reduced man and morality to the laws of inorganic nature. In this worldview, man cannot intervene in the course of nature which is now understood mechanically. He can become the master and lord of nature by adapting himself to the natural laws. According to Borkenau, this is a modern version of Stoic morality.[8] This disconcertment and the attempt to overcome the resulting pessimism is what led to the emergence of materialistic and capitalistic society. Borkenau writes:

> The Stoic viewpoint, the view of the external world as something alien whose fatal necessity we can only perceive but not change, namely the elementary fact of the relationship between the individual and the external world in capitalism which is the foundation of Descartes's thought, has been laid down at the beginning of his development.[9] (Borkenau, 1934, p. 299)

In this worldview, man and nature have lost any meaning and they are in an all-encompassing process of mass production. But, furthermore, this view of the world as obeying unchangeable mechanical rules sanctions the existing social order and prevents any endeavour to bring about a change, to revolt. It thus reflects the ideology of the ruling class. As Herbert Marcuse (1898–1979), another thinker related to the Frankfurt School, says in his collection of essays on Critical Theory:

> But in the contemporary form of social organization, the domination of nature through rational methods of production as envisioned by Descartes was neither joined to nor directed by the sovereign reason of the associated individuals. The fate of bourgeois society announces itself in its philosophy. When the liberated individual as the subject of practice actually sets himself to shaping the conditions of his life, it sees himself subjected to the laws of

the commodity market, which operates as blind economic laws behind his back. At most, his first step, the beginning of his career, can appear free, as though dictated by his own reason. All subsequent ones are prescribed him by the conditions of a commodity-producing society, and he must observe them if he does not want to go under.

Post-Cartesian idealism retains this fundamental philosophical idea of the bourgeois period, the idea that the 'organization' of existing things in accordance with their comprehended potentialities is a function of the free, critical reason of the individual. (Marcuse, 2009, pp. 35–6)

All this looks like an immense sociopolitical theoretical edifice which towers higher above what Descartes ever stated. French philosopher Paul-Yves Nizan (1905–1940) seems to draw an even more audacious conclusion from what Descartes explicitly said. Nizan writes:

In truth, 'The Discourse on Method', in which Descartes fully explained himself for the first time, constitutes a philosophical coup de force. It is something more than the 'Ethics' because it is the historic manifesto of bourgeois intelligence, just as the 'Summa' of Saint Thomas was the manifesto of feudal intelligence, and as the works of Marx were to be the manifesto of proletarian intelligence. (Nizan, 2013)

Max Scheler (1874–1928) leads his reading of Descartes in other direction. In his famous work *Die Stellung des Menschen im Kosmos* (*Man's Position in the Cosmos*) he attacks Descartes's dualism and his theory on the association of mind and body in the pineal gland. The body, human and non-human, is permeated with soul, Scheler argues. The 'waking consciousness' (*Wachbewußtsein*) emerges out of the blood glands, which determines, inter alia, also the racial characteristics (*Rassencharaktere*) of the person, according to him (2016, p. 69). This is by no means a Freudian slip on Scheler's part. Conceiving the human body as permeated with soul means no longer saying that different human beings are equal in their reasoning powers. Now, even the human mind, not only the human body, is bound with race. In his essay '*Das Nationale im Denken Frankreichs*' (The National in the French Thought), Scheler makes a distinction between French and German philosophy, based on their different national characters. Upon the basis of that distinction, Scheler discusses the philosophy of Descartes. According to him, Descartes's concept of truth as *verum quod clare et distincte percipitur* (truth perceived as clear and distinct) cannot by any means reflect the truth about reality, but rather the French critical mind and its subjective urge for achieving clarity. Likewise, Scheler contends, the statement *cogito ergo sum* does not convey any truth about reality but rather, in a nutshell, the art and spirit of the *ancien régime*. It reflects the cruel distance from which, later, Voltaire, Diderot, and Balzac observed and portrayed the human being. Scheler argues further that the Cartesian ego is detached from the world. This view gives birth to the conception of animals, plants, and even man in his purely bodily state of existence, as a machine without soul and rational motivation. Scheler sums up, It is the 'French thought, Gallic excess kat'exochen [par excellence]!' (Scheler, 1963, p. 142).[10] According to him, all the intermediate realms between God and man collapsed in Descartes: '*Causae secundae* [secondary causes] are consumed by the *causa prima* [primary cause]' in the same way that all classes and their liberty were consumed by the monarch in the French development of the state (ibid.). Scheler writes:

> And just as in face of '*l'etat c'est moi*' ['the state is me'] (the analogy of the '*cogito ergo sum*' in political philosophy) eventually all society becomes a uniform democratic mass, so the thinking subjects become in the face of God 'equal' as far as the mind's *idées innées* ['innate ideas'] are concerned.[11] (Ibid.)

Lacking the 'scholarly' apparatus which Scheler uses in his discussion, Franz Josef Böhm (1903–1946), a pupil of Heinrich Rickert and protégé of Ernst Krieck, traces his entire philosophy back to the *Volk*. In his book *Anticartesianismus: Deutsche Philosophie im Widerstand* (Anti-Cartesianism: German Philosophy in Resistance) he writes: 'With Descartes, the place of the Western man, in whom *völkisch* rootedness and universal expansion are united, becomes occupied by the European man – a full realization of rationality with no existence and history' (Böhm, 1938, p. 55).[12] 'Europe' no longer refers to the people in the way 'Western World' (*Abendland*) does: 'Western World' refers to people with history and tradition, whereas 'Europe' is a neutral geographical term, according to Böhm. Since humans now exist as isolated substances, the community of shared blood and fate (*Gemeinschaft*) collapses and humans exist instead in a society (*Gesellschaft*) which is a random gathering of people. Without community, sacrifice becomes impossible, he says.

> The decay of a community can never be definitely repaired and we know
> from our past that also natural fundaments of the community fall prey to
> decay if the *ethos* of sacrifice – which is what makes the community exist as
> *binding* reality – decays.[13] (Ibid., p. 217, italics in original)

At about the same time, Edmund Husserl (1859–1938) saw in Descartes
the model for carrying out his phenomenological research. Husserl views
the human subject as transcendental subjectivity, the source of meaning.
In order to reach out to that transcendental subjectivity, Husserl carries out
what he calls ἐποχή (epoché) – inhibition of all judgements and assessments
concerning reality, also called 'bracketing' (*ausklammern*) – and then a series
of methodical reductions which lead from meaning to its constitution. Husserl
discerns parallels between his phenomenological method and Descartes's
hyperbolical doubt which also leads to the subject, although not to the
transcendental subjectivity. Even before delving into Husserl's philosophy, as
we shall later do, we must admit that the gap between Husserl and Descartes
is immense. Husserl shares with Descartes the wish to provide science with
a firm foundation. Yet Husserl inquires after the original constitution of
meaning; reality as such does not interest him. Descartes, on the contrary,
looks for *fundamentum inconcussum* (firm foundation) whose reality cannot
be cast in doubt. Transcendental subjectivity as the source of meaning
in Husserl's philosophy constitutes meaning within the temporal flux of
consciousness with horizons open to the past and the future. Transcendental
subjectivity itself is also temporal, according to Husserl. Thus, it turns out that
it has nothing in common with the a-temporal ego in Descartes's philosophy.
Most important, Descartes's worldview is mechanical, whereas Husserl's
is teleological. Despite this substantial difference between Husserl's and
Descartes's philosophy, Husserl keeps claiming that Descartes paved the way
for his phenomenology and that Descartes's philosophy is his model. As it
turns out, Husserl's insistence to adhere to Descartes's philosophy is *political*.
Husserl saw the disaster of the First World War and in the mid-1930s the great
danger coming from National Socialism and the impending war. He must have
thought that the only answer to National Socialism and loss of rationality is the
rationalism and objectivism of the Enlightenment as embodied in Descartes's
philosophy. As François Azouvi writes:

By 1914 the myth [of Descartes as representative of the French spirit and nature] was sufficiently well developed for official philosophers to incorporate it. Among those who did so were Alain, Bergson, Delbos and Boutroux. To counter German barbarism, France offered the visage of Descartes: a clear, measured mind ('the French genius is in no way exclusive but remains essentially human'), an enemy of jargon and of vast, pretentious constructions ('nothing could be farther from the truth than the argument that has been made by some people in France and accepted by many, that the Cartesian spirit, typical in this respect of the French spirit, is excessively constructive and deductive'), the founder of the democratic ideal. ('It is on the fact that we are all reasonable beings, and that, as Descartes said, "reason in its entirety is within each one of us," that we base the right of each person to the respect of all and the inviolability of the individual', Bergson declared to the Comité France-Amérique in April 1913). This Descartes was mustered into service against the 'monstrous deployments of intelligence and soul that Germany is making at the present time'. As irrationality was unleashed on the other side of the Rhine, what better response could French philosophers offer than Cartesian rationalism? Despite the now commonplace view to the contrary, this rationalism was characterized by flexibility, moderation, and a feeling for reality. (Azouvi, 1998, p. 517)

At the same time, Husserl's worldview is teleological. In it, he and Descartes play a central role in realizing the European end, τέλος (telos, end). His worldview is Eurocentric, and other peoples, non-European, are inferior races in his eyes.

The research in the present book is historical. It deals with various readings of Descartes and reactions to him. As far as I know, Descartes never explicitly referred to any political matter, except once, in a letter to Princess Elisabeth of Bohemia who handed him a copy of Machiavelli's *The Prince* and asked him about his opinion (Pallandt and Descartes, 2007, pp. 139–49). It seems to me also extremely difficult to point at any implicit political intention in Descartes's work. In a consummate work on Descartes, Richard Kennington shows the political subtext in Descartes's work (Kennington, 2004). Many texts, which we will be discussing in the present study, may seem at first glance as objective dealing with the Cartesian philosophy. They, however, may reveal political commitment and viewpoint in a close and critical reading.

Progress is the leading idea of the Enlightenment. Philosophers such as Marquis de Condorcet (1743–1794) and François-Jean Lefebvre de la Barre

(1745–1766) identified progress with Descartes (Israel, 2006, pp. 572–3). Chapter 1 deals with Pierre-Joseph Proudhon (1809–1865), Georges Sorel (1847–1922), and Martin Heidegger (1889–1976), and with their discussion of Descartes, progress, technology, and truth. Proudhon sees in progress the key to anarchy and revolution which he wishes to take place. This leads him to reformulate Descartes's statement *cogito ergo sum*. On the contrary, Sorel regards progress as the means of the ruling noble class, and later the bourgeois class, to consolidate their position. Thus, Sorel sees in Descartes the main representative of these classes which, according to him, should be toppled. Both Proudhon and Sorel share the Enlightenment's view on progress. However, they disagree with Descartes and the Enlightenment about the desired end of that progress. Heidegger, on the contrary, discards the idea of progress as a worldview altogether. His vantage point is rather the eschatological revelation of Being.

Pierre-Daniel Huet (1630–1721), in his *Censura Philosophiae Cartesianae* (*Against Cartesian Philosophy*), shows logically how the subject cannot intuit itself as a thinking subject (*res cogitans*) (Huet, 2003, pp. 67–112). The ego is perceived from an external perspective and therefore cannot be formulated in the first person: *ego cogito, ego sum*. A similar claim against Descartes is raised by Franz Xaver von Baader (1765–1841). Baader reformulates Descartes's statement *cogito ergo sum* and says instead '*cogitor (a deo) ergo sum*' (I am thought or conceived by God, therefore I exist). Baader expands his critique of Descartes to the entire secular society which sets the human subject at its centre instead of God. It is an alienated society which lacks love to God and man. From this viewpoint, he treats the question of freedom, authority, church, state, and the proletariat. Chapter 2 deals with Baader.

It was François-Pierre-Gonthier Maine de Biran in the eighteenth century (1766–1824) who felt uncomfortable with the Cartesian a-temporal ego, being conceived as *res cogitans* (Henry, 1975). Maine de Biran introduced time, movement, and sensuality into the sphere of the thinking subject and thus undermined the whole Cartesian conception of subject. Edmund Husserl (1859–1938) does the same in his phenomenology. The ego in Husserl's phenomenology constitutes meaning in time and exists within the temporal flux of consciousness. In his later works, Husserl reiterates time and again that Descartes is his model for conducting phenomenological research. Chapter 3 shows how Husserl deviates altogether from Descartes's philosophy in all presumable respects. It suggests that Husserl still adheres to Descartes as a model, because he probably assumed that Cartesian rationalism is the only conceivable antidote to the cultural maladies of the West in the aftermath of the First World War and the rise of National Socialism to power. At the same time, in Husserl's teleological worldview, he and Descartes realize the end, *τέλος*, of the European man. This is a Eurocentric worldview in which other, non-European peoples and nations, are regarded as inferior races.

Martin Heidegger followed in the path of Husserl's phenomenology. In *Being and Time*, his *opus magnum*, he professes to prepare the way to raise the forgotten question about the meaning of Being. This undertaking requires a sweeping deconstruction of modern and medieval philosophy in order to reach back to the era in which the question about the meaning of Being still mattered, namely, in ancient Greece. Chapter 4 shows how this deconstruction of Western philosophy produces alternatives to the main aspects of Descartes's philosophy as they are unfolded in his *Meditations on First Philosophy*. In place of the a-temporal thinking substance Heidegger posits a temporal human-Dasein. Whereas Descartes discarded tradition and history as a reliable source of meaning, the human-Dasein in *Being and Time* relies on tradition and history in projecting meaning. Descartes views time as made up of a succession of 'nows'. In *Being and Time* this view is replaced with the eschatological experience of time (*Augenblick*). Cartesian dualism is replaced by the organic unity of meaning which Heidegger calls 'Dasein'. Descartes's view of truth as *adaequatio intellectus et rei* (correspondence between the mind and reality) is replaced by truth as *ἀλήθεια* (*aletheia*, truth), that is, disclosure. History and tradition are reauthorized in *Being and Time* and the human-Dasein knowingly succumbs to them and takes them upon itself as its destiny. *Being and Time*, seen as a response to the Cartesian worldview, will turn out to be a scathing social and political critique of modern mass society which is alienated to itself and to its tradition. Against it, Heidegger poses the ancient Greek and early Christian society with their experience of knowledge as *φρόνησῐς* (*phronesis*, practical knowledge) and *νοῦς* (*nous*, intuition), truth as *ἀλήθεια*, and time as *καιρός* (*kairos*, moment of revelation), and *ἔσχατον* (*eschaton*, apocalyptic end). We will then discuss Heidegger's lectures on Nietzsche from the early- and mid-1940s and the 'notorious' *Black*

Notebooks in which Cartesianism is presented as the source out of which all the human disasters in modern times such as unrestrained technology, racism, nationalism, arms race, overuse of power, and barbarism emerged.

The intellectual revolution which took place in the seventeenth century led not only to the creation of a new science, that is, mathematical science, and did not only pave the way for modern technology, new division of labour and consequently modern economy; it also gave birth to a new type of man. This led to revolution in morality and society. In a world ruled by mechanical law there is no longer room for spontaneous change and divine intervention. In a world ruled economically, man is seen only in light of his productivity. Chapter 5 deals with Franz Borkenau (1900–1957) and his analysis of Descartes's philosophy in light of Marxist analysis of society, technology, and economy.

One of the implications of Cartesian dualism is that the mind, contrary to the body, has no race, nationality or gender. Reason according to Descartes is the essence of the human being. We have already seen in the example of Max Scheler what may happen if we discard that dualistic view of man and see the body and mind as an inseparable unity. In this respect, if the *Volk* makes up the essence of man, Cartesian philosophy poses a serious danger to our culture. Chapter 6 deals with Franz Josef Böhm (1903–1946), supporter of the *völkisch* philosophy, who discerns in Cartesianism the enemy of the German *Volk*, culture, and society, and calls upon philosophers to wage war against it.

***

As we have seen, progress is one of the main ideas which is associated with Descartes and the Enlightenment. Chapter 1 deals with three different views on progress by Pierre-Joseph Proudhon, George Sorel, and Martin Heidegger. For Proudhon, progress should not stop at any point but rather lead to perpetuum mobile which dismantles all static governing structures and possession of power. We should say *Moveor, ergo fio* (I move, therefore I become), instead of *cogito ergo sum* (I think, therefore I exist), Proudhon says. This should lead to dynamic anarchy. For Sorel, progress, as Descartes conceives it, is the political means of the aristocracy to oppress the lower classes. Sorel suggests replacing the ideal of progress with mythological heroism as an intellectual basis to overthrow the ruling class. For Heidegger, progress is the main symptom of the degenerate Western civilization and culture. Heidegger views and analyses progress from an eschatological point of view.

Notes

1 On this matter, see Joisten (2014).

2 For a detailed discussion of Vico's critique of Descartes see Berlin (1980). See also Grassi (1976) and Horkheimer (1987).

3 'Einer aus dem Haufen: / Cogito, ergo sum. Ich denke, und mithin so bin ich, / Ist das eine nur wahr, ist es das andere gewiss. / Ich: / Denk ich, so bin ich! Wohl! Doch wer wird immer auch denken? / Oft schon war ich, und hab wirklich an gar nichts gedacht!.'

4 'Das in dem cogito begriffene sum heißt also nur: sum qua cogitans, ich bin als denkend, d.h. in dieser bestimmten Art des Seins, welche denken genannt wird, und die nur eine andere Art zu sein ist als z.B. die des Körpers, dessen Art zu sein darin besteht, daß er den Raum erfüllt.'

5 It is not clear where the line between Descartes and his philosophy and 'Cartesianism' runs. See Müller (2007, pp. 383–4).

6 'Insofern freie Selbstentfaltung die Grundlage aller Kunst und zwingende Schlußfolgerung die Grundlage aller Wissenschaft ist, muß man daher unbedingt anerkennen, was schon ausgesprochen wurde; daß die Philosophie nicht eine Wissenschaft sondern eine Kunst ist. Man hat jetzt den Satz des Descartes cogito, ergo sum umzukehren in sum, ergo cogito; das heißt: ich bin–in einer ganz bestimmten, ein für allemal und nur mir gegebenen Form, in meiner Individualität! Mit Descartes fängt die kritische Periode der Philosophie an; mit seinen Nachfolgern, die bis heute reichen, wird sie auch aufhören; nunmehr kommt die künstlerische Periode derselben. Philosophie muß volksthümlich sein; sie kann nur volksthümlich sein, wenn sie individuell ist; die bisherige deutsche Philosophie ist daran gescheitert–denn Niemand wird behaupten, daß irgend ein philosophisches System noch heute in Deutschland lebendig sei–daß sie jene wahrhaft künstlerischen Forderungen entweder garnicht oder nur in beschränktestem Maße erfüllt. Der Volksgeist verleugnete die Philosophie, weil die Philosophie den Volksgeist verleugnet hatte.'

7 'Wenn der Mensch Gedanke Gottes (keineswegs der Gottgedanke von sich selbst), wenn also der Mensch von Gott gedacht ist und ohne dieses von Gott Gedachtwerden nicht wäre, so kann er auch seines Seins nur gewiss sein, indem

er sich von Gott gedacht weiss. Daher genügt nicht das Cogito ergo sum, sondern nur das Cogitor (a deo) ergo sum.'

8 'Das Individuum ist nicht mehr rein qualitativ bestimmtes Glied eines Standes, der seinerseits eine verständliche Funktion im Ganzen des Lebens hätte; es steht dem geschichtlich-gesellschaftlichen Leben als etwas Fremdes und von ihm gänzlich Unbeinflußbaren gegenüber. Dieses Geschehen ist für es "Natur", aber nicht mehr im Sinne der Identität des Strebens der menschlichen Seele mit der Natur: "Natur" ist jetzt das Fremde, das, was der Mensch so wenig von innen heraus verstehen kann, wie das kontingente Geschehen im Bereich des Anorganischen. Dieser "Natur" kann der Mensch sich entgegenstellen und untergehen, oder sie hinnehmen und dadurch zwar nicht Glück, wohl aber Leidlosigkeit erreichen. In diesem letzten Punkte trennt sich Descartes von der stoischen Lehre. Er stellt ihrer Insensibilität die Möglichkeit von Glück als Resultat der richtigen Philosophie gegenüber; er meint damit Vollender des alten Stoizismus zu sein' (Borkenau, 1934, p. 299).

9 'Der stoische Standpunkt, die Betrachtung der Außenwelt als etwas Fremdes, dessen fatale Notwendigkeit zu erkennen und nicht zu ändern ist, die Grundtatsache des Verhältnisses von Individuum und Außenwelt im Kapitalismus also, ist der Ausgangspunkt von Descartes' Denken, liegt von Anfang seiner Entwicklung an fest.'

10 'Ein französischer Gedanke, ein gallischer Exzeß kat'exochcn!'

11 'Und wie vor dem "l'etat c'est moi" (dem staatsphilosophischen Analogon des "cogito ergo sum") schließlich alle Gesellschaft eine demokratisch gleichförmige Masse wird, so werden die denkenden Ichs auch vor Gott "gleich" an der Vernunftmitgift der idées innées.'

12 'Mit Descartes tritt an die Stelle des abendländisch gebundenen Menschen in seiner Einheit von volkhafter Verwurzelung und universalem Ausgreifen der europäische Mensch – die Schöpfung einer unwirklichen und geschichtslosen Rationalität.'

13 'Der Verfall einer Gemeinschaft ist nie endgültig aufzuheben, und wir wissen es aus unserer Vergangenheit, daß auch die natürlichen Fundamente einer Gemeinschaft der Auflösung anheimfallen, wenn das *Ethos* des Opfers verfällt, das die Gemeinschaft als *verpflichtende* Wirklichkeit erst existent macht.'

1

Progress: Pierre-Joseph Proudhon, Georges Sorel, and Martin Heidegger

Progress

To the followers of Descartes, such as Marquis de Condorcet (1743–1794) and François Poullain de la Barre (1647–1723), Enlightenment is *progress*, and progress is best represented by Descartes. Descartes promises us progress which will make us the lords and masters of nature. Most importantly, it is progress in medicine, the science which is supposed to ensure us long and healthy life. Descartes writes:

> But as soon as I had acquired some general notions in physics and had noticed, as I began to test them in various particular problems, where they could lead and how much they differ from the principles used up to now, I believed that I could not keep them secret without sinning gravely against the law which obliges us to do all in our power to secure the general welfare of mankind. For they opened my eyes to the possibility of gaining knowledge which would be very useful in life, and of discovering a practical philosophy which might replace the speculative philosophy taught in the schools. Through this philosophy we could know the power and action of fire, water, air, the stars, the heavens and all the other bodies in our environment, as distinctly as we know the various crafts of our artisans; and we could use this knowledge – as the artisans use theirs – for all the purposes for which it is appropriate, and thus make ourselves, as it were, the lords and masters of nature. This is desirable not only for the invention of innumerable devices which would facilitate our enjoyment of the fruits of the earth and all the goods we find there, but also, and most importantly, for the maintenance of health, which is undoubtedly the chief good and the foundation of all the other goods in this life. For even the mind depends so much on the temperament and disposition of the bodily organs that if it is possible to find

some means of making men in general wiser and more skillful than they have been up till now, I believe we must look for it in medicine. (Descartes, 1985a, pp. 142–3)

In order to achieve this prosperity, we should first of all release reason from the fetters of all the prejudices which man has inherited through tradition and education, to cast into doubt also the existence of God and to put trust in nothing but reason. This is the first step which Descartes takes in the *Meditations* and which leads him to the pure subject, the purified *res cogitans* (thinking thing). Methodically seen, it may turn out to be impossible to cast everything in doubt. As Wittgenstein put it: 'If you tried to doubt everything you would not get as far as doubting anything. The game of doubting itself presupposes certainty' (Wittgenstein, 1969, §115). Politically seen, it is revolutionary to want to destroy everything we consider to be valid in one thrust of the sword, instead of gradually replacing the wrong judgements with right judgements. This abrupt demolition of everything upon which our society is built is what unsettled people who were opposed to the French Revolution, such as Edmund Burke (1729–1797) (Burke, 1951). On the other hand, it attracted people like Condorcet who saw in prejudices the main obstacle on the way to achieve progress and prosperity. Prejudices lead to wars, to religious intolerance, tyranny, despotism, and stagnation in science, says Condorcet. In the *Sketch*, which he entitled *Prospectus d'un tableau historique des progrès de l'esprit humain* (Leaflet of the Historical Chart of the Progress of the Human Mind) (Condorcet, 2013), he views man as 'infinitely perfectible'. He also discusses the negative influences of prejudices and superstitions on progress throughout history. 'The history of this form of prejudice and its influence on the fate of the human race must figure in the picture that I have undertaken; and nothing will serve better to show the extent to which happiness depends upon the progress of reason' (ibid., p. 18). Condorcet divides the history of human progress into ten epochs and entitles the ninth one 'From Descartes to the Foundation of the French Republic' (ibid., p. 89). Progress, as he says, is global, and is found in all branches of life: 'But this progress in politics and political economy was caused primarily by the progress in general philosophy and metaphysics, if we take the latter word in its broadest sense' (ibid., p. 95). It is thanks to the Cartesian method that one could bring progress to all branches of knowledge and life, he contends (ibid., pp. 96–7). It is by means of the Cartesian method that we overcome the prejudices of the masses which have corrupted reason (ibid., p. 98). Philosophers of all nations should join together to combat all sorts of errors and tyrannies (ibid., p. 102). In conclusion he writes, 'We see the rise of a new doctrine which was to deal the final blow to the already tottering structure of prejudice: the doctrine of the infinite perfectibility of the human race of which Turgot, Price and Priestley were the first and the most brilliant apostles' (ibid.).

François Poullain de la Barre uses the Cartesian method to show that there is no difference between the sexes (Barre, 2002). Man and woman are completely equal, because the mind has no gender. This is indeed great progress, thanks to Descartes, as Albistur and Armogathe note in their *Histoire du féminisme en France du Moyen Age à nos jours* (History of Feminism in France from the Middle Ages to Our Days) (Albistur and Armogathe, 1977): 'Sans Descartes, il n'y aurait pas eu Poullain de la Barre; sans Poullain de la Barre, l'histoire du Féminisme aurait piétiné longtemps encore' [Without Descartes, Poullain de la Barre would not have been; without Poullain de la Barre, history of feminism would have trodden long time.]' (cited in Barre, 2002, p. 33). Following Descartes, de la Barre writes:

> We, however, propose to examine this idea [the equality of the sexes] by applying the rule of truth: accept nothing as true unless it is supported by clear and distinct ideas. Thus, we find that the common prejudice is founded on mere popular hearsay, and that the two sexes *are* equal. Women have the same gifts of intelligence and energy as men. (Ibid., p. 50, italics in original)

There is however no progress without regress; the one cannot be conceived without the other. Our experience and history provide sufficient reasons to doubt progress. They can be conceived only out of definite *perspective*, out of which something is seen as positive or negative. Jean-Jacques Rousseau (1712–1778) was perhaps the first to distrust at length the idea of progress.[1] In his *Discourse on the Sciences and Arts*, 1750, Rousseau protests against the damage which sciences cause to the natural disposition of man and the distance they create between him and the *fatherland* (Rousseau, 1997, p. 8). In

Emile, or On Education, 1762, he criticizes medicine in a way which sounds like a critique of Descartes's view of medicine:

> I have no intention of enlarging on the vanity of medicine here. My object is only to consider it from the moral point of view. I can nevertheless not prevent myself from remarking that men make concerning its use, the same sophisms as they make concerning the quest for truth. They always assume that in treating a sick person, one cures him and that, in seeking a truth, one finds it. They do not see that it is necessary to balance the advantage of a cure effected by the doctor against the death of a hundred sick persons killed by him, and the usefulness of a truth discovered against the harm done by the errors which become current at the same time. Science which instructs and medicine which cures are doubtless very good. But science which deceives and medicine which kills are bad. Learn, therefore, to distinguish them. That is the crux of the question. If we knew how to be ignorant of the truth, we would never be the dupes of lies; if we knew how not to want to be cured in spite of nature, we would never die at the doctor's hand. (Rousseau, 1979, p. 54)

Later we see a critique of progress in the fifth act of *Faust* by Goethe. Faust takes on the role of a modern colonialist who empties nature of its essence and finally rules over people in a tyrannical way by subjugating everything to his plans (Schmidt, 2001, p. 229). In a letter to a friend, dated 1825, Goethe uses his review of a performance of Gaspare Sponitini's opera *Alcidor* to criticize the entire social phenomenon of progress: 'Everything is now ultra, everything rushes ahead (*transzendiert*) with no pause, in thought as well as in action. Nobody knows himself, nobody conceives the element in which he hangs and acts, the material on which he works' (cited in Jaeger, 2004, p. 60). A definite perspective is presumed in any evaluation of progress and regress. Thus, we can always ask about the interest and motivation behind defining something as progressive or regressive. Our evaluation seems to be never free of ideology. As Hans Blumenberg puts it, the idea of progress 'is rather the continuous self-justification of the present, by means of the future that it gives itself, before the past, with which it compares itself' (Blumenberg, 1983, p. 30).

Is any attempt to bypass the barrier of ideological perspective doomed to failure and meaningless talk? In his *Theses on the Philosophy of History*,

Walter Benjamin criticizes the phenomenon of progress as ideological, that is, exploitation of the working class. He concludes his essay with the following words:

> We know that the Jews were prohibited from investigating the future. The Torah and the prayers instruct them in remembrance, however. This stripped the future of its magic, to which all those succumb who turn to the soothsayers for enlightenment. This does not imply, however, that for the Jews the future turned into homogeneous, empty time. For every second of time was the strait gate through which Messiah might enter. (Benjamin, 1968, p. 264)

Furthermore, is the eschatological view, that is, salvation which is implied in Benjamin's text, the only way to bypass the barrier of ideological perspective? To what extent is it not itself ideologically biased? Or, vice versa, to what extent is the scientific worldview not a secularized conception of salvation? In the following definition of progress given by Friedrich Schlegel (1772–1829), we see the origin of the scientific view of progress evolve out of the religious view. 'The revolutionary wish to realize the kingdom of God is the elastic point of progressive education and the beginning of modern history' (Schlegel, 1798, p. 60).[2] To what extent then is the scientific conception of progress different from the religious conception of the Old Testament as *praeparatio evangelica* (preparation of the Gospel)? As J. W. Burrow shows, science, that is, scientific progress, has been conceived as a new religion. 'But science was not only to provide the ground of social ethics; its practice and principles were themselves an ethic – the highest, prescribing duties and claiming undeviating allegiance, like a religious vocation' (Burrow, 2000, p. 53). Friedrich Nietzsche (1844–1900) did not see any difference between religion and the scientific idea of progress. They both equally represent the worst, namely, slave morality (*Skaleven-Moral*). Against that corrupted morality Nietzsche posits the master morality (*Herren-Moral*). The morality of the masters is characterized, inter alia, through reverence to the monumental in the past, and not through the expectation of the future. In *Beyond Good and Evil*, §260, Nietzsche writes:

> A profound reverence for age and origins – the whole notion of justice is based on this double reverence – a faith and a prejudice in favor of forefathers and against future generations is typical of the morality of the powerful. And

when, conversely, people with 'modern ideas' believe almost instinctively in 'progress' and 'the future', and show a decreasing respect for age, this gives sufficient evidence of the ignoble origin of these 'ideas'. (Nietzsche, 2002, p. 155)

Nietzsche's alternative to that idea of progress, which yields the rejection of history and tradition, is the eternal return of the same (*ewige Wiederkunft*). Given a limited mass of material and an infinite span of time, each combination will repeat itself to infinity. This view leads to the confirmation of the present, to *amor fati* (love of destiny).[3] I will now turn to three different readings of Descartes in which the idea of progress stands at the centre of the discussion.

Proudhon

Pierre-Joseph Proudhon (1809–1865) gave both Descartes's *cogito* and the common scientific conception of progress a twist in order to explicate and promote his philosophical anarchism. In his text *Philosophie du progrès, programme*, 1853 (*The Philosophy of Progress*), Proudhon contrasts progress with the absolute. In Proudhon's text, 'absolute' stands for any one-sided claim and theory. Progress is the process which demolishes all one-sidedness. Anything which lies one-sided outside dialectical progress is prejudice, according to him. Progress demolishes it and thus brings us freedom. Both terms, 'progress' and 'prejudice', undergo a substantial change, a metamorphosis, under Proudhon's hand. Prejudice can no longer refer only to what is not established or proved by means of scientific procedure. It rather refers to the dogmatic one-sidedness which should be destroyed by dialectical movement. Likewise, progress no longer stands for scientific progress, but rather for the global dialectical movement which starts within our conception of reality and extends to reality itself.

The notion of Progress, carried into all the spheres of consciousness and the understanding, become the base of practical and speculative reason, must renew the entire system of human knowledge, purge the mind of its last prejudices, replace the constitutions and catechisms in social relations, teach to man all that he can legitimately know, do, hope and fear: the value of his ideas, the definition of his rights, the rule of his actions, the purpose of his existence ... The theory of Progress is the railway of liberty. (Proudhon, 2009, pp. 7–8)

Anything which stands opposed to this dialectical movement is permeated with one-sided dogmatism, and any one-sidedness, which Proudhon dubs 'Absolute', should be demolished by progress. 'Everyone, blaspheming against Progress, is allied to the Absolute' (ibid., p. 11). Progress, according to him, is the most basic principle of the mind. 'Progress, in the purest sense of the word, which is the least empirical, is the movement of the idea, *processus*; it is innate, spontaneous and essential movement, uncontrollable and indestructible, which is to the mind what gravity is to matter' (ibid.).[4] Proudhon goes on to criticize the common utilitarian use of the term progress. Progress in the true sense of the word is the destruction of any immutable order.

> Progress, once more, is the affirmation of universal movement, consequently the negation of every immutable form and formula, of every doctrine of eternity, permanence, impeccability, etc., applied to any being whatever; it is the negation of every permanent order, even that of the universe, and of every subject or object, empirical or transcendental, which does not change. (Ibid., p. 12)

Progress, according to Proudhon, has the same evidential status as the *cogito*. It is, furthermore, the true sense of the *cogito*. Progress also serves, as the *cogito* does, to clear the view of all prejudices, by which Proudhon means one-sided statements within a static system: it sweeps away all one-sidedness by means of the dialectical movement. For Proudhon, however, it turns out that Descartes himself was captivated by one-sided metaphysical prejudices. This is the reason why Descartes looked for *aliquid inconcussum* (something firm) and was unable to see that the true meaning of the self is not a static substance, but rather *movement*, *becoming* which is the real meaning of *sum* (I am) in Latin, הָיָה (ha'ya, was) in Hebrew, and εἶναι (einai, to be) in ancient Greek, according to Proudhon. Thus, instead of *cogito ergo sum*, Descartes should have said '*Moveor, ergo fio*, I move, therefore I become!' (ibid., p. 13). 'Movement exists: this is my fundamental axiom. To say how I acquired the notion of movement would be to say how I think, how I am' (ibid., p. 17). Contrary to Descartes, Proudhon does not seek to found sciences, but rather to establish the right attitude towards all social, political, and religious orders.

So the notion of Progress is provided to us immediately and before all experience, not what one calls a criterion, but, as Bossuet says, a favorable prejudice, by means of which it is possible to distinguish, in practice, that which it may be useful to undertake and pursue, from that which may become dangerous and deadly, – an important thing for the government of the State and of commerce. (Ibid., p. 13)

It may seem that Proudhon would allow for some sort of government despite its being static order. But eventually he would more probably allow none:

Thus, whether you take for the dominant law of the Republic, either property, like the Romans, or communism, like Lycurgus, or centralization, like Richelieu, or universal suffrage, like Rousseau, – whatever principle you choose, since in your thought it takes precedence over all the others, – your system is erroneous. There is a fatal tendency to absorption, to purification, exclusion, stasis, leading to ruin. There is not a revolution in human history that could not be easily explained by this. (Ibid., p. 14)

From Descartes's *cogito* nothing remains in Proudhon's theory. The Cartesian philosophy is a dogmatic philosophy, subject to prejudices on immovable substance lying at the foundation of everything, which refuses to acknowledge progress, real dialectical progress. Thus, this philosophy fails to capture the meaning of the revolution.

Such is the situation that France finds itself in, not only since the revolution of February, but since that of 1789, a situation for which I blame, up to a certain point, the philosophers, the publicists, all those who, having a mission to instruct the people and form opinion, have not seen, or have not wanted to see, that the idea of Progress being from now on universally accepted, – having acquired rights from the bourgeoisie, not only in the schools, but even in the temples, – and raised finally to the category of reason, the old representations of things, natural as well as social, are corrupted, and that it is necessary to construct anew, by means of that new lamp of the understanding, science and the laws. (Ibid., p. 16)

Abstracted substance, the atom, does not exist according to Proudhon. 'I do not occupy myself with that *caput mortuum* [worthless residue] of beings, solid, liquid, gas or fluid, that the doctors pompously call SUBSTANCE; I do not even know, as much as I am inclined to suppose it, if there is something which responds to the word substance' (ibid., p. 24). Multitude of substances, of empty mathematical points, could not make up society. Only by means of progress we can explain the emergence of a group of people, of 'the superior individuality of the collective man' (ibid., pp. 24–5).

From Descartes's original philosophy nothing has remained in Proudhon's reading. Cartesian philosophy represents the social order which Proudhon strives to undermine. At the end of the day, it is not even clear why Proudhon chose to rely on Descartes's philosophy. It is never clear whether Proudhon is talking about progress as principle or rather of progress as empirical change or whether he confuses both. As a principle, it threatens to undermine itself, being itself static; as empirical change it does not suffice to serve as a first principle and thus to constitute a philosophical view. Likewise, it is not clear out of which perspective Proudhon looks at progress. He admits that he is an anarchist (ibid., p. 31). Does it imply that the destruction of all order is the perspective out of which he looks at progress? Or does he rather have a different social and political order in his mind? It seems that at this point also Proudhon is not clear. He writes:

> In order to pull society from the vicious circle where it has suffered death and passion for so many centuries, it is necessary, I insist, to enter resolutely on the path of progression and of association; to pursue the reduction of rent and interest to zero; to reform credit, by raising it from the entirely individualist notion of loan to the thoroughly social one of reciprocity or exchange; to liquidate, according to that principle, all public and private debts; to purge all mortgages, to unify taxation, to abolish octrois and duties, to create the patrimony of the people, to insure inexpensive products and rents, to determine the rights of the laborer, to remake corporate and communal administration, to reduce and simplify the allocations of the State. (Ibid., p. 33)

This passage seems to suggest that Proudhon has in mind a better society and political order to which progress should lead. So, eventually, he shares with the Enlightenment the idea of progress. He however has in mind a different end to which it should lead.

Sorel

Two books which appeared a few years before the First World War, *Les illusions du progrès* and *Réflexions sur la violence* (*The Illusion of Progress and*

Reflexions on Violence) by Georges Sorel (1847–1922), criticized the idea of progress as the most illustrious representative of the bourgeois worldview.[5] As John Stanley writes in the introduction to the English translation of *The Illusions of Progress*, Sorel's main target was European capitalism and parliamentary socialism, whose leading idea was progress. Sorel conceived progress as ideology (Sorel, 1969, p. xii). This is an ideology of modern times, and it did not exist in ancient times and the Middle Ages. As Johan Huizinga writes:

> In the Middle Ages, Christian faith had so strongly implanted in all minds the ideal of renunciation as the base of all personal and social perfection, that there was scarcely any room left for entering upon this path of material and political progress. The idea of a purposed and continual reform and improvement of society did not exist. Institutions in general are considered as good or as bad as they can be; having been ordained by God, they are intrinsically good, only the sins of men pervert them. What therefore is in need of remedy is the individual soul. (Huizinga, 1987, p. 36)

As Hannah Arendt explains:

> But to go back to the assumption of unlimited progress, the basic fallacy was early discovered. It is well known that not progress per se, but the notion of its limitlessness would have made modern science unacceptable to the ancients. It is less well known that the Greeks had some reason for their prejudice against the infinite. (Plato discovered that everything permitting of a comparative is by nature unlimited, and limitlessness was to him as to all Greeks the cause of all evils. Hence, his great confidence in number and measurement: it sets limits on what of itself (pleasure, for instance) 'does not and never will contain and derive from itself either beginning (ἀρχή) [arche] or middle or end (τέλος) [telos]'. (Arendt, 1978, p. 58)

As John Stanley writes:

> Optimism pervades modern progressivism, not only about the future but about all things human.... Modern progressivism is a different approach. The latter depicts history as a line – occasionally broken to be sure – destined to rise in an upward direction of indefinite perfectibility. This linear rather than cyclical concept of history is perhaps the most important single attribute of the contemporary view of progress. (Sorel, 1969, p. xviii)

For Sorel, progress is an ideology which has been created by the bourgeoisie. His purpose is to destroy that ideology which is the foundation of the dominating class. Thus, contrary to Proudhon, progress does not give birth to a new creation, but rather consolidates the position of the ruling class and the status quo. Progress promotes quietism, in his eyes. Why should we do something or act, if we are always promised a progress which will better our life? Instead of the *ideology* of progress, Sorel suggests *mythology*. Heroism and struggle, as we know them from Homer, will lead to action, according to him. For him, Descartes is the father of corrupt and static bourgeois ideology. Sorel writes:

> According to Brunetière, the idea of progress heavily depended on two important Cartesian theses related to knowledge: knowledge can never be separated from its application, and it is always increasing. It seems, indeed, that we ought immediately to infer limitless progress from such premises as these, but I think it is wrong to attribute to them the scientific scope that a modern writer could give them. In the seventeenth century, they originated from political ideology rather than true science, so that, in measuring their historical importance, we should start by observing the political phenomena. (Ibid., p. 13)

Sorel goes on to depict the politics that gave progress its prestigious place:

> From the time of Descartes, it was easily seen that the new model of governments, with their concentrated power and their regular administration, were in a position to execute their plans in a most precise way and that they could thus realize a union of theory and practice. Furthermore, the royal power seemed infinite. So many extraordinary changes since the Renaissance had taken place because of the will of the sovereign power, especially in religious matters, that nothing seemed beyond the power of the king. (Ibid.)

Descartes, according to Sorel, became the philosopher of the salons, for it is that philosophy which promises to provide the answer to everything. His physics does not leave room for any activity of the mind, Sorel claims. Likewise, nobility had very little respect for tradition and Cartesian philosophy demolished tradition:

> All Descartes did in formulating his famous rule of methodical doubt was to introduce aristocratic modes of thought to philosophy. Brunetière very

correctly notes that writers of noble origins have very little respect for traditions. It seems that this similarity of Cartesianism and the skepticism so dear to the hearts of men of quality was one of the major reasons for the success of the new philosophy. (Ibid., p. 19)

The Cartesian philosophy enabled the people of the salon to talk about any subject without any knowledge of it (ibid.). On close examination, we notice, Sorel claims, that Cartesianism reflects perfectly the mood at the salon:

Cartesianism was resolutely optimistic, a fact which greatly pleased a society desirous of amusing itself freely and irritated by the harshness of Jansenism. Furthermore, there is no Cartesian morality, for Descartes reduced ethics to a rule of propriety prescribing respect for the established usages; since morals had become quite lenient, this was very convenient. Descartes never seemed to have been preoccupied with the meaning of life. As a former student of the Jesuits, he must not have reflected very much on sin, and his disciples were able, like Renan, to suppress it. Sainte-Beuve said that Descartes relegated faith, 'like the gods of Epicurus, into some sort of intermediate realm of thought'. This suited those who hoped to be freed from the yoke of Christianity. (Ibid., p. 20)

Thus, as Sorel sums up, Descartes's physics may turn out to be wrong. Cartesianism, however, stands for the state of mind of the French aristocracy. Therefore, it will always maintain (ibid., p. 21). Cartesianism means progress which in turn only has political meaning, according to Sorel.

For our democrats, as well as for the sophisticated Cartesian intellects, progress consists neither in the accumulation of technical methods nor even of scientific knowledge. Progress is the adornment of the mind that, free of prejudice, sure of itself, and trusting in the future, has created a philosophy assuring the happiness of all *who* possess the means of living well. (Ibid., p. 22)

The idea of progress, he goes on to say, simply consolidates democracy on the foundations of the *ancien régime* (ibid., p. 25). Sorel understands that under Cartesianism the mood of the French aristocracy as well as the means of the wealthy people were to consolidate their status by subjugating the weak under the pretension of bringing progress. It seems, however, that Sorel does not by any means deny the idea of progress altogether, but rather the progress as we know it, namely, as the political means used by the strong to rule over the weak. Sorel suggests mythology as alternative to progress. For he thinks that mythology would succeed in driving people out of their apathy and mobilize them to combat the ruling elites. It means that, eventually, he also shares with the Enlightenment the idea of progress, but in his eyes it should lead to a different end, towards a better society.

Heidegger

With Heidegger, the question regarding progress gets a different meaning, since he looks at it from a completely different vantage point than the course of events in history as seen by Proudhon and Sorel. As it turned out, Proudhon and Sorel accepted the leading idea of progress, but they expected a different outcome than the one which resulted from the Enlightenment. In his text *Die Zeit des Weltbildes* (The *Age of the World Picture*), Heidegger rejects the idea of progress altogether. As he writes, 'If, then, we wish to grasp the essence of contemporary science we must first free ourselves of the habit of comparing modern with older science – from the perspective of progress – merely in terms of degree' (Heidegger, 2001, p. 58). Heidegger's alternative vantage point is eschatology. That is to say, progress as the essence of modern times is seen and discussed from the perspective of the destiny of Being. It demands courage (*Mut*) to transcend to this point of view and reflect (*Besinnung*) on the destiny of Being (Heidegger, 1977, p. 75). The content of that reflection is the history of Western philosophy or metaphysics as it is seen from that 'supra-temporal' perspective which, according to Heidegger, is the destiny of Being.[6]

> Reflection on the essence of modernity places thought and decision within the sphere of effectiveness belonging to the authentically essential forces of the age. These forces work, as they work, beyond the reach of everyday evaluation. With respect to such forces there is only preparedness for the resolution or else the evasive turning to the ahistorical. (Heidegger, 2001, p. 73)

The first question that comes to mind is what that history of Being or its destiny means? In other words, what is destined and determined by

it? Destined and determined, Heidegger replies, is the way in which we
conceive truth. He discusses two different conceptions of truth. The first is
correspondence between the mind and the object: *adaequatio intellectus et
rei*. This conception of truth did not start with Descartes. But since Descartes,
correspondence should be conceived clearly and distinctly. The emphasis here
is on the knowing subject. Its mind should be purged in order to achieve that
correspondence between the mind and reality. Descartes reaches it by means
of his methodological doubt. This truth is related to entities (*Seiende*) alone,
and never to Being. According to Heidegger, this way of thinking of truth
characterizes the entire Western philosophy with the exclusion of the pre-
Socratic thinkers. Descartes brought the application of this conception of truth
to its extreme in that he defines the human as *res cogitans* (thinking thing),
nature as *res extensa* (extended thing), whose essence can be captured only in
mathematical terms, and true perception as clear and distinct. According to
Heidegger, the inception of this conception of truth can already be discerned
in Plato and Aristotle. The second conception of truth is disclosure, ἀλήθεια
(*aletheia*, truth). The emphasis here is not on the subject, but rather on the
emergence of Being out of its oblivion. The conception of truth determines
our worldview and attitudes towards life, objects, other people, and history.
There are three different epochs in Heidegger's description of the history of
Being, three different conceptions of truth: ancient Greek, medieval, and
modern. The Middle Ages are only mentioned en passant, but never discussed
in detail (Heidegger, 1977, pp. 76, 81–2, 90). These epochs are discussed by
Heidegger from an eschatological point of view, from the perspective of the
destiny of Being, by which these different conceptions of truth are determined.
As Heidegger says, the task is to grasp, in advance, the essence of the age from
its concept of truth. Only thus can Being be experienced as destiny which
determines the human understanding of entities (Heidegger, 2001, p. 73).

Modern times are characterized by conceiving truth as correspondence
between the mind and the object. This perception should be clear and distinct,
that is, formulated mathematically. It began with Descartes. As Heidegger says:

> Modern knowledge (*neuzeitliches Wissen*) of nature, especially the
> technological ruling over – and making use of nature, is essentially implied
> by the mathematical way of thinking. We owe the French thinker Descartes

the decisive start of the foundation and outlining of the mathematical knowledge in a fundamental sense.[7] (Heidegger, 1983, p. 19)

Descartes did not choose this role; it is rather the destiny of Being, the destiny of Western modern science and society, which allotted him that role. Although history is fatally determined, which means that there is no room for free choice, Heidegger's discussion of modern philosophy turns out to be a sharp critique, sometimes a caricature, of modern Western science and society.

Heidegger begins his discussion about the notion of truth in modern times by specifying its main characteristics. According to him, there are five main characteristics of modern times. The first characteristic is its science and the second characteristic is technology that makes use of machines (*Machinentechnik*). This kind of technology is the most obvious outgrowth of Western technology which Heidegger traces back to modern metaphysics, that is, the modern conception of truth (Heidegger, 1977, p. 75). The third characteristic is aesthetics as the means to approach the work of art as an object. The fourth is culture as the way to realize the highest value of the human being. The fifth is the loss of gods (*Entgötterung*). This does not imply atheism, according to him. It is rather a Christianized worldview in which the first cause of everything is conceived as independent and absolute. On the other hand, Christianity becomes *Weltanschauung* and thus adapts itself to modern times. The human being, now conceived as *res cogitans*, stands at the foundation of all these characteristics: he is the measure and yardstick of clear and distinct perception and consequently of developing modern science and technology. Likewise, the perception of artwork as object goes back to the ego as substance, as *res cogitans* (thinking substance). Culture is the means to cultivate that thinking substance. Finally, the centrality of the subject now occupies the place of God.

Heidegger does not directly tackle the question regarding the conception of truth in modern times, but rather continues to the description of the characteristics of modern science. By 'science' he refers first of all to natural sciences (*Naturwissenschaften*) as also to humanities (*Geisteswissenschaften*) and especially to history.

The essence of modern science, Heidegger claims, is research (*Forschung*). This research follows the scheme or projection (*Entwurf*) which determines in advance the only legitimate way in which things can be conceived in any research. This projection, this projected blueprint, is of mathematics as the only legitimate way to describe the results of the experiments. Wilhelm Dilthey (1833–1911), who anticipated Husserl's phenomenological account of modern science and Heidegger's analysis of it in many respects, describes this projection of mathematical meanings which enables in turn the development of modern science:

> Since Galileo, the conception of natural science was bound with the recognition of its method. In accordance with the mathematical natural science, the subordination of experiences in observation and experiment under simple mathematical law in some kind of combination of these two factors became the principle of the method. As this procedure has been applied to the recognition of the universe, a philosophical method of the construction of the given phenomena then emerged through logical, mathematical, and metaphysical terms and propositions, which bear their evidence in themselves.[8] (Dilthey, 1921, p. 453)

Everything should now be conceived and formulated in exact mathematical terms. This is what gives modern science its accuracy and precision and distinguishes it from the medieval *doctrina* (doctrine) and *scientia* (knowledge) as well as from the ancient ἐπιστήμη (episteme, understanding), which did not have the ideal of mathematical perfection, as Heidegger claims (Heidegger, 1977, p. 76). As he writes concerning modern physics, in this worldview all kinds of motion are equal and every point in time is the same. This is the perspective from which every event is seen (Heidegger, 2001, p. 60).

Thus, all the events in nature which are perceived (*in Vorstellung kommen sollen*) are determined in advance as a quantity of spatio-temporal motion (*Bewegungsgröße*) (Heidegger, 1977, p. 79). Research is the first characteristic of modern science, and it becomes what it is through the projection (*Entwurf*) and rigorousness (*Strenge*) of the scientific method (*Verfahren*). Method is the second essential characteristic of modern science. By means of method, rules and laws are applied to the diverse and changing things and thus they are perceived objectively. Carrying out experiments is what characterizes modern science and distinguishes it from ancient and medieval observation (*Beobachtung*). It is however not experiment which makes modern science what it is. On the contrary, experiment is possible only after rules and laws have been projected (ibid., p. 81). The same holds true for humanities in modern times, as Heidegger claims (ibid., pp. 82–3).

Each branch of knowledge is founded on the projection of a specific kind of object (physical, biological, chemical, etc.). Thus, modern science is characterized by specialization which enables progress in research in a specific branch of science. This modern science is characterized by constant activity within an institution (*Betrieb*) (ibid., p. 83). Hence, according to Heidegger, science must become institutionalized in order to be recognized (ibid., p. 63).

That constant activity (*Betreiben*) is characterized by a lack of reflection (*Besinnung*) on the origin of its meaning (Heidegger, 1977, pp. 96–7). This emergence of specification makes one type of man – the scholar – disappear. At the same time, it gives birth to another type of man, the researcher, who wanders from one conference to another to present his papers.[9] This is a caricature which Heidegger makes of contemporary academic life, which in modern times evolved out of the conception of truth and the development of science. In the appendix of The Age of the World Picture, he continues to mock modern science in its relation to mass consumption and popular culture.

> The growing importance of the publishing business is not merely based on the fact that the publishers (through, for example, the book trade) have a better eye for the needs of the public, or that they understand business better than do authors. Rather, their distinctive work takes the form of a process of planning and organizing aimed, through the planned and limited publication of books and periodicals, at bringing the world into the picture the public has of it and securing it there. The predominance of collected works, sets of books, journal series, and pocket editions is already the result of this work on the part of the publishers. This work coincides, in turn, with the aims of researchers, since these not only become more easily and rapidly known and respected through series and collections, but also, along a wider front, immediately achieve their intended effect. (Heidegger, 2001, p. 74)

Projection, rigorousness, method, and organization make up the essence of research. Research as the way of knowledge in modern times reckons (*zieht zur Rechenschaft*) to what extent a given entity (*Seiendes*) is accessible to representation (*Vorstellen*). In natural science, research calculates the entity by means of prediction (*vorausberechnen*). In humanities, in history, research calculates the entity by means of accounting (*nachrechnen*) of what happened in the past. With his intentional repetition of verbs and nouns, which are related to calculation through their root, Heidegger wants to convey the idea that in modern times, only perception in terms of mathematics, of calculation, is valid.[10] It is no longer the presence of Being (*das Anwesende*) that sways, but rather grasping (*Begreifen*), which Heidegger equates with seizure (*Ergreifen*) and attack (*Angriff*) (Heidegger, 1977, p. 108). He explains that in the prediction of nature (*Vorausberechnung*) and the retrodiction (*Nachberechnung*) of history, nature and history are seen in the same way. They are both an object of representation, since only what can be represented really exists (Heidegger, 2001, pp. 65–6).

Research as the way of gaining knowledge in modern times reifies (*vergegenständlichen*) the entities in that it posits them in front of man, so that he can calculate them and then use and exploit them. Thus, Heidegger hyphenates the verb 'to represent' (*vor-stellen*), which now means, in its new form, setting or positing in front. In his lectures on Nietzsche, he writes, 'Descartes uses at an important point the verb *percipere* (*per-capio*) – to take possession of something, to seize something, and, in fact, at this point, in the sense of setting-for-oneself (*Sich-zu-Stellen*), of representing to oneself' (Heidegger, 1961, p. 151).[11]

This new conception of entity and the mathematical access to it as the only valid one was born with Descartes, according to Heidegger, and it determined the way in which Being as a whole, truth and human being, have been conceived since then in Western philosophy and thought (Heidegger, 1977, p. 87). Human being became a *subject* (ibid., p. 88). This implies, as he says, that when man becomes the primary *subjectum*, he becomes the sole standard of Being and truth. This view became possible following a transformation in the understanding of Being as a whole (Heidegger, 2001, pp. 66–7).

The outcome of this transformation in the conception of 'Being as a whole' Heidegger calls 'world-picture' (*Weltbild*). It means that the world is now conceived as a picture or image, as a reflection. Something exists only insofar as it is conceived from the human perspective of representing-producing (*Vorstellend-herstellend*) (Heidegger, 2001, pp. 67–8).

In other words, something exists as long as it can be represented by the subject. The reality of something consists in its being represented. Man becomes a representing subject and as such the centre of the cosmos. The world becomes a represented or perceived object. It is a correspondence between the representing subject and the represented object which should be conceived clearly and distinctly. From this point, Heidegger continues to criticize modern Western civilization and society. The conception of man as subject leads to the following questions: whether man is an isolated 'I' (*ich*) or collective 'us' (*wir*) of the society; whether man is conceived as a personality in the community or rather a group member in the corporation; whether man is conceived as a representative of the state, people, and nation or rather of humanity in general. It leads likewise to the battle against individualism for the sake of the community (Heidegger, 1977, pp. 92–3). This conception of man as subject – which Heidegger traces back to Descartes – and the world as an object gives birth to anthropology and to humanism as ways to define and study man (ibid., p. 99). Anthropology presupposes a firm definition of man. Therefore, it can never ask who this man is and how his existence should be understood. Raising that question would destroy anthropology, Heidegger claims. This conception of man brings forth what he calls *Weltanschauung*. He explains the fundamental event of modernity as the victory of the notion of world as a picture. From now on, 'picture' means the collective image of the representing production (Heidegger, 2001, p. 71).

As it turns out, representation becomes the essence of existence. That is, something exists only if it can be represented, set in front of the human perception (*vor-gestellt*), clearly and distinctively, and described in mathematical terms. This is the foundation of modern technology and production which becomes the only way to look at and relate to Being. Things now exist only to the extent that they can be part of the technological process of production. Heidegger writes:

> For the sake of this battle of worldviews, and according to its meaning, humanity sets in motion, with respect to everything, the unlimited process of calculation, planning, and breeding. Science as research is the indispensable form taken by this self-establishment in the world; it is one of the pathways along which, with a speed unrecognized by those who are involved, modernity races towards the fulfillment of its essence. With this

battle of worldviews modernity first enters the decisive period of its history, and probably the one most capable of enduring. (Ibid.)

This change is mainly seen in the prevalence of the gigantic (*Riesenhaft, das Riesige*) in all realms of life and the attempt to make it small, to overcome, and bring it closer to us by means of technology, as for example, the attempt to overcome gigantic distances by means of airplanes, satellites, and radio waves. Representation is the essence of Being in modern times, according to Heidegger. It evolved out of the conception of truth as correspondence. This is the key to understanding the emergence of modern technology and progress. In ancient Greece, on the contrary, truth was understood differently. It was conceived as non-concealment (*Unverborgenheit*), whereas its opposite was conceived as concealment (*Verborgenheit*) (Heidegger, 1977, p. 105).

> One of the oldest expressions of Greek thinking about the being of beings reads: 'τὸ γὰρ αὐτὸ νοεῖν ἐστίν τε καὶ εἶναι' [*to gar auto noein estin te kai einai*, for the same thing can be thought and exist]. This statement of Parmenides means: the apprehension of beings belongs to being since it is from being that it is demanded and determined. The being is that which rises up and opens itself; that which, as what is present, comes upon man, i.e., upon him who opens himself to what is present in that he apprehends it. The being does not acquire being in that man first looks upon it in the sense of representation that has the character of subjective perception. Rather, man is the one who is looked upon by beings, the one who is gathered by self-opening beings into presencing with them. To be looked at by beings, to be included and maintained and so supported by their openness, to be driven about by their conflict and marked by their dividedness that is the essence of humanity in the great age of Greece. In order to fulfill his essence, therefore, man has to gather ('λέγειν') [*legein*] and save ('σῴζειν') [*sozein*], catch up and preserve, the self-opening in its openness; and he must remain exposed to all of its divisive confusion. Greek humanity is the receiver (*Vernehmer*) of beings, which is the reason that, in the age of the Greeks, the world can never become picture. (Heidegger, 2001, pp. 68–9)

In other words, in ancient Greece, human being was not conceived as a subject, as an ego, which was supposed to correctly represent things. Thus, technological progress could not be achieved at that time. Later, Heidegger compares Descartes's ego with Protagoras's ἐγώ (ego, I). Both refer to man.

In Protagoras, man dwells (*verweilt*) within the vicinity of disclosed entities. He explores or hearkens to them (*vernimmt*). This exploration is grounded in *dwelling* or *lingering* (*Verweilen*), which means that man does not rush to anywhere. Man's main concern is not progress, as in Descartes, but rather Being in its revelation (*Unverborgenheit*) (Heidegger, 1977, p. 104).[12] Heidegger however reserves his assessment of ancient Greece and says that Plato's εἶδος (eidos, image) can be seen as anticipating the conception of man and truth in modern times (ibid., p. 91). He equates Descartes's metaphysics with Platonic-Aristotelian metaphysics and argues against them that they all were focused on entities (instead of on Being) (ibid., pp. 98–9).

The various conceptions of truth are determined by the destiny of Being. We have not chosen them. They rather forced themselves upon us. We cannot change that fate. We can only make ourselves free by means of posing questions and by special reflection (*Besinnung*) in which this fate is seen only as one of many other possibilities, Heidegger says (ibid., p. 111). His description of the modern era very often turns out to be a critique of modern society and culture.

> Man has become the *subiectum*. He can, therefore, determine and realize the essence of subjectivity – always according to how he conceives and wills himself. Man as the rational being of the Enlightenment is no less subject than man who grasps himself as nation, wills himself as people (*Volk*), nurtures himself as race and, finally, empowers himself as lord of the earth. Now in all these fundamental positions of subjectivism, too, different kinds of I-ness and egoism are possible; for man is always defined as I and thou, we and you. Subjective egoism for which – usually without knowing it – the I is pre-determined as subject can be beaten down through the insertion of the I into the we. Through this, subjectivity only gains in power. In the planetary imperialism of technically organized man the subjectivism of man reaches its highest point from which it will descend to the flatness of organized uniformity and there establish itself. This uniformity becomes the surest instrument of the total, i.e., technological, dominion over the earth. (Heidegger, 2001, p. 84)

The many allusions to Descartes, in whom Heidegger discerns the major culprit in the development of that decadence, and the centrality of the ego in his philosophy are obvious. Heidegger concludes by contending that the truth of Being will be conceived once man ceases to see himself as a representing subject which is focused on entities as represented objects.[13]

***

Cogito ergo sum is associated with Descartes's philosophy no less than the idea of progress: the procedure of casting everything in doubt until one reaches rock bottom, *fundamentum inconcussum,* the Archimedean point, upon which everything should be built anew from scratch. Franz Xaver von Baader discerns in Descartes's *cogito*, in the Cartesian egocentrism, the source of all maladies plaguing modern civilization: secularization, tyrannical regimes, exploitation of the working class, and alienation. As an alternative to the *cogito ergo sum*, Baader suggests *cogitor ergo sum*: 'I am thought (by God), thus I exist.' Hence, he calls for a return to God and Christian faith, to the centre of human life, as a solution for the maladies of European civilization. Chapter 2 deals with Franz Baader, who was an extremely influential figure in his time but is nowadays almost entirely forgotten.

Notes

1 On Rousseau and the Enlightenment, see Graeme (2006, pp. 16–35).
2 'Der revolutionäre Wunsch, das Reich Gottes zu realisieren, ist der elastische Punkt der progressiven Bildung und der Anfang der modernen Geschichte.' See Löwith (1964).
3 See Nietzsche (2017, p. 63). On that topic see above all Löwith (1957).
4 On p. 38 Proudhon writes, 'What can the theory be which, after having posited Progress as the condition *sine qua non* of nature and mind, is forced to admit that it finds for that Progress neither term nor object, and which would contradict itself if it admitted either?'
5 See Löwith (1964, p. 20). On Descartes and Sorel, see Sternhell, Sznajder, and Asheri (1995, pp. 71–8).
6 'Supratemporal' is set in inverted commas, because Heidegger's point of view is eschatological. Thus, it is neither 'temporal' nor 'not-temporal'.
7 'Das neuzeitliche Wissen von der Natur, zumal die technische Beherrschung und Nutzung derselben, ist wesentlich mitgetragen durch die mathematische Denkweise. Der entscheidende Beginn der Begründung und Vorzeichnung des

im grundsätzlichen Sinne mathematischen Wissens wird dem französischen Denker Descartes verdankt.'

8 'Von Galilei ab war mit dem naturwissenschaftlichen Denken das Bewußtsein über dessen Methoden verbunden, und der mathematischen Naturwissenschaft entsprechend wurde die Unterordnung der Erfahrungen in Beobachtung und Experiment unter einfache Verhältnisse mathematischer Gesetlichkeit in irgendeiner Art von Zusammensetzung dieser beiden Faktoren zum Prinzip der Methode. Indem nun dies Verfahren auf die Erkenntnis des Universums angewandt wurde, entstand die philosophische Methode der Konstruktion der gegebenen Erscheinungen durch logische, mathematische und metaphysische Begriffe und Sätze, welche ihre Evidenz in sich selber tragen.'

9 Compare the following: 'Da die Wissenschaften zunehmend und, wie es scheinen will, unaufhaltsam einer "Technisierung" und "Organisation" zustreben müssen (vgl. zum Beispiel die Art und Rolle der internationalen Kongresse), um ihren seit langem festgelegten Weg bis zu seinem Ende zu gehen, und da andrerseits die "Wissenschaften" dem öffentlichen Anschein nach zuerst und allein das "Wissen" besitzen und darstellen, vollzieht sich gerade in den Wissenschaften und durch sie die schärfste Entfremdung gegenüber der Philosophie und zugleich der vermeintlich überzeugende Nachweis ihrer Entbehrlichkeit' (Heidegger, 1983, p. 18).

10 Rechenschaft = accountability, reckoning; vorausberechnen = to predict, literally: to calculate in advance; nachrechnen = to recalculate. See Heidegger (1977, pp. 86–7).

11 'Descartes gebraucht an wichtigen Stellen für cogitare das Wort percipere (per-capio) – etwas in Besitz nehmen, einer Sache sich bemächtigen, und zwar hier im Sinne des Sich-zu-Stellens von der Art des Vor-sich-stellens.'

12 Compare: 'Jeder Subjektivismus ist in der griechischen Sophistik unmöglich, weil hier der Mensch nie Subjectum sein kann; er kann dies nicht werden, weil das Sein hier Anwesen und die Wahrheit Unverborgenheit ist' (Heidegger, 1977, p. 106).

13 'Es ist das Sein selbst, dessen Wahrheit der Mensch dann übereignet wird, wenn er sich als Subjekt überwunden hat, und d. h., wenn er das Seiende nicht mehr als Objekt vorstellt' (Heidegger, 1977, p. 113).

2

Franz Baader: *Cogitor ergo sum*

In his reading of Descartes, the German philosopher Franz Xaver von Baader says that instead of *cogito ergo sum* we should say *cogitor (a deo), ergo sum*. The first person form in *active* mode (*cogito* = I think) is replaced with the first person in the *passive* form (*cogitor* = I am thought). 'I am thought – *by God* (*a deo*)', Baader adds – 'therefore I exist'. The transition from *cogito* to *cogitor* can be seen as a necessary transition entailed logically by the *cogito* itself, as we shall see later on. Yet, Baader is not interested in logical necessity. For him, it is rather a socially, religiously, and politically crucial matter: Descartes's *cogito* represents a world with no God, which is centred upon the human subject, whereas Baader's *cogitor* represents a world whose centre is God. Thus, logic will not give us the key to understand Baader's statement. We should rather become acquainted with the religious, social, and political agenda, which Baader promotes by means of his attack on Descartes. Likewise, we will have to discuss his attitude towards nihilism, the church, and the proletariat to get the full picture. In a letter, composed close to the time of his death, Baader wrote, 'It is my mission to put an end to Cartesianism in philosophy' (cited in Geldhof, 2005, p. 249).

From the introduction by Gerd-Klaus Kaltenbrunner to Baader's *Sätze aus der erotischen Philosophie* (Propositions from the Erotic Philosophy) we glean the following general statements about Baader: He was born on 27 March 1765 and died on 23 May 1845 in Munich. He was a philosopher, a physician, an expert on mining construction, an alchemist, an inventor, an industrialist, a social politician, a pioneer of the reunification of the Christian confessions, a forerunner of the idea of a Russian imperium stemming out of the Christian world responsibility, a mediator between the German, Baltic, and Slavic spiritual worlds, a prophet of the 'holy alliance' between the proletariat and the priesthood, and an interpreter and continuator of the thought of Meister Eckhart, Tauler, and Saint-Martin. Among Baader's admirers, we encounter Goethe, Novalis, Schelling, Alexander von Humboldt, Hegel, Lenau, Kierkegaard, Hermann Hesse, and Ernst Jünger. Leo Löwenthal, a member of the Frankfurt School, wrote his doctoral dissertation on Baader. According to Löwenthal, Baader is the only outstanding opponent of Karl Marx. He influenced Russian philosophy from Solovyov to Berdyaev. He promoted ecosophy (*Ökosophie*) with the goal of integrating man with the cosmos and developed a visionary metaphysics of sexuality (*Geschlechtigkeit*) on an androgynous basis (Kaltenbrunner, 1991).

Baader's writings are complicated and demanding. As Friedrich Schlegel, Ludwig Tieck, and other contemporaries noted, 'In personal conversation, it is easy to understand Baader. However, his writings are fraught with difficulties (*dornig*)' (ibid., p. 16).

Baader is a conservative thinker, yet he is not the muse of the restoration of absolute feudalism or a forerunner of the Nazi movement (ibid., p. 36). In 1792, he began a stint of four years in England. Fifty years before Friedrich Engels, he had been exposed to the misery of the proletariat in England as well as to early movement of socialism (ibid., pp. 39–40). Long before Marx and Engels, he talked about the problem of the proletariat. As Johannes Sauter (1891–1945), the German philosopher of law, said, 'In his economy, Marx has taken the material from Baader; in his social science, he has taken the form from Hegel; in both cases, he is lacking the spirit' (quoted in Löwenthal, 1923, p. 51).[1]

The solution to the misery of the proletariat is seen by Baader in what he calls 'theodemocracy' (*Theodemokratie*). He demands that we treat one another 'royally and not slavishly, and nobody should strive to rule over others, but rather to seek to act above all through love, like God, towards others' (cited in Kaltenbrunner, 1991, p. 43).[2] As he points out, all members of the social organism, the king included, owe their existence to the grace of God (ibid.). He is concerned by the disappearance of God and religion from the centre of human existence as other conservative thinkers. Joseph de Maistre, a contemporary conservative thinker whom Baader admired, demands a restoration of ecclesial dominance as the only conceivable antidote to the chaotic state brought about by the French Revolution. He writes:

The French revolution is not like anything that was ever witnessed in the world in bygone times. It is essentially satanical. Never will it be wholly extinguished except by the contrary principle, and never will the French people resume their place until they have acknowledged this truth. The priesthood ought to be the principal object of the sovereign's care. (Maistre, 1850, p. xxiii)

Thus, de Maistre concludes, 'If there be anything evident to reason as well as to faith, it is, that the universal Church is a monarchy' (ibid., p. 2). On the contrary, Baader does not want a church monarchy. He rather demands a 'world corporation', a 'world community', and a 'world guild' (Baader, 1991, p. 47). Back to the socio-economical problem, as care provider for the proletarians, he wants to see 'neither police officers nor officials at all nor advocates in the narrow sense, but rather priests who should provide not only pastoral care (*Seelsorge*) but also socio-political physical care (*Leibsorge*)' (ibid., p. 49).[3]

Questions regarding religion and church were by no means secondary in nineteenth-century Western Europe. As historian Jürgen Osterhammel contends, religion should occupy the centre stage of nineteenth century history. The historian Olaf Blaschke argues that we should think of the nineteenth century as a second confessional era (Howard, 2017). Baader was one of those first Christian outsiders in the nineteenth and early twentieth centuries who were anti-clerical. His arguments against Rome were later revived by people of the Old Catholic Church such as Ignaz von Döllinger (Kaltenbrunner, 1991, p. 53).[4]

Locating the ego at the centre of reality and letting God vanish or move to the periphery leads to nihilism, according to Baader. Dieter Arendt shows that the term 'nihilism' occurred for the first time in the writings of Friedrich Heinrich Jacobi, in his letter to Fichte.[5] According to Jacobi, in order to get rid of the mysterious, sensual *Ding-an-sich*, the empirical residue in rational philosophy, Fichte traced everything back to the ego, to the human reason. The ego, the human reason, has become the sole source of reality. Thus, Jacobi concludes, 'everything except [reason] has transformed into nothing and only it [reason] remains' (cited in Arendt, 1970, p. 41).[6] The foundation of his claim, Arendt argues, is a Christian religious one; nothing exists but human reason (ibid., pp. 63–4). Kierkegaard, in his dissertation, describes the progress which leads into nihilism: 'The more the I is sunk in contemplation of the I in criticism, the thinner and dryer I became, until finally the I became a ghost, equally immortal as the aurora man' (ibid., p. 67).[7] Prior to Kierkegaard, Baader was the first who openly attacked nihilism from a conservative-catholic standpoint (ibid., pp. 63–4). Baader identifies the danger of nihilism in the detachment of reason from the objective forms of religion. Giving up the regulative role of faith, free perception and science have become, according to him, a 'destructive and annihilating neology'. The collapse of faith yielded, according to him, a 'destructive, scientific nihilism' and a 'non-scientific, separatist pietism' or 'obscurantism' (ibid., p. 64). In that break between science and religion, he identifies the problem of his time which he wants to solve (ibid., pp. 64–5). The solution, Arendt claims, is to be found in a synthesis between emancipated subjectivity and respected objectivity or between individualism and traditionalism. Contrary to Descartes's start *a primis fundamentis* (from first foundations) (Descartes, 2013, p. 17) and Kant's call *sapere aude*, 'have the courage to use your own mind!' (Kant, 1850, p. 3),[8] Baader writes that the problem of our time is 'to secure the term Authority in ecclesial, political, and scientific respect against the older and new skepticism or protest' (Baader, 1970b, pp. 269–70).[9]

Thus, similar to Jacobi and Kierkegaard, Baader sees nihilism as the product of the human subject's hubris as it is embodied in Cartesian philosophy. Johann Kaspar Schmidt (1806–1856), better known as Max Stirner, in his work *Der Einzige und sein Eigentum* (*The Ego and Its Own*), gives this hubris perhaps the most extreme expression as he turns everything into a property of man: 'Thoughts had incarnated, became ghosts as God, Kaiser, Pope, Fatherland, etc.' (cited in Arendt, 1970, p. 72).[10] In the following passage, Stirner sums up his general attitude towards Fichte:

> When Fichte says: 'The I is everything', this seems to completely harmonize with my statements. Yet, not the I *is* everything, but rather the I *destroys* everything and only the I who eliminates himself, the never existing I, the *final* I, is a real I. Fichte talks about the absolute I. I, on the contrary, speak about myself, the transitory I.[11] (Ibid., italics in original)

As we shall presently see, Baader is not the only one who rejects the Cartesian *cogito* which in turn should be replaced by *cogitor*. He writes:

If man is a thought of God (by no means the thought of God himself), if namely man is thought by God and he could not exist without being thought by God (*dieses von Gott Gedachtwerden*), then he can be certain of his existence only as long as he knows that he is thought by God. Therefore, the *Cogito ergo sum* [I think, therefore I exist] does not suffice, but rather only *Cogitor (a deo) ergo sum* [I am thought (by God), therefore I exist].[12] (Baader, 1860, p. 238)

In his critique of Descartes's *cogito*, Immanuel Kant emphasizes the *first person* element in the *cogito* to show that it is no syllogism, no inference of empirical proposition from a major premise, that is to say, of existence from essence. Kant writes:

The 'I think' is, as already said, an empirical proposition and contains within itself the proposition 'I exist'. But I cannot say: everything that thinks exists. For then the attribute of thinking would turn all essences, which the thought possesses, to necessary essences. Therefore, my existence cannot also be seen as inferred from the proposition 'I think', as Cartesius claimed. If it could, then the major premise, i.e. 'everything that thinks exists', must have preceded it. On the contrary, my existence is identical with thinking.[13] (Kant, 1889, p. 342)

The validity of the proposition 'I think therefore I exist' is necessarily bound up with the *first person* form in active mode. It is important to dwell at this point before turning back to Baader. Bernard Williams notes that the peculiarity of the proposition 'I think, therefore I exist' consists in its being self-verifying and incorrigible. Williams writes:

The unspecific proposition 'I am thinking' is, like 'I exist', self-verifying, and its incorrigibility can be traced to that; but 'I am uncertain whether God exists' or 'it seems to me as though I can see a red patch' are not self-verifying, and if they are incorrigible (as Descartes believes) then it is for a quite different sort of reason. One thing that helps to bring out the difference between this kind of proposition and a self-verifying one, is that these can be used to tell a lie. 'It all looks fuzzy', 'I feel cheerful', 'I believe what you say', can all in various ways be used to deceive, but 'I exist', and the others, for obvious reasons, cannot. The difference does not of course suggest that the evident kind of proposition is less certain than the self-verifying one, but it illustrates how the basis of its certainty is something different. (Williams, 2005, p. 65)

The first person form in an active mode is a *conditio sine qua non* for this proposition to be self-verifying and incorrigible. As Williams puts it, 'If there were someone else to comment on Descartes's state of mind, they would refer to the same state in the third person as Descartes refers to it in the first person, but their statements would not possess his certainty' (ibid., pp. 65–6).

Following this, by replacing the *cogito*, 'I think', with *cogitor*, 'I am thought', Baader gives up the most important component in Descartes's proposition that makes it work, that is to say, the first person form in active mode. *Cogitor* means that my self-certainty is achieved through reference to something else; I exist because I am thought by somebody else or by God as in Baader's text. Baader writes:

> In truth, the inquiring mind does not come to rest until it gets to the perception of the perceiving, i.e. of its being perceived, or, as Plato says, until its eye encounters an eye that sees its seeing. Therefore we argue that one of the basic principles of man is that in perceiving and knowing he knows himself in something that perceives and knows him, as willing in something that wills him and as acting in something that enacts him.[14] (Baader, 1855a, p. 339)

This passage is complicated and it refers to mystical experience: humans know themselves in God or in so far as they are reflected in God, and God is reflected in them in a unification which is achieved (in Christ). In a beautiful passage, Baader describes that mutual relationship between me and God:

> When the beloved gives herself to me, I become indebted (*ihr schuldig*) to her, and when I give myself to her (being faithful to her), she becomes indebted to me. Likewise, God cannot give Himself to me, if I do not give myself to Him, submit myself, rely on or have faith in Him. He can however not abandon me, if I, having faith in Him, give myself to Him, and He hereby becomes equally indebted to me.[15] (Baader, 1831, p. 11)

Baader is not the only one who holds that the *cogito* is inconsequential and thus must become *cogitor*. The most obvious reason for the shift from *cogito* to *cogitor*, from the first person form in active mode to the first person in passive mode, is that the *cogito* is a product of reflection: once I reflect, there emerges a split between the reflection and its object. That is, in reflection, thinking becomes a thinking thing (*res cogitans*) which is not identical with the reflecting act or the reflecting person. Thus, the Austrian philosopher Alois Riehl (1844–1921) concludes his discussion of Descartes with the following revision of the *cogito*-proposition: '*cogito, ergo sum et est*', that is, 'I think, therefore I am and it is'. Similarly, Arthur Schopenhauer says: '*cogito, ergo est*', that is, 'I think, therefore it is' (cited in Funke, 1960, pp. 169–70). Nietzsche makes the following observation regarding the *cogito*:

> 'It is thought; therefore there should be thinking'; Cartesius' argument boils down to this. This means to presuppose as 'a priori true' our belief in the notion of substance: – as long as something is thought, something 'that thinks' must exist – this is simply a formulation of our grammatical habit which ascribes agent to act, in short, a logical-metaphysical postulate is already being made here – and not only perceived.[16] (Cited in Funke, 1960, p. 171)

Yet, these readings of Descartes are different in their essence from Baader. For him, *cogitor* refers to the dependency of human finitude on God's infinitude. It is first of all a religious, social, and political matter. Disregarding this dependency leads to hubris, as we saw. Finite being is always dependent and thus cannot really become an independent *fundamentum inconcussum* (firm foundation). In Schelling's reading of Descartes, human dependency also leads to God. Schelling writes:

> The *sum* which is included in the *cogito* means only *sum qua cogitans* [I am as thinking], I exist as thinking, that is, *in this given way* of existence which is called thinking, and it is only a different kind of existence than, for example, that of the body whose kind of existence is to occupy space ... The *sum* which is included in the *cogito* does not, therefore, have the meaning of an independently existing I, but only the meaning of 'I exist *in a certain way*', that is, to exist as thinking, in this way which one calls thinking. Therefore, the *ergo sum* cannot imply an existing I in an independent way, but only I exist in some way.[17] (Schelling, 1861, p. 10, italics in original)

The 'I think' turns out to exist only to some extent, that is, as long as it thinks, according to Schelling. Thus, it cannot imply independency and cannot provide complete certainty. He then goes on to say that the 'I think' is a product of reflection on thinking that takes place in me. It means that this reflection is independent of thought. Hence, I may be wrong regarding thinking as I may be wrong regarding any other objects. Put differently, as much as I cannot say with certainty regarding 'my' body that it is *mine*, I cannot say regarding 'my' thinking that it is *mine* (ibid., pp. 11–12). Hence, 'I think' is also subject to doubt (ibid., p. 23). That is, the 'I think' cannot stand for itself, independently, but always refers to something else, otherwise, it could never be understood. This leads eventually to God, according to Schelling. Return to God, however, should not be the only possible implication, as we can see in Feuerbach's reading of Descartes.

Feuerbach explains that the path to the *cogito*, to the mind as pure spirit, is the doubt, *dubitatio*, of anything which Descartes has held so far to be true and valid. The pure mind is reached by means of casting everything in doubt. In this procedure of casting everything in doubt the mind separates itself from anything which is foreign to it, *res aliena* (foreign thing), and thus achieves itself as a pure *res cogitans* (Feuerbach, 1906, pp. 202–3). He claims that in order to appeal to popular opinion Descartes says that doubt is only a means to achieve pure mind, and doubt can be disposed of once we have reached our purpose (ibid., p. 203). But the truth, he says, is rather the opposite. 'The highest principle of philosophy is the existence of our mind – and what is this thinking other than doubt?' (ibid., p. 204).[18] In other words, casting doubt is the procedure by means of which the mind separates itself from anything which does not essentially belong to it and thus becomes pure. He sums up and says that the mind is not an immaterial thinking substance because 'immateriality' is appended to it as a general predicate. On the contrary, the mind is immaterial because it doubts (ibid., p. 207).[19]

Feuerbach refers to the Cartesian Louis de la Forge of the seventeenth century who says, '[Descartes] does not say with the scholastic (with scholastic philosophy) that [immateriality] makes up the mind, namely, that it is mind only because it is not extended; he says, on the contrary, that it is immaterial because it is mind, that is, a thinking substance.' Thus, if the essence of the mind is doubt, it cannot stand only on its own but entails reference to something else from which it receives its definition as a thinking substance. In Feuerbach, it is world-history; the *cogito* is a product of world-history out of which it emerges. The philosopher can never detach himself from this world-history and become independent, relying only on the *cogito*. As Feuerbach says:

The philosopher is preceded by the mind and the general viewpoint of philosophy that commences with this doubt. The philosopher does not choose this philosophy such as seating himself on a chair which he could *ad libitum* leave and then occupy again. On the contrary, he finds himself put there by the mind (*Geist*) of world-history and its philosophy, and therefore it is a necessary viewpoint.[20] (Feuerbach, 1906, p. 187)

In other words, the self-certainty which is supposed to be achieved in the *cogito* by means of doubt is not self-sufficient and independent but is rather dependent upon world-history.

Baader, by contrast, is not primarily interested in epistemological and ontological questions, but rather in social, religious, and political questions. He writes, 'With his "cogito, ergo sum", Cartesius has initiated atheism in that he posited the human reflection (*Nachdenken*) before God's prime-thought (*Urdenken*)' (cited in Betanzos, 1992, p. 60).[21] He expands a little on this matter:

There is a kind of a prime-knowledge (*Urwissen*) of God which is founded upon the fact that we primarily stand within God's consciousness (*in Gottes Bewußtsein urständen*). Theosophy knows that 'in the final analysis, there is something higher than man which is his authority'.[22] (Baader, 1991, p. 19)

'Authority' and 'atheism' are two keywords in the two quotations above. Yet, Baader does not succumb to mystical experience and blind submission to authority. He rather talks about prime knowledge (*Urwissen*) and uses the verb *cogitare*, although in the passive mode. All this requires further elucidation.

'Scientific knowledge' and 'prime knowledge' should not exclude one another. There are various ways to conceive their relationship. Descartes himself leaves us with a broad leeway to various interpretations. Scholars who want to show that God is the source of scientific-knowledge, usually refer to the *Olympica*. This is Descartes's report on the dreams which he had on the night of 10 November 1619. These dreams occurred during the time when he began composing his *Discourse*. In the *Olympica*, he tells us that, convinced he had just discovered the foundations of science, he went to bed that night filled with inspiration. He then had three consecutive dreams in which, according to some interpretations, the spirit of truth wanted to reveal to him the treasures of all sciences.[23] Thus, for example, Étienne Gilson writes:

At least at the time of the *Olympica*, he places a certain inspiration at the origin of philosophy, a point to which Descartes never returned, neither to reaffirm it, nor to deny it. The 'inspiration' in question is divine: the sentiment experienced by Descartes that he was invested by God with the mission of constituting the body of the sciences and thus, as a consequence, to establish true wisdom. (Cited in Kennington, 2004, p. 79)

It follows, according to Gilson, that Descartes could not think of unaided reason as the highest instance in matters of truth and validity. According to Richard Kennington, this reading of Descartes is broadly accepted (ibid., pp. 79–80). The German philosopher and historian, Walter Schulz, writes, 'In reality the whole modem metaphysic derives from Christianity' (ibid., p. 80). In his classical studies on Descartes, Jacques Maritain writes:

Although the only thing he [Descartes] really cherished was his physics – it was for his physics, above all, that he wrote the *Meditations*, in order to assure the success of mechanism by binding its fate to that of knowledge of the soul and God – he believed quite sincerely that by his philosophy he was serving the interests of religion; still more, he was convinced he had given to the world a philosophy more Christian, more satisfying to the sentiments of the Christian reader. (Maritain, 1944, p. 37)

Maritain interprets the dreams of Descartes as the birth of science out of divine revelation. He writes, 'It is an outflowing of the science of God in our spirit, a sort of angelic geometry' (ibid., pp. 47–8).

For Baader, the focus lies elsewhere. He does not seek to found scientific knowledge. His main interest is religious and social. As we shall presently see, he is also interested in the co-existence of scientific knowledge and prime knowledge. Hence, Baader writes, 'I am thought, therefore I think, or: *I am willed (loved), therefore I am*' (cited in Betanzos, 1992, p. 61).[24] Human love, as human thought, is not a primary-love, but rather counter-love, Ἀντέρως (anteros), as in Plato (ibid.). Man loves – or is supposed to love his fellow – because he is loved by God. Perception and love are two basic principles in Baader's philosophy, but love stands higher. 'The heart stands above thought', Baader writes, and 'love is the origin of any perfection' (ibid.).[25] They can only be understood when they are bound with authority and submission.

Let us start with the social aspect of Baader's view. The key term here is *Sozietät.* 'Fellowship' is perhaps the best English translation of that term. The Cartesian worldview yields a mechanical, indifferent relationship between isolated subjects, whereas love, as the principle of the unity among humans and between them and God, leads to fellowship. Fellowship is an *organic* unity among people and between them and God, whereas the Cartesian worldview is an inorganic accumulation of atom-like subjects. As Franz Hoffmann explains Baader's view:

> The difference between the organic body and inorganic accumulation consists in that in the latter, the parts exist indifferently one next to another, whereas in the former, no part can exist without the other. The grand kingdom of God has no other sense other than bringing the creatures of the all universe into a true organic community (*Innung*), since only in that community (*Gemeinschaft*) God has become everything in everything.[26] (Cited in Löwenthal, 1923, p. 43)

In positing the subject at the centre, Cartesianism destroys the principle of love and leads to the creation of inorganic accumulation (ibid., pp. 43–4). The Cartesian principle of inorganic accumulation is a principle of *hatred* and it sets people against one another. It lies at the base of all kind of despotism and slavery, modern democracy and liberalism included (ibid., pp. 45–6),[27] since they likewise lack love as the basic principle. 'Only love makes really free (liberal), for only the lover does not detach the right (the ruling) from duty (serving), possessing from being possessed or letting oneself be possessed' (ibid., p. 52).[28] In the social contract theories, Baader asserts, everything comes down to despotism and anarchy (ibid., pp. 58–9).

Baader writes, 'No human governance emerges and exists out of a mere fear without respect, out of a mere egoistic interest without love, out of a mere possession and acquisition without justice' (ibid., p. 46).[29] Concerning the Cartesian ego, he says, '*non audiam, non serviam, non credam, non orem*' ('neither listens, nor serves, nor believes, nor prays'). He then concludes that we need to destroy in ourselves the ability to doubt (*posse dubitare*) (Baader, 1855b, p. 105).

> To be free in knowing (*Erkennen*) is not to be one who dissociates himself from any authority or pretends to dissociate himself, but instead … to be

one who does not attend to any authority except that which sets him free either mediately or immediately, since it founds his knowledge.[30] (Cited in Löwenthal, 1923, p. 48)

In this sense, we should also understand the term 'subject', Baader claims. *Subicere* in Latin means to submit, to subject (Geldhof, 2005, p. 241). Subjection, according to him, is the first condition of any understanding.

> No manifestation, namely, no thinking is possible without subjugation. Knowing and understanding transcend the finitude. True entity exists only for the thought, there is nothing perceptible that could exist for itself; it should have its ground in the infinite.[31] (Baader, 1855b, p. 43)

Since Baader's main concern is social rather than ontological and epistemological, we should now turn to the question concerning freedom. Submission, according to him, does not exclude freedom but rather enables it. According to him, when love is seen as the basic principle, as in fellowship, humans are like organs in a body without which they could never be free, and the body itself could never exist without God at the centre: 'Only in the central organ of the organism, every organ has its ground and freedom against all the other particular organs' (cited in Löwenthal, 1923, p. 71).[32] He calls this centre 'central heart': human life, as *communal* rather than isolated life, is not independent but rather owes its existence to God.

> If there were no central heart (Coeur-Centre), and if humans could not communally exist and maintain (*restauriren*) their life out of this heart and in it, they could likewise never exist depending only on each other (*von einander*); they must have rejected one another, as it actually occurs.[33] (Baader, 1831, p. 44)

This condensed passage contains the substance of Baader's social, religious, and political views. Let me elaborate on this. Due to its finitude, the human subject can never stand on its own, it can never be self-positing, in Fichte's words. Thus, the *cogito* leads by necessity to *cogitor*. Highly influenced by Baader, Søren Kierkegaard shows how the self finds out about its dependency on God in what Kierkegaard calls 'despaired defiance' (*verzweifelter Trotz*). In defying any dependency, the self is referred to the instance against which it claims to be independent, that is, the higher force from which it is derived.[34]

This demonstration of human dependency on God by no means contradicts Descartes's view. As Walter Schulz explains:

> Descartes proves God … as it were *e contrario*: I want once to find out whether I can get by without God … But exactly that attempt fails at the insight into my finitude. The evidence of one's own finitude is the inner sense of the argument.[35] (Cited in Rosenau, 2000, p. 138)

Now, even if this dialectical move is valid and the human subject turns out to be dependent, it by no means leads to God. As we saw in Feuerbach's secular worldview, it can likewise lead to world-history out of which the subject emerges. It is the same story with love. Baader claims that only love can serve as the principle of fellowship or what he calls *Societät*. It is a love of God that requires the complete submission which yields that fellowship.

The question is why love, as a principle of fellowship, must be dependent upon God, according to Baader. Why cannot it be love among people without reference and submission to God? The long tradition of dialogue philosophy is not exclusively religious. In Feuerbach's *Grundsätze der Philosophie der Zukunft* (*Principles of the Philosophy of Future*), a secular outline of the future philosophy, §59, we read the following: 'The *essence* of man can be maintained only in community, only in *unity between man and man* – a unity which is founded upon the difference between me and you' (Feuerbach, 1906, p. 318).[36] In §62, he writes, 'The *true* dialectic *is not a monolog of the lonely thinker within himself,* it is rather *a dialog between me and you*' (ibid., p. 319, italics in original).[37]

The question is why Baader insists upon God's love and submission to God as the only way to achieve fellowship. Why does he argue that without God's love people can never live peacefully together, can never be free, but rather wrong one another and turn society into dictatorship? The answer is that without submitting ourselves to God, without giving up the hubris of the *cogito*, of the self-centred subject, we will by necessity submit our self to the self of other people or subject other people to our self. Thus, submitting ourselves in love to God is a necessary precondition for a free and just society, according to Baader.

Yet, submission to God is mediated by the church or occurs within its scope as political institutions. So how can we avoid the huge danger of ecclesiastical tyranny, oppression, and dictatorship? Baader is well aware of that problem. We have mentioned his rejection of pietism as a blind sentimental submission as well as his high influence on Ignaz von Döllinger. Döllinger was the main figure in the revolt against ultramontanism in time of Pope Pius the IX and the first Vatican Council. This led to the establishment of the Old Catholic Church (*Altkatholiche Kirche*) which accepts the authority of the Bible but not of the Vatican. Baader distinguishes between true and false authority. His distinction sheds light on Döllinger's thesis as well. According to him, false authority, to which he refers to as heathen (*heidnisch*), demands complete submission of the subject to the ruler. It is tyranny. On the contrary, true authority, to which he refers to as Christian, demands complete submission of both the ruler and the subject to God (Baader, 1991, pp. 164–5). That is, both the believer and the church as a temporal political institution must submit themselves to the authority of God. Thus, the relationship between the ruler and the subject is a mutual service (*Dienst*) which is achieved through submission of both to God. This is the only meaning of fellowship as a free and fair society.

> Service does not make us unfree and humiliated but rather [only] that service which destroys respect and love; service out of love (*Liebesdienst*) is hence setting free, honoring and elevating, and therefore nothing can be more foolish than to want to make people free through lack of service and love whereby one would make them become a disobedient riffraff (*hörloses Gesindel*).[38] (Baader, 1831, p. 33)

Baader calls this social organization 'theodemocracy' in which we 'treat one another royally and not slavishly, and nobody should strive to rule over the others, but rather to seek to act above all through love, like God, in the others' (cited in Kaltenbrunner, 1991, p. 43).[39] Submitting oneself does not imply lack of freedom as long as it is done out of love. 'The identity of duty and love demonstrates itself already in that both express conjunction' (Baader, 1831, p. 18).[40]

We can now attend to the question about the relationship between knowledge, faith, and love. Baader writes:

> The claim that love yielded knowledge, rather than knowledge love, should express the superiority of feeling as a *force* over knowledge as *resistance*. Thence: wherever you find true knowledge, there is love.[41] (Cited in Betanzos, 1992, p. 61, italics in original)

Baader does not call for a rejection of scientific knowledge and disregard of reason. He represents neither mysticism nor ultramontanism, but rather a more complicated stance towards knowledge and authority. As Dieter Arendt states, Baader wants a synthesis between emancipated subjectivity and respected objectivity, in other words, between individualism and traditionalism. In his address at the inauguration ceremony of the Ludwig-Maximilian University in Munich in 1825, Baader says:

> I am very pleased with the world-historical meaning of the distance which Ludwig-Maximilian University took from both nihilism and obscurantism of our time, that is, to act with success against the misuse of the intelligence, which is destructive to religion, as well as against the equally bad inhibition of its use [i.e. of intelligence] partly out of fear of knowledge and partly out of contempt toward knowledge.[42] (Cited in Arendt, 1970, p. 65)

The fear of knowledge, according to Baader, leads to pietism, whereas the misuse of intelligence leads to nihilism (Baader, 1970b, pp. 267–8). In a letter dated 1824, he refers to his view of knowledge with regard to Hegel's disciples: 'They do not know that there is perception (image, poetic) which *precedes* the concept (*Begriff*), one [perception] which follows and one which is simultaneous with its [i.e. concept] emergence' (Baader, 1970a, p. 292, italics in original).[43] 'Concept', *Begriff*, refers to the ruling abstraction in rational philosophy which produces a picture of emptied reality. On the contrary, figurative language and poetry provide us with a picture of reality in its meaningful fullness.[44]

This explanation can by no means satisfy those who expect from Baader a satisfying theoretical alternative to Descartes's view of perception or to a rational theory of knowledge. Baader, however, is not interested in epistemology but rather in the forms of religion, politics, and society which in his view emerged out of Cartesianism, such as rationalism and Enlightenment, the French Revolution, secularism, and the modern state. Fighting Cartesianism means for him to stand against all the maladies of Western civilization which emerged out of it.

***

Edmund Husserl, the father of phenomenology, declares time and again that Descartes is the father of phenomenology who enabled, through his discovery of the *cogito*, the phenomenological breakthrough into the realm of meaning. Yet, we see Husserl blaming Descartes for all the evil afflicting Western civilization. In Chapter 3, we will see, on the one hand, Husserl praising Descartes time and again, and on the other hand, diverging from him in every respect. We see how Husserl's dealing with Descartes's philosophy becomes a political matter, a critique of the degraded European culture, which Husserl calls to revive, along with the dismissal of non-European cultures.

Notes

1 'In seiner Wirtschaftslehre hat Marx von Baader das Material, in seiner Gesellschaftslehre von Hegel die Form übernommen–der Geist ist ihm beidemal entwichen!'

2 'Wir sollten "einander königlich und nicht sklavisch behandeln und keiner über den andern zu herrschen begehren, sondern vorzüglich durch Liebe, wie Gott, in andere zu wirken suchen."'

3 ' "Weder Polizeibedienstete noch überhaupt Bedienstete, noch Advokaten im engeren Sinne," sondern Priester, die sich nicht nur um pastorale "Seelsorge," sondern auch um sozialpolitische "Leibsorge" bemühen sollen.'

4 On the relationship between Baader and Döllinger, see Howard (2017, p. 71).

5 See Arendt (1970, p. 105), footnote 45.

6 'Alles außer ihr [Vernunft] in Nichts verwandelt wird und sie [Vernunft] allein übrig läßt.'

7 'Je mehr im Kritizismus das Ich in die Betrachtung des Ich versank, umso magerer und dürrer ward dieses Ich, bis es damit endete, daß das Ich ein Gespenst ward, unsterblich gleich Auroras Mann.'

8 'Sapere aude! Habe Mut dich deines eigenen Verstandes zu bedienen!'

9 'Den Begriff der Autorität in kirchlicher, politischer und wissenschaftlicher Hinsicht gegen jeden ältern und neuern Zweifel oder Protest festzustellen.'

10 'Die Gedanken waren für sich leibhaftig geworden, waren Gespenster wie Gott, Kaiser, Papst, Vaterland usw.'

11 'Wenn Fichte sagt: "Das Ich ist Alles," so scheint dies mit meinen Aufstellungen vollkommen zu harmonieren. Allein nicht das Ich *ist* Alles, sondern das Ich *zerstört* Alles und nur das sich selbst auflösende Ich, das nie seiende Ich, das *endliche* Ich ist wirklich Ich. Fichte spricht vom "absoluten" Ich. Ich aber spreche von Mir, dem vergänglichen Ich.'

12 'Wenn der Mensch Gedanke Gottes (keineswegs der Gottgedanke von sich selbst), wenn also der Mensch von Gott gedacht ist und ohne dieses von Gott Gedachtwerden nicht wäre, so kann er auch seines Seins nur gewiss sein, indem

er sich von Gott gedacht weiss. Daher genügt nicht das *Cogito ergo sum*, sondern nur das *Cogitor (a deo) ergo sum*.'

13 'Das: Ich denke, ist, wie schon gesagt, ein empirischer Satz, und hält den Satz: Ich existire, in sich. Ich kann aber nicht sagen: Alles, was denkt, existirt; denn da würde die Eigenschaft des Denkens alle Wesen, die sie besitzen, zu notwendigen Wesen machen. Daher kann meine Existenz auch nicht aus dem Satze: Ich denke, als gefolgert angesehen werden, wie Cartesius dafür hielt (weil sonst der Obersatz: Alles, was denkt, existiert, vorausgehen müsste) sondern ist mit ihm identisch.' See Simon (2003, pp. 52–3).

14 'In der That ruht der forschende Geist nicht, bis er zu solch einem Erkennen eines Erkennenden, d. h. seines Erkanntseins, durchgedrungen ist, oder, wie Plato sagt, bis sein Auge einem sein Sehen sehenden Auge begegnet. Wir behaupten darum, dass es eine der Grundüberzeugungen des Menschen ist, dass er, als schauend und er kennend, sich in einem ihn Schauenden und Erkennenden, als wollend in einem ihn Wollenden, als wirkend in einem ihn Wirkenden begriffen weiss.'

15 'Indem nämlich die Geliebte sich mir giebt, bin ich mich ihr schuldig worden, und indem ich mich der Geliebten gebe (ihr glaubend) ist sie sich mir schuldig geworden. Aber auch Gott kann sich mir nicht geben, wenn ich mich ihm nicht gebe, lasse, mich auf ihn verlasse oder ihm glaube. Er kann sich aber auch mir nicht entziehen, wenn ich, ihm glaubend, mich ihm gebe, und er sich mir hiemit gleichsam schuldig geworden ist.'

16 ' "Es wird gedacht: folglich gibt es Denkendes"; darauf läuft die Argumentation des Cartesius hinaus. Aber das heißt unseren Glauben an den Substanzbegriff schon als "wahr a priori" ansehen: – daß, wenn gedacht wird, es etwas geben muß, "das denkt," ist eine einfache Formulierung unserer grammatikalischen Gewöhnung, welche zu einem Tun einen Täter setzt, kurz, es wird hier bereits einlogisch-metaphysisches Postulat gemacht – und nicht nur konstatiert.'

17 'Das in dem cogito begriffene sum heißt also nur: sum qua cogitans, ich bin als denkend, d.h. in dieser bestimmten Art des Seins, welche denken genannt wird, und die nur eine *andere* Art zu sein ist als z.B. die des Körpers, dessen Art zu sein darin besteht, daß er den Raum *erfüllt*, d.h. von diesem Raum, den er einnimmt, jeden andern Körper ausschließt. Das in dem cogito eingeschlossene sum hat also nicht die Bedeutung eines unbedingten Ich bin, sondern nur die Bedeutung eines "Ich bin *auf gewisse Weise*," nämlich eben als denkend, in dieser Art zu sein, welche man denkend nennt. Daher kann auch in dem Ergo sum nicht enthalten sein: Ich bin unbedingter Weise sondern nur: Ich bin auf gewisse Weise.'

18 ' "Das oberste Princip der Philosopie ist das Dasein unseres Geistes"– was ist dies Denken anders, als Zweifeln?'

19 'Der Geist ist nicht immateriell und denkt, als wäre die Immaterialität für sich ein Prädicat, oder das allgemeine Prädicat; und ebensowenig denkt er, weil er immateriell ist; sondern er ist immateriell, weil und insofern er denkt.'

20 'Es ist ihm vorausgesetzt ferner der Geist und der allgemeine Standpunkt der mit diesem Zweifeln anhebenden Philosophie, auf den sich der Philosoph nicht willkürlich setzt, wie auf einen Stuhl, den er *ad libitum* verlassen und dann wieder besetzen kann, sondern auf den er von dem Geiste der Weltgeschichte und seiner Philosophie sich gesetzt findet, und der darum ein nothwendiger Standpunkt ist.'

21 'Cartesius mit seinem: "Cogito, ergo sum" [hatte] den Atheismus angebahnt, indem er das Nachdenken der Creatur dem Urdenken Gottes vorsetzte.'

22 'Es gibt eine Art Urwissen von Gott, das darin gründet, daß wir in Gottes Bewußtsein urständen. Theosophie weiß, daß "in letzter Instanz nicht der Mensch dem Menschen Autorität ist," sondern ein Höheres.'

23 See Sanderson Haldane (1905, pp. 51–2).

24 'Ich werde gedacht, darum denke ich, oder: *ich werde gewollt (geliebt), darum bin ich.*'

25 ' "Das Herz steht über dem Denken" und "Liebe ist Quelle aller Vervollkommnung." '

26 'Darin besteht gerade der Unterschied des Organischen vom Unorganischen so faßt Hoffmann Franz Baaders Gedanken zusammen, daß die Teile im lezteren gleichgiltig nebeneinander bestehen, im ersteren aber kein Teil ohne den anderen zu existieren vermag – Das große Reich Gottes hat nun keinen anderen Sinn, als die Geschöpfe des gesamten Universums in eine warhaft organische Innung zu bringen, weil nur in dieser lebendigen Gemeinschaft Gott Alles in Allem geworden ist.'

27 See also 'Die Anhänger des Liberalismus sehen nicht ein, – daß, so wie der Teufel, indem er den wahren Gott weglügt, sich selber dafür als Gott anlügt, auch der Liberale ein verkappter Despot ist, oder daß der Liberalismus für nicht mehr als eine Fabel erklärt werden kann, dessen Moral der Servilismus ist, weil – die Losmachung oder Lossagung von der legitimen Autorität, welche der Liberalismus bezweckt, uns zwar nicht vom Dienen losmacht, wohl aber die Freiheit, die Ehre und die Liebe im Dienste uns nimmt, und unsfolglich einem servilen, unfreien, ehr- und lieblosen Diensteu nterwirft' (Löwenthal, 1923, p. 52).

28 'Nur die Liebe macht wahrhaft freisinnig (liberal), denn nur der Liebende trennt das Recht (das Herrschen) nicht von Pflicht (dem Dienen) das Besitzen nicht vom Besessensein oder Sichbesitzenlassen.'

29 'Durch bloße Furcht ohne Achtung, durch bloßes eigennütziges Interesse ohne Liebe, durch bloßen Besitz und Erwerb ohne Recht entsteht und besteht kein menschlich Regiment.'

30 'Frei im Erkennen ist nicht jener, welcher von jeder Autorität sich lossagt oder sich loszusagen vorgibt, sondern frei im Erkennen ist jener, welcher auf keine andere Autorität hört, als auf die ihn unmittelbar oder mittelbar befreiende, weil sein Erkennen begründende.'

31 'Keine Manifestation, also kein Denken ist möglich ohne Subjection. Das Wissen und Erkennen geht über die Endlichkeit hinaus. Das wahre Dasein ist nur für den Gedanken, es gibt kein Ding, das als erkennbar für sich bestehen könnte, es muss im Unendlichen seinen Grund haben.'

32 'Nur im Zentralorgan des Organismus jedes einzelne Organ begründet und also frei gegen alle übrigen einzelnen Gliedmaßen ist.'

33 'Gäbe es kein Centralherz (Coeur-Centre), und könnten die Menschen nicht gemeinschaftlich sich von und in diesem Herzen substantiren und restauriren, so würden sie auch nicht wechselseitig sich von einander substantiren können, und ein Mensch müßte den andern, wie es denn auch geschieht, von sich ausspeien.'

34 'Er will so gern vor Gott er selbst sein, jedoch nicht in bezug auf diesen festen Punkt, worin sein Selbst leidet, da will er verzweifelt nicht er selbst sein; er hofft, daß die Ewigkeit ihn wegnehmen werde, aber hier in der Zeitlichkeit kann er sich, wie sehr er auch darunter leidet, nicht entschließen, diesen Punkt anzunehmen und sich gläubig darunter zu demütigen. Und doch bleibt er im Verhältnis zu Gott, und dies ist seine einzige Seligkeit; es würde ihm das Schrecklichste sein, Gott entbehren zu sollen, "das wäre zum Verzweifeln"' (Kierkegaard, 1849, pp. 72–3). See Rosenau (2000, pp. 125–42).

35 'Descartes beweist Gott … gleichsam e contrario: ich will einmal erproben, ob ich ohne Gott auskomme … Aber eben dieser Versuch scheitert an der Einsicht in meine Endlichkeit. Der Beweis der eigenen Endlichkeit ist der innere Sinn der Argumentation.'

36 'Das *Wesen* des Menschen ist nur in der Gemeinschaft, in der *Einheit des Menschen mit dem Menschen* enthalten – eine Einheit, die sich aber nur auf die *Realität des Unterschiedes* von Ich und Du stutzt.'

37 'Die *wahre* Dialektik ist *kein Monolog des einsamen Denkers mit sich selbst*, sie ist ein *Dialog zwischen Ich und Du.*'

38 'Nicht der Dienst macht unfrei und erniedrigt, sondern nur jener Dienst, welcher Achtung und Liebe tilgt; der Liebesdienst ist darum der befreiende und ehrende oder erhebende, und nichts kann thöricher seyn, als die Menschen durch Dienstlosigkeit, und folglich Lieblosigkeit, frei machen wollen, womit man sie nur zum hörlosen Gesindel machen würde.'

39 'Wir sollten "einander königlich und nicht sklavisch behandeln und keiner über den andern zu herrschen begehren, sondern vorzüglich durch Liebe, wie Gott, in andere zu wirken suchen."'

40 'Die Identität der Pflicht und Liebe zeigt sich übrigens schon dadurch, daß beede eine Verbindung aussagen.'

41 'In der Behauptung, die Liebe habe das Wissen hervorgebracht, nicht das Wissen die Liebe, will die Superiorität des Gefühls als *force* über das Wissen als *resistence* ausgedrückt werden. Daher: wo du wahres Wissen findest, da ist auch Liebe.'

42 'Ich freue mich ... auf die weltgeschichtliche Bedeutung der Hierherverlegung der Ludwig-Maximilian-Universität sowohl dem Nihilismus als auch dem Obscurantismus unserer Zeit, d. h. sowohl dem für die Religion destructiven Mißbrauch der Intelligenz als auch der gleich schlechten theils aus Wissensscheue theils aus Verachtung des Wissens hervorgehenden Inhibition ihres Gebrauches mit Erfolg entgegen zu wirken.'

43 'Sie wissen nicht, daß es eine Vorstellung (Bild, Poesie) *vor* dem Begriff und Eine auch nach und mit dessen Eintritt gibt.'

44 For a detailed treatment of Baader's critique of rational epistemology and his alternative see Schmitz (1975, pp. 14–22).

3

Edmund Husserl: The crisis of the European man

In his lectures of 1923/4 *First Philosophy*, part I, Husserl names the three groundbreakers (*Wegeröffener*) of Western philosophy. Descartes occupies the second place after Plato (Orth, 2000, pp. 286–7).

> His *Meditations de prima philosophia* [Meditations on First Philosophy] signifies in the history of philosophy thereby a completely new beginning in that it made the attempt, in an unprecedented radicalism, to discover the absolutely necessary beginning of philosophy and at the same time to create that beginning out of absolutely and completely pure self-knowledge (*Selbsterkenntis*).[1] (Ibid., p. 287)

In 1929, in a lecture at the Sorbonne entitled 'Cartesian Meditations' in which Husserl presented his own philosophy, he says of Descartes that he is the crown witness (*Kronzeuge*) of the phenomenological study of consciousness as first philosophy (ibid., p. 286). Descartes, according to him, broke through naive objectivism and realism and opened up the way to phenomenology and to transcendental subjectivism, to the ego as the only apodictic evidence (Husserl, 1973, p. 5). In doing so, Descartes thought that he had established a firm foundation for the sciences. According to Husserl, any attempt to lay a firm foundation for science must return to Descartes and thus embark on the same undertaking. Hence, Husserl allocates Descartes a special place in his detailed and meticulous historical reflections which are an integral part of his phenomenology. The following quotation is taken from the opening words of Husserl's *Paris Lecture*, which he later expanded to *Cartesian Meditations*:

> I have particular reason for being glad that I may talk about transcendental phenomenology in this, the most venerable abode of French science. France's

greatest thinker, René Descartes, gave transcendental phenomenology new impulses through his *Meditations*; their study acted quite directly on the transformation of an already developing phenomenology into a new kind of transcendental philosophy. Accordingly one might almost call transcendental phenomenology a neo-Cartesianism, even though it is obliged – and precisely by its radical development of Cartesian motifs – to reject nearly all the well-known doctrinal content of the Cartesian philosophy. (Husserl, 1982, p. 1)

At the same time, Husserl says of Descartes that he is the inaugurator of 'all the great evil' in modern philosophy and culture (Husserl, 1956, p. 73; Orth, 2000, p. 286). As we will see, Husserl diverges from Descartes in every respect. The gap between the two philosophies is unbridgeable. In the *Crisis* texts, Husserl talks about his attitude to Descartes as 'equivocal' (*Doppeltdeutigkeit*).[2] In some respects, Descartes is Husserl's forerunner, and in others he is not, according to Husserl. As the following passage from Husserl's *Crisis* may suggest, Husserl's evaluation of Descartes may contain, besides philosophy, other considerations as well:

> The negative practical-ethical (political) skepticism lacks, also in all latter times, the original Cartesian motive: to press forward through the hell of the quasi-skeptical epoché, of which nothing can be more radical, to the entrance gate at the heaven of the absolute rational philosophy and to build it up systematically by itself.[3] (Husserl, 1976, p. 78)

The question concerning the urge to philosophize is about the *decision* to give up any practical issues and turn to reflection. This decision is preceded by nothing (no practical or other considerations), thus it is hard to refer to and characterize it. In Heidegger's lecture 'What is Metaphysics?' this decision befalls the philosophizing person. As he puts it succinctly, *Das Nichts selber nichtet* (The nothing itself annihilates) (Heidegger, 1976, p. 114). In his worldview, philosophy is not a doctrine but rather that urge to philosophize which befalls man. He calls this *Ereignis* 'event' – his translation for the Greek καιρός (kairos, moment of revelation). In the *Sixth Cartesian Meditation*, an expansion of Husserl's text by Eugen Fink which Husserl authorized, Fink refers to phenomenology as *Urereignis*, 'primordial event' (Fink, 1988, p. 124). Husserl himself aligns the phenomenological procedure with 'religious conversion' (*religiöse Umkehrung*) (Luft, 2002, pp. 122–3). As Hedwig Conrad-Martius, Husserl's disciple in Göttingen who belonged in his closest circle, writes, 'In the phenomenological circle, the soil has been made fertile for the perception of the transcendence, of revelations, and of God Himself.' Some of the members in that circle, she goes on to explain, converted to Christianity, some remained Jews or undenominational. 'But all of them have been somehow touched by the existence of other worlds whose essence – as the essence of many other things – suddenly dawned on them' (cited in Schlickel, 1998, p. 9).[4]

For scholars like Alfred Schulz (see Kennington, 2004, p. 80), Jacques Maritain (1944, p. 37), and Étienne Gilson (see Kennington, 2006, p. 79), Descartes's decision to philosophize goes back to divine revelation in the dreams which he had. In the *Meditation*, to which Husserl mainly refers, the decision to philosophize goes back to Descartes's own will to provide science with firm foundations:

> Some years ago I was struck by how many false things I had believed, and by how doubtful was the structure of beliefs that I had based on them. I realized that if I wanted to establish anything in the sciences that was stable and likely to last, I needed – just once in my life – to demolish everything completely and start again from the foundations. (Descartes, 2004, p. 1)

Descartes's radical doubt brings him eventually to the thinking ego which he cannot cast in doubt and even God cannot take from him:

> Even then, if he [God] is deceiving me I undoubtedly exist: let him deceive me all he can, he will never bring it about that I am nothing while I think I am something. So after thoroughly thinking the matter through I conclude that this proposition, I am, I exist, must be true whenever I assert it or think it. (Ibid., p. 5)

Husserl praises Descartes for this course of thought and its urge to give science a firm and lasting foundation and the consequent return to the ego as the only apodictic evidence (Husserl, 1973, p. 4). He thus calls upon us to follow Descartes in his path that leads to solipsism, to the isolated ego (ibid., p. 7). Husserl writes:

> As radically meditating philosophers, we now have neither a science that we accept nor a world that exists for us. Instead of simply existing for us, that is,

being accepted naturally by us in our experiential believing in its existence, the world is for us only something that claims being. (Husserl, 1982, p. 18)

So far, Husserl seems to follow Descartes's procedure as the only way to attain truth: to cast everything in doubt in order to reach the isolated ego. Let us read a bit further in Husserl's *Cartesian Meditations*:

> But, no matter what the status of this phenomenon's claim to actuality and no matter whether, at some future time, I decide critically that the world exists or that it is an illusion, still this phenomenon itself, as mine, is not nothing but is precisely what makes such critical decisions at all possible and accordingly makes possible whatever has for me sense and validity as 'true' being – definitively decided or definitively decideable being. And besides: If I abstained – as I was free to do and as I did – and still abstain from every believing involved in or founded on sensuous experiencing, so that the being of the experienced world remains unaccepted by me, still this abstaining is what it is; and it exists, together with the whole stream of my experiencing life. Moreover, this life is continually there *for me*. (Ibid., p. 19, italics in original)

For Husserl, the world remains the same as it was before he applied the ἐποχή (epoché, suspension of judgement) to it. The only difference is seen in the new formulation of the judgement regarding the world, namely, that the world continues to exist as before without any change – but now it exists *for me*. What is the change that this 'for me' signifies? To what extent does the world now seem different? For Descartes, everything is different once reality has been cast in doubt and it is no longer clear whether it really exists or is rather a dream. Husserl, on the contrary, claims that his study is altogether independent of the question whether the world exists or not.[5] This fleshes out the difference between Descartes's and Husserl's basic views on philosophy and its goal: Descartes asks about the validity of our perception of reality as such, whereas Husserl asks about the *meaning* of reality – as it is *for me*. Husserl's ἐποχή has thus a completely different function than the Cartesian doubt, the ἐποχή is supposed to lead us into a realm of meaning and its origin, whereas the Cartesian doubt leads us to the isolated ego. Regarding the solipsism into which Descartes runs and his following attempt to prove the existence of the external world, Husserl writes that Descartes was by necessity led into this problem, since he missed the genuine sense of the reduction to the transcendental ego and concentrated solely on the attempt to overcome dualism and epistemological skepticism (ibid., p. 83).[6]

The Cartesian system creates a body–mind dualism, a distinction between the ego as *res cogitans* (thinking thing) and reality as *res extensa* (extended thing). This distinction is crucial for Descartes and an integral part of his system, since without it he could never achieve validity. On the other hand, once he reached validity within the mental sphere, he must find a good solution to the body–mind dualism to enable a reliable access of the mind to the physical reality. For Husserl, whose research is about meaning, the body–mind dualism does not exist.

In Husserl's view, Descartes was not radical enough in his procedure of casting everything in doubt. Consequently, the way to the ego remained blocked for him. He formulates his rejection of Descartes in different ways. One of them is that the *ego cogito* is meaningless, a postulate which is never experienced (*erlebt*) (Landgrebe, 1963, p. 173). More specifically, he explains to what extent Descartes was not radical enough: the *ego cogito* is for Descartes a 'tiny remainder' of the world which he should also have cast in doubt, but he did not. The aim of the reduction, as Husserl argues against Descartes, is not to rescue a 'tag-end of the world', namely, the indubitable ego, from which the existence of external reality can be inferred by means of arguments. Descartes must have made this fateful error because his inquiry was determined by the prejudices according to which the ego is *substantia cogitans* (thinking substance), *mens sive animus* (mind or spirit), which is the point of departure for inference according to the principle of causality. The only way to avoid this fatal error, Husserl claims, is to adhere to radical phenomenology, that is to say, to 'intuition' or evidence which is given in the sphere of the ego opened to us through the ἐποχή, and to assert nothing which we do not see (Husserl, 1982, p. 24).

'Radicality', according to Husserl, means to cast everything in doubt, and to apply the ἐποχή also to the *ego cogito* which is part of the world, whereas the subject, the source of any meaning, is transcendental – transcendental subjectivity (Husserl, 1976, p. 82). Descartes, instead, stuck to a 'tag-end' (*ein kleines Endchen der Welt*) (Husserl, 1982, p. 24) and thus did not transcend reality. The ego as transcendental subjectivity, according to Husserl, is not a substance, but rather activity which constitutes meaning within a temporal flux (ibid., p. 81). As Husserl claims, Cartesian 'evidence', that is to say, the proposition 'ego cogito, ego sum' remained empty, since Descartes did not clarify the meaning of the ἐποχή and furthermore overlooked the fact that the ego can explicate itself in infinity and systematically through transcendental experience (ibid., p. 31).

Descartes has not been radical enough and thus he failed to achieve transcendental subjectivity. He ended up with the ego, a thinking thing, a remainder of the world. Husserl, on the contrary, reached transcendental subjectivity which is transcendental to the world. It is the source of any meaning. Thus, it cannot be referred to as an existing thing in the world. It is far from being clear what Husserl means by transcendental subjectivity. He says that it is not an empty point or pole (ein *leerer Punkt oder Pol*). By that, he refers to the Cartesian *ego cogito* which serves as a postulate, geometrical point in Descartes's system. On the contrary, he describes transcendental subjectivity as having character and habits (Husserl, 1973, p. 26).[7] It has a 'personal character' (ibid., p. 101), and is a 'substrate of habits' (ibid., p. 102). The ego, Husserl contends, is not an empty pole of identity, identical substance, just as the object, in turn, is not an identical substance. On the contrary, in accordance with the law of 'transcendental generation', with every act emerging from it, the ego acquires a new objective sense, a new enduring feature. Thus, as Husserl says, if in judging something I decide for the first time in favour of something and not of something else, from now onwards I am the one who made this decision, although the act of this decision no longer exists (Husserl, 1982, p. 66).

This ego or subjectivity is very different from what Descartes had in mind. The question is why Husserl keeps seeing Descartes as his model, calling his phenomenological procedure 'neo-Cartesianism'. The following concise passage accentuates this sharp discrepancy: 'But perhaps, with the Cartesian discovery of the transcendental ego, *a new idea of the grounding of knowledge* also becomes disclosed: the idea of it as a transcendental grounding' (ibid., p. 27, italics in original). Descartes's grounding was by no means transcendental but rather geometrical – Descartes did not seek the transcendental source of meaning, as Husserl does, but rather *fundamentum inconcussum* (firm foundation). Husserl argues against Descartes that the bare identity of the 'I am' is not the only indubitable thing given to us. There is, on the contrary, a 'universal apodictically experienceable structure of the ego which is given with any experience such as the immanent temporal form (ibid., p. 29). This claim by Husserl illustrates the unbridgeable gap between him and Descartes.

As we saw, Husserl argues against Descartes that he was not radical enough in his endeavour. Hence, he did not reach transcendental subjectivity. Being radical enough, according to Husserl, means to cast in doubt or to apply the ἐποχή to mathematics and logic as well. Descartes accepted mathematics and logic as true and valid and thus does not apply his radical doubt to them. (Descartes applies the *genius malignus* [malicious demon] argument to mathematics, but never seriously deals with it.) The question is how we are supposed to proceed once mathematics and logic are inactivated, once no deductive inference is allowed, no causal relationship, no logical standard to distinguish between the true and the false?

Husserl rejects the two premises which Descartes did not cast in doubt: the validity of mathematics, geometry, and logic and their methodical procedure. The foundation of science, he claims, lies deeper than deduction (Husserl, 1973, p. 49). To the question how we are now supposed to proceed, Husserl responds that we possess the general idea of science led and determined by an end, τέλος (Husserl, 1982, p. 8).

All sciences have been overthrown, but their leading idea, their τέλος, remains as our *pis aller* which enables us to continue. Husserl extracts from all sciences, from their ever continuing striving for improvement and accuracy, their idea of perfection, of τέλος, as the leading idea of his procedure. This regulative idea imposes upon us the constant demand to strive to achieve evidence; to make our knowledge evidently true (Husserl, 1973, p. 51). Unknowingly, Descartes himself was led by that idea (ibid., p. 52). Husserl rejects the priority of methodical procedure and logical standard and introduces teleology instead. He unfolds a teleological worldview, a Hegelian one, in which each science and each philosophy has its share, and only in Husserl's phenomenology it reaches its end and becomes transparent to itself.[8] Historically seen, in this teleological worldview, each science strives to achieve a better grounding or understanding of itself. Yet, only phenomenology attains the full understanding of itself, full transparency (Husserl, 1982, p. 153).

In the *Crisis*, Husserl resorts to Hegelian terminology to describe this teleology.[9]

It is a direction, as I shall try to show here, toward a *final form* of transcendental philosophy – as *phenomenology.* This also contains, as a suspended moment (*aufgehobenes Moment*), the *final form of psychology* which uproots the naturalistic sense of modern psychology.[10] (Husserl, 1970, p. 70, italics in original)

The father of rational philosophy, Descartes, would never accept teleology as a legitimate philosophical explanation – the idea of science and knowledge as such, the regulative idea that governs them from on high (Husserl, 1973, p. 50). Husserl writes that all sciences, although different from one another, strive to realize this one idea (Husserl, 1982, p. 9).

With the introduction of teleology, science turns out to be for Husserl a *cultural* and *political* matter, and as we shall later see, a European matter which emerged in ancient Greece – the cradle of European culture and thought. This is a significant divergence from Descartes.

Before we return to that matter, let us see how different is Husserl's notion of the ego from Descartes's. In Descartes, the mind is an isolated substance and it refers to *reality* by means of ideas. This access to reality should be secured in order to have a firm foundation of science. In Husserl, on the contrary, reality is part of the ego's constituted world of meaning. Thus, the world remains the same after applying the ἐποχή to it. The mind, according to him, is intentional. It always intends something. The ego is a network of acts of intention, *cogitationes*, and their intended objects are the *cogitata* (Husserl, 1973, pp. 13–16). Once transcendental subjectivity has been reached, studying it means to explore the various acts of intentions. In this framework, the Cartesian body–mind dualism does not exist. Instead of a body–mind dualism, Husserl talks about 'psychophysical unity'. The bodily aspect of the ego has a share in constituting meaning. As Husserl says, among the bodies which I encounter within the field of my experience, I come across my own body as singled out from the rest in that it is the only body to which I ascribe sensation, the only body which I directly rule in each of its organs. I perceive with my hands and my eyes. I thus experience myself as a psychophysical unity (Husserl, 1982, p. 96).

Let us discuss one more cardinal point in which Husserl diverges from Descartes altogether. The certainty and validity of the statement *ego cogito sum* is bound with the present tense; the statement would not work in the future or the past tense. The problem which Descartes confronts is to explain how the myriad of present moments being indifferent to each other could be connected into one temporal span. Descartes resorts to God to solve this problem:

> Perhaps I have always existed as I do now. In that case, wouldn't it follow that there need be no cause for my existence? No, it does not follow. For a life-span can be divided into countless parts, each completely independent of the others, so that from my existing at one time it does not follow that I exist at later times, unless some cause keeps me in existence – one might say that it *creates me afresh* at each moment. Anyone who thinks hard about the nature of time will understand that what it takes to bring something into existence is also needed to keep it in existence at each moment of its duration. (Descartes, 2004, p. 15; italics added)

As we saw earlier, according to Husserl, the Cartesian ego is an empty geometrical point which we can never experience (*erleben*). The same applies to the 'Cartesian present'. In his view, present, on the contrary, is a changing stream of consciousness. This stream is not made up of indifferent moments connected one to another. The moments are rather connected by means of a meaningful *synthesis*. Synthesis of meaning is, according to him, the prime character of the ego. The main task of phenomenology is to explore this character.[11] Within the Cartesian framework, there is no room for such a synthesis.

> If we consider the *fundamental form of synthesis*, namely *identification*, we encounter it first of all as an all-ruling, *passively* flowing synthesis, in the form of the *continuous consciousness of internal time*. Every subjective process has its internal temporality. If it is a conscious process in which (as in the perception of the dice) a worldly object appears as a cogitatum [thought], then we have to distinguish the *objective temporality that appears* (for example: the temporality of this dice) from the *'internal' temporality of the appearing* (for example: that of the dice-perceiving). This appearing 'flows away' with its temporal extents and phases, which, for their part, are continually changing appearances of the one identical dice. Their unity is a unity of synthesis: not merely a continuous connectedness of cogitationes [thoughts] (as it were, a being stuck to one another externally), but *a connectedness that makes the unity of one consciousness*, in which the unity

of an intentional objectivity, as 'the same' objectivity belonging to multiple
modes of appearance, becomes '*constituted*'. (Husserl, 1982, pp. 41–2, italics
in original)

This last step demolishes altogether Descartes's definition of truth as a clear
and distinct perception (*clara et distincta perceptio*). The ego can no longer be
regarded as a thinking substance, since it turned out to be a temporal stream
of intentions. Likewise, the object can no longer be regarded as an extending
substance, since it is perceived (*erschaut*) in endlessly open horizons of
possible facets – some of them have been revealed in the past and others will
be revealed in the future (Husserl, 1973, p. 18). The temporal perspectives are
intermingled in the stream of consciousness.

In the *Second Meditation*, Descartes observes how a piece of wax can
assume endless forms and states of fluidity and solidity while at the same time
it must refer to the same substance that remains identical throughout all the
material changes (Descartes, 2004, p. 7). In Husserl's view, on the contrary, this
is impossible: the object is never perceived isolated, but always in a synthesis
of open horizons. Consciousness is, as Husserl puts it, an endlessly Heraclitian
stream which is synthetically organized (Husserl, 1973, p. 18). His assistant,
Ludwig Landgrebe, remarks that discovering the horizons in the acts of
consciousness led Husserl away from Descartes and modern philosophy and
consequently made him admit the dependency of consciousness on history
and tradition and thus to give up the idea of a firm foundation for science.[12]

Seeing an object in a meaningfully arranged horizon stretching to the
past and the future (what Husserl calls *Erwartungshorizont*) means to see it
embedded in a network of potentialities and actualities. Thus, Husserl does
not talk about 'objects' but rather about 'units of meaning' (*Sinneseinheiten*)
(ibid., p. 19).[13] Husserl writes:

> The horizons are 'predelineated' potentialities. We say also: We can *ask
> any horizon what 'lies in it'*, we can *explicate* or unfold it, and '*uncover*'
> the potentialities of conscious life at a particular time. Precisely thereby
> we uncover the *objective sense meant implicitly* in the actual *cogito*,
> though never with more than a certain degree of foreshadowing. This
> sense, the cogitatum qua cogitatum [thought as thought], is never present
> to actual consciousness (*vorstellig*) as a finished datum; it becomes
> 'clarified' only through explication of the given horizon and the new

horizons continuously awakened (*stetig neu geweckte Horizonte*). The predelineation itself, to be sure, is at all times imperfect; yet, with its *indeterminateness*, it has a *determinate structure*. For example: the dice leaves open a great variety of things pertaining to the unseen faces; yet it is already 'construed' in advance as a dice, in particular as colored, rough, and the like, though each of these determinations always leaves further particulars open. This leaving open, prior to further determinings (which perhaps never take place), is a moment included in the given consciousness itself; it is precisely what makes up the 'horizon'. (Husserl, 1982, p. 45, italics in original)

As we have seen, nothing remains of the original Cartesian philosophy: the question whether the world exists or not is no longer a concern for Husserl; both maths and logic are cast in doubt; we get teleology instead of mechanical causation; the ego is not a thinking substance but rather a stream of consciousness; the object is not an extended substance but rather a network of perspectives which are perceived within open and ever-changing horizons; and finally, time is regarded as a stretch and not as a now-point. The question is why Husserl calls his procedure Cartesian and keeps saying that he follows in the path of Descartes.

Husserl's viewpoint is teleological. In a letter from 10 July 1935, Husserl tells Roman Ingarden about his lecture in Vienna (which is included in the *Crisis*): ' "Philosophy and the Crisis of the European Humanity." First Half: The Philosophical Idea of the European Humanity (or "of European Culture") Explained out of the Teleological-Historical Sources (out of Philosophy).'[14] Now that we know that his view is teleological, we can ask why Descartes occupies such a key position in this teleological story.

Husserl's last texts and lectures are compiled under the title *Crisis of the European Sciences and Transcendental Phenomenology*. The question which immediately comes to mind is why 'European'? Eugen Fink, Husserl's close disciple and his assistant by the time of the work on the *Crisis*, pointed out to Husserl the political aspects of 'European' and, in order to avoid political allusions, suggested instead 'The Problem of Humanity' (Husserl, 1993, p. xx). Husserl did not accept his suggestion and maintained the 'European'. For him, Descartes is thus seen as a representative of European culture and civilization which is in a state of crisis. By 'crisis' Husserl means the situation in which, despite their significant progress, the sciences no longer bear any meaning for us.[15] They have lost their meaning and are in a state of crisis, since they lost their source in the activity of human subjectivity and the idea of science which gave birth to the European sciences. This leads to scepticism and the loss of faith in universal philosophy and reason (Husserl, 1976, pp. 10–11). The 'crisis' of which Husserl is speaking is thus *existential*. The term 'crisis', which he uses, is not accidental. As Hans Sluga shows, in the wake of the loss of the First World War, 'crisis' became a prevalent general mood in pre-Nazi Germany and the Third Reich that demanded a heroic decision to stand up and react to the crisis (Sluga, 1993).[16] 'Decision' (*Entscheidung*) is a term which occurs often in Landgrebe's text when he talks about the phenomenological ἐποχή.

In Husserl's view, history consists of epiphanies of reason as end, as ἐντελέχεια (entelecheia, completion, perfection). Reason manifests itself, according to him, only in the *European* tradition, and not the Chinese one, for example (Husserl, 1976, p. 72). The first manifestation of reason, according to him, occurred in ancient Greece with Plato's theory of ideas and the rise of mathematics. In modern times, according to him, it is Descartes in whom the manifestation of reason occurs most obviously and in whom this manifestation was more intensive. Hence, a special place is allocated to Descartes in recounting this history of epiphanies in the European tradition (ibid., p. 18). Husserl writes about his 'historical' reflections:

> It is to carry forward, through his own self-reflection, the self-reflection of his forebears and thus not only to reawaken the chain of thinkers, the social interrelation of their thinking, the community of their thought, and transform it into a living present for us but, on the basis of the *total unity* thus made present, to carry out a *responsible critique*, a peculiar sort of critique which has its ground in these historical, personal projects, partial fulfillments, and exchanges of criticism rather than in what is privately taken for granted by the present philosopher. (Husserl, 1970, pp. 71–2, italics in original)

The epiphany of reason, Husserl argues, of general and eternal forms, implies the birth of science, of accuracy, of a striving for adequacy, of more control over one's destiny, over one's self and other selves (Husserl, 1976, §12).

> Philosophy in its ancient origins wanted to be 'science', universal knowledge of the universe of what is; it wanted to be not vague and

relative everyday knowledge –δόξα ['doxa', 'opinion', 'belief'] – but rational knowledge –ἐπιστήμη ['episteme', 'knowledge', 'understanding']. But the true idea of rationality, and in connection with that the true idea of universal science, was not yet attained in ancient philosophy – such was the conviction of the founders of the modern age. (Husserl, 1970, p. 65)

The foundation of our thought lies in ancient Greece, Husserl claims. Ancient Greek philosophy and science tolerated various kinds of knowledge in which full certainty was impossible to attain. In modern times, on the contrary, philosophy could no longer tolerate them, and thus it gave birth to method and subjectivity which were supposed to guarantee the validity and truth of science and knowledge (Husserl, 1976, §14). It was Descartes, he says, in whom reason revealed itself as having these characteristics (ibid., p. 75). It was Descartes who turned to transcendental subjectivity by means of his radical doubt or, as Husserl calls it, ἐποχή, but sidestepped and did not explore it (ibid., §17). Descartes was neither aware of his achievement nor guilty of his failure to explore transcendental subjectivity. He rather embodied a stage in the teleological development that led to Husserl's phenomenology. Husserl's reflections on Descartes are hermeneutical in nature – he extracts from Descartes's texts things which Descartes neither said nor was aware of (ibid.). Since Descartes at one and the same time revealed the ego and covered it up, we should both return to and go beyond his philosophy, according to Husserl. In Husserl's view, Descartes serves as the father of modern times and the forerunner of phenomenology. At the same time, the current 'European' crisis goes back to his philosophy but also to the avoidance of transcendental subjectivity. He returns to Descartes, since his philosophy is the cause of the present malady but it also points us to the recovery – the return to transcendental subjectivity. This malady is exclusively European and not human in general. As Husserl argues in one of the *Crisis* lectures:

> In this lecture I shall venture the attempt to find new interest in the frequently treated theme of the European crisis by developing the philosophical-historical idea (or the teleological sense) of European humanity. As I exhibit, in the process, the essential function that philosophy and its branches, our sciences, have to exercise within that sense, the European crisis will also receive a new elucidation. (Husserl, 1970, p. 269)

In Husserl's view, European history, culture, and civilization are detached from the rest of humanity. 'The European nations are sick; Europe itself, it is said, is in crisis', Husserl (1970, p. 270) says.

> As already indicated in our introductory statements, a remarkable teleology, inborn, as it were, only in our Europe, will become visible in this way, one which is quite intimately involved with the outbreak or irruption of philosophy and its branches, the sciences, in the ancient Greek spirit. We can foresee that this will involve a clarification of the deepest reasons for the origin of the portentous naturalism, or, what will prove to be equivalent, of modern dualism in the interpretation of the world. Finally this will bring to light the actual sense of the crisis of European humanity. (Ibid., p. 273)

But what is 'European' in Husserl's view? Are colonized states in Africa, Asia, and America 'European'? He replies:

> We pose the question: How is the spiritual shape of Europe to be characterized? Thus we refer to Europe not as it is understood geographically, as on a map, as if thereby the group of people who live together in this territory would define European humanity. In the spiritual sense the English Dominions, the United States, etc., clearly belong to Europe, whereas the Eskimos or Indians presented as curiosities at fairs, or the Gypsies, who constantly wander about Europe, do not. Here the title 'Europe' clearly refers to the unity of a spiritual life, activity, creation, with all its ends, interests, cares, and endeavors, with its products of purposeful activity, institutions, and organizations. Here individual men act in many societies of different levels: in families, in tribes, in nations, all being internally, spiritually bound together, and, as I said, in the unity of a spiritual shape. (Ibid.)

As Jacques Derrida poignantly remarks on this passage:

> The retention of the English colonies in 'spiritual' Europe would be proof of a ludicrous enough kind – by the comic load weighing down this sinister passage – of a philosophical non-sequitur whose gravity can be measured in two dimensions: (1) It is apparently necessary, therefore, in order to save the English dominions, the power and culture they represent, to make a distinction between, for example, good and bad Indians. This is not very 'logical', either in 'spiritualist' logic or in 'racist' logic. (2) This text was delivered in 1935 in Vienna! (Derrida, 1991, pp. 120–1)

In Husserl's posthumous texts we find the following: 'Papua has no biography in a full sense, and the Papua tribe has no history of life, no history of people' (Husserl, 1993, p. 57). The European nations, he holds, are characterized by the ideal of a universal philosophy; this is their end (*Endgestalt*), τέλος, which directs them (Husserl, 1976, p. 319; 1993, pp. 58–9). In expanding on that matter, he sounds like a common *völkisch* thinker:

> However, upon more consistent and internally directed observation we notice new, peculiar interrelations and differences. No matter how hostile they may be toward one another, the European nations nevertheless have a particular inner kinship of spirit which runs through them all, transcending national differences.

> There is something unique here that is recognized in us by all other human groups, too, something that, quite apart from all considerations of utility, becomes a motive for them to Europeanize themselves even in their unbroken will to spiritual self-preservation; whereas we, if we understand ourselves properly, would never Indianize ourselves, for example. (Husserl, 1970, pp. 274–5)

'Europe' designates a spiritual unity which refers back also to a physical and historical birthplace. Husserl writes:

> Spiritual Europe has a birthplace. By this I mean not a geographical birthplace, in one land, though this is also true, but rather a spiritual birthplace in a nation or in individual men and human groups of this nation. It is the ancient Greek nation in the seventh and sixth centuries B.C. Here there arises a *new sort of attitude* of individuals toward their surrounding world. And its consequence is the breakthrough of a completely new sort of spiritual structure, rapidly growing into a systematically self-enclosed cultural form; the Greeks called it *philosophy*. (Ibid., p. 276, italics in original)

The cure of the crisis starts, according to Husserl, by return to the origin of the European civilization.

> In times as ours, times of skeptical uncertainty, in which the goal (*Zwecksinn*) of philosophy has become entirely questionable, the philosopher will always be time and again required to reflect about it [i.e. that goal], about the sense and possibility of his entire undertaking. And this can be carried out only through query into the historical origins of that undertaking which has

been bequeathed to us in the continuity of a thousand years.[17] (Husserl, 1993, p. 47)

As we have seen, there is a huge gap between Husserl and Descartes. We can think neither of a natural development from the one to the other nor of a bridge between them. It is rather Husserl's political and ideological worldview which brings them together – they are both directed by the European τέλος, by the ideal of the European man. Non-European peoples and nations are not part of that teleological story. As Derrida puts it:

> It is useful to recall that the reference to spirit, to the freedom of spirit, and to spirit as European spirit could and still can ally itself with the politics one would want to oppose to it. And this reference to spirit, and to Europe, is no more an external or accidental ornament for Husserl's thought than it is for Heidegger's. It plays a major, organizing role in the transcendental teleology of reason as Europocentric humanism. (Derrida, 1991, p. 121)

***

Being and Time, Martin Heidegger's *opus magnum*, can be read as an alternative to Descartes's *Meditations on First Philosophy* in which Heidegger professes to offer a deeper, more original meaning to the main components in Cartesian philosophy: subject, object, essence, existence, space, and time. A careful reading of *Being and Time* reveals an implicit political critique of European civilization, which is founded on Cartesianism, and its excessive, uncontrolled use of technology. Heidegger's later writings reveal a scathing critique of Cartesianism in which he discerns the foundation of totalitarianism, excessive use of technology and arms race, misuse of power and weapons, fascism and world wars. In Chapter 4, we will focus first on Heidegger's early philosophy, especially *Being and Time*, and its sociopolitical critique of Descartes. We will then turn to Heidegger's later writings and see how he traces back all the maladies of modern European civilization and culture to Descartes.

Notes

1 'Seine *Meditationes de prima philosophia* bedeuten in der Geschichte der Philosophie dadurch einen völlig neuen Anfang, daß sie in einem bis dahin

unerhörten Radikalismus den Versuch machen, den absolut notwendigen Anfang der Philosophie zu entdecken und dabei diesen Anfang aus der absoluten und völlig reinen Selbsterkenntnis zu schöpfen.'

2 See also 'Damit wird eine verborgene Doppeldeutigkeit der Cartesianischen Gedanken zu Tage treten; es zeigen sich zwei Möglichkeiten, diese Gedanken zu fassen, sie auszubilden, wissenschaftliche Aufgabenzu stellen, von denen für Descartes nur die eine die vorweg selbstverständliche war. So ist der Sinn seiner Darstellungen faktisch (als der seine) eindeutig; aber leider stammt diese Eindeutigkeit daher, daß er den originalen Radikalismus seiner Gedanken nicht wirklich durchführt, daß er nicht wirklich alle seine Vormeinungen, nicht wirklich in allem die Welt der Epoché unterwirft ("einklammert"), daß er, auf sein Ziel verschossen, gerade das Bedeutsamste nicht herausholt, was er im "ego" der Epoché gewonnen hatte, um rein an diesem ein philosophisches θαυμάζειν zu entfalten' (Husserl, 1976, p. 80).

3 'Es fehlte dem negativistisch praktisch-ethisch (politisch) eingestellten Skeptizismus auch in allen späteren Zeiten das originale Cartesianische Motiv: durch die Hölle einer nicht mehr zu übersteigernden quasi-skeptischen Epoché hindurch zum Eingangstor in den Himmel einer absolut rationalen Philosophie vorzudringen und diese selbst systematisch aufzubauen.'

4 'Im phänomenologischen Umkreis wurde der Boden fruchtbar gemacht für die Erkenntnis von Transzendentem, von Offenbarungen, und von Gott selbst ... ' 'Aber all wurden irgendwie berührt von der Existenz jenseitiger Welten, deren Wesen – wie das Wesen vieler anderer Dinge – plötzlich in Sicht trat.'

5 See also 'Jetzt aber handelt es sich um eine sozusagen absolut subjektive Wissenschaft, eine Wissenschaft, deren Gegenstand in seinem Sein von der Entscheidung über Nichtsein oder Sein der Welt unabhängig ist' (Husserl, 1973, p. 69).

6 See also 'Das Universum wahren Seins fassen zu wollen als etwas, das außerhalb des Universums möglichen Bewußtseins, möglicher Erkenntnis, möglicher Evidenz steht, beides bloß äußerlich durch ein starres Gesetz aufeinander bezogen, ist unsinnig' (Husserl, 1973, p. 117).

7 See also 'Jede Evidenz stiftet für mich eine bleibende Habe. Auf die selbst erschaute Wirklichkeit kann ich *immer wieder* zurückkommen, in Ketten neuer Evidenzen als *Restitutionen* der ersten Evidenz; so z.B. bei der Evidenz immanenter Gegebenheiten etwa in Form einer Kette anschaulicher Wiedererinnerungen mit der offenen Endlosigkeit, die, als potentiellen Horizont, das *Ich kann immer wieder* schafft. Ohne dergleichen Möglichkeiten wäre für uns kein stehendes und bleibendes Sein, keine reale und ideale Welt. Eine jede ist für uns aus der Evidenz bzw. der Präsumption, evident-machen und gewonnene Evidenz wiederholen zu können' (Husserl, 1973, pp. 95–6).

8 See also 'Jeder Versuch, von den historisch gewordenen Wissenschaften her zu besserer Begründung, zu einem besseren Sich-selbst-verstehen nach Sinn und Leistung zu kommen, ist ein Stück Selbstbesinnung des Wissenschaftlers. Es gibt aber nur eine radikale Selbstbesinnung, das ist die phänomenologische' (Husserl, 1973, p. 179).

9 See also 'Es ist, wie ich hier versuchen werde zu zeigen, eine Ausgerichtetheit auf eine Endform der Transzendentalphilosophie–Phänomenologie -, in der als aufgehobenes Moment die Endform der Psychologie liegt, die den naturalistischen Sinn der neuzeitlichen Psychologie entwurzelt' (Husserl, 1976, p. 71).

10 Carr translates *aufgehobenes Moment* as 'suspended moment'. This may be misleading, since the meaning of *aufheben* here is 'to supersede an inferior stage' and yet to 'retain' it – both functions are essential components of teleology. Compare Hegel: 'Die ursprünglich bestimmte Natur des Individuums hat ihre positive Bedeutung, an sich das Element und der Zweck seiner Tätigkeit zu sein, verloren; sie ist nur *aufgehobnes Moment*, und das Individuum ein Selbst; als allgemeines Selbst' (Hegel, 1990, p. 323, italics added).

11 See also 'Erst die Aufhellung der Eigenheit der Synthesis macht die Aufweisung des *cogito*, des intentionalen Erlebnisses, als Bewußtsein-von, macht also die bedeutsame Entdeckung Franz Brentanos, daß die Intentionalität der deskriptive Grundcharakter der psychischen Phänomene sei, fruchtbar und legt die Methode einer deskriptiven – wie transzendental-philosophischen, so natürlich auch psychologischen – Bewußtseinslehre wirklich frei' (Husserl, 1973, p. 79).

12 ' "Philosophie als Wissenschaft, als ernstliche, strenge, ja apodiktisch strenge Wissenschaft – der Traum ist ausgeträumt" ' (Landgrebe, 1963, p. 187). See also 'Natürlich bewegt sich die Forschung in verschiedenen Stufen. Sie wird nicht etwa dadurch gehindert, daß hier das Reich des subjektiven Flusses ist und daß es ein Wahn wäre, hier in einer Methodik der Begriffs- und Urteilsbildung verfahren zu wollen, die für die objektiven exakten Wissenschaften die maßgebende ist. Gewiß, das Bewußtseinsleben ist im Fluß, und jedes *cogito* ist fließend, ohne fixierbare letzte Elemente und letzte Relationen' (Husserl, 1973, p. 20). See also 'Die Philosophie mit dem Zeithorizont der Weltvergangenheit (der unserer Welt) ist gegenwärtige jetzt wirkliche Philosophie als die aus ihren Vergangenheiten gewordene. – Diese Vergangenheiten sind aber horizonthaft unbekannt, sind für uns nicht als vorgegebene Seinsgewißheiten der gewesenen Philosophien, sondern ein Horizont möglicher Seinsgewißheiten. Deren erste Klärung ist Evidentmachung der Möglichkeiten als solcher, die sich unter beschränkender Bindung an die vereinzelten dokumentierten Überlieferungen ergeben' (Husserl, 1993, p. 47).

13 See also 'Die transzendentale Subjektivität ist nicht ein Chaos von intentionalen Erlebnissen, sondern eine Einheit der Synthese, und einer vielstufigen Synthese,

in der immer neue Objekttypen und Einzelobjekte konstituiert sind' (Husserl,
1973, p. 22).

14 ' "Die Philosophie und die Krisis des europäischen Menschentums." Die erste
Hälfte: die philosophische Idee des europäischen Menschentums (oder "der
europäischen Kultur") aus teleologisch-historischen Ursprüngen (aus der
Philosophie) aufgeklärt' (Husserl, 1976, p. xiii.).

15 See also 'Es ist eine Krisis, welche das Fachwissenschaftliche in seinen
theoretischen und praktischen Erfolgen nicht angreift und doch ihren ganzen
Wahrheitssinn durch und durch erschüttert'(Husserl, 1976, p. 10).

16 'No doubt Heidegger appeals to a historial decision supposing the experience
of a *krinein*. No doubt he also wants to awaken Europe and philosophy to
their responsibility before the task of the question and the originary question
of grounds. No doubt he is suspicious, in the first instance, that a certain
technoscientific objectivity represses and forgets the question. No doubt Husserl
too asks himself, "How is the spiritual configuration of Europe" (*die geistige
Gestalt Europas*) characterised?'(Derrida, 1991, p. 60).

17 'In einer Zeit wie der unseren, einer Zeit skeptischer Unsicherheit, in welcher
der Zwecksinn <der> Philosophie ganz und gar fraglich geworden ist, wird der
Philosoph immer wieder ernstlich genötigt sein, sich auf diesen, auf den Sinn
und die Möglichkeit seines ganzen Vorhabens zu besinnen. Und wie könnte dies
anders geschehen als durch eine Rückfrage in die geschichtlichen Ursprünge
dieses uns Philosophen in der Kontinuitat von jahrtausenden übermittelten
Vorhabens?'

4

Martin Heidegger: *Homo est brutum bestiale*

Scholars usually distinguish between the earlier and the later Heidegger, utilizing the term *Kehre* (turn) to draw a line between the earlier Heidegger, whose main concern was the human Da-sein, and the later Heidegger, whose main concern was the history of Being or the ways in which Being has been understood in Western thought. In both periods, Descartes occupies a central position. We will first concentrate on *Being and Time*, Heidegger's opus magnum. It turns out that *Being and Time* can be regarded as a direct response to Cartesian philosophy. There are two famous studies on Heidegger's *Being and Time*, one by Robert B. Brandom (2002, pp. 298–376) and one by Hubert L. Dreyfus (1990), which profess to find in *Being and Time* a new epistemology and pragmatic theory of judgement, which work better than the traditional epistemology and pragmatic theory in solving problems such as psychophysical dualism and providing a better theory of judgement and justification. There is also a serious study by Ernst Tugendhat on the concept of truth in Husserl and Heidegger (Tugendhat, 1967). People who are familiar with Heidegger's texts in the original, before and after *Being and Time*, as well as with his unique terminology and explicit allusions to early Christian eschatological literature, know that the epistemological aspect and interest are only marginal and inessential in the earlier Heidegger. His main concern is the renewal of the question concerning the meaning of Being, which had sunk into oblivion. There is critique, a sharp critique indeed, of Descartes in *Being and Time*, and it is mainly a cultural critique of modern society which emerged out of modern rationalism whose main representative is Descartes. It is by no means an alternative epistemology and pragmatic theory. As we shall see, modern Western society is viewed as a mass culture which has lost any access to the self, truth, and history. It is alienated from its history and tradition. We will next turn to the later Heidegger, to the role of Descartes in the lectures on Nietzsche from the 1940s and the 'notorious' *Black Notebooks*. Here Heidegger's cultural critique becomes a scathing political critique. He traces back the emergence of nationalism, Communism, Nazism, racism, and barbarism to Descartes and the rationalism which he represents.

There are only three paragraphs dedicated explicitly to Descartes in *Being and Time*. In the second part of *Being and Time*, which Heidegger only outlined but never published, the second section was to have been dedicated to Descartes: 'The Ontological Foundation of Descartes's *cogito sum* and the Incorporation of Medieval Ontology in the Problem of the *res cogitans*' (Heidegger, 1996, p. 35). *Being and Time* as a whole can even be regarded as a response to Descartes, as an attempt to rescue man from the alienation of the ego to itself and to its existence.[1] Herbert Schnädelbach remarks concerning Descartes's philosophy: 'Hence, we find ourselves with Descartes in a hopelessly split world, conceptually alienated from external nature and from our own body' (Schnädelbach, 2000, p. 188).[2]

The difference between Descartes and Heidegger is substantial: Descartes strives to lay down a firm foundation for natural sciences, whereas Heidegger professes to renew the forgotten question concerning the meaning of Being. Yet, we can easily discern overlapping paths. Descartes is focused on the human ego which serves as the source of validity to assure a firm foundation for the natural sciences. Heidegger, in preparing the way to renew the question concerning the meaning of Being, concentrates on the human Da-sein in what he calls 'fundamental ontology' (*Fundamentalontologie*) (Heidegger, 1967, pp. 6–7).[3] Despite the substantial differences, we can discern some interesting parallels between Da-sein and the ego. Descartes writes in the *Second Meditation*:

> Yet apart from everything I have just listed, how do I know that there is not something else which does not allow even the slightest occasion for doubt? Is there not a God, or whatever I may call him, who puts into me the thoughts I am now having? But why do I think this, since I myself may perhaps be the author of these thoughts? In that case am not I, at least, something? But I have just said that I have no senses and no body. This is the sticking point: what follows from this? Am I not so bound up with a body and with senses that I cannot exist without them? But I have convinced

myself that there is absolutely nothing in the world, no sky, no earth, no minds, no bodies. Does it follow that I too do not exist? No: if I convince myself of something then I certainly existed. But there is a deceiver of supreme power and cunning who is deliberately and constantly deceiving me. In that case I too undoubtedly exist, if he is deceiving me; and let him deceive me as much as he can, he will never bring it about that I am nothing so long as I think that I am something. So after considering everything very thoroughly, I must finally conclude that this proposition, *I am, I exist,* is necessarily true whenever it is put forward by me or conceived in my mind. (Descartes, 1996, pp. 36–7)

The ego is 'filled' up with its existence, everything can be subtracted from it except its existence. Likewise, the human Da-sein is determined first of all in regard to existence. Understanding of Being (*Seinsverständnis*), Heidegger says, defines the being of Da-sein (*Seinsbestimmtheit*). He thus concludes that the ontic distinction of Da-sein is due to its being ontological, that is to say, stemming from its understanding of Being (Heidegger, 1967, p. 12).

Da-sein means the understanding of Being. We cannot set them apart. According to Heidegger, Descartes, in laying the firm foundation for science, failed to clear up the *sum,* the existence of the *res cogitans,* or more precisely, the meaning of Being (*Seinsinn*) (Heidegger, 1967, p. 24).[4]

The study of the 'sum' constitutes the first part of *Being and Time.* The study commences with the average daily understanding of Being in working and using tools. This will be the first step in understanding man out of his Being, as Heidegger promised to do, and not as a *res cogitans,* as Descartes does. In order to distance himself from Descartes, Heidegger asserts that he will *not* proceed deductively in his inquiry (Heidegger, 1967, pp. 8, 11). At the same time, Heidegger talks in a manner that reminds us of Descartes: the inquiry after the meaning of Being is supposed to provide philosophy and the sciences with a stable foundation which reminds us of Descartes's search after *fundamentum inconcussum* (firm foundation). The question regarding the meaning of Being, Heidegger contends, aims at the a priori conditions of the various sciences and, furthermore, at the a priori conditions of the ontology preceding these sciences. For without a clarification of the meaning of Being, any ontology remains meaningless (ibid., p. 11).

In Descartes, the first person *cogito, ergo sum* is the point of reference of any truth and validity. Similarly, the first person is implied in the definition of Da-sein: 'always my own', *je meines* in German. Its essence is defined as 'being always my own', *Jemeinigkeit* (Heidegger, 1967, pp. 41–2). Despite Heidegger's attempt to bypass the *ego cogito sum* as the basic point of reference, he ends up with a rather similar point of reference. Heidegger takes great pains to distinguish human Da-sein from the Cartesian ego as a thinking thing. For Heidegger, ego is the outcome of the failure to raise the question concerning the meaning of Being. Since Descartes, *res cogitans* has been seen in Western tradition as the only way to look at the existence of man. Thus, an unyielding destruction of the Western philosophical tradition is required. It will reveal, as Heidegger argues, the tacit ontological foundations of Descartes's philosophy. It will also demonstrate the reason why Descartes had to neglect the question regarding the meaning of Being and why he thought that the absolute certainty attained with the *cogito* excused him from inquiring after the meaning of Being (ibid., p. 24).

Descartes likewise demands an unyielding destruction right at the beginning of his *Meditations*:

> I realized that it was necessary, once in the course of my life, to demolish everything completely and start again right from the foundations if I wanted to establish anything at all in the sciences that was stable and likely to last. (Descartes, 1996, p. 12)

Heidegger concentrates on language as the basic channel of communication in which the meaning of Being becomes distorted. Thus, language is the main target of the destruction. He also claims that the original meaning of any proposition may get lost through circulation and communication in language, and thereby lose its link to the original experience (Heidegger, 1967, p. 36).

Since Descartes, man is exclusively regarded as a substance. This is the main obstacle to study the human Da-sein. The first stage of the destruction is directed towards the Cartesian notion of man as a thinking thing. This destruction is carried out as a return to man's understanding of Being in his daily occupations (*durchschnittliche Alltäglichkeit*) (Heidegger, 1967, pp. 50–1), to what Heidegger calls 'world'. Da-sein is 'being-in-the-world' (*In-der-Welt-sein*). By this term he designates Da-sein's first understanding of Being in a mode of familiarity, being at home, in the midst of its familiar surroundings (ibid., p. 54). In this mode of familiarity, Da-sein is immersed in its vicinity and there is no gap between subject and object. The dualism of subject and object is a remote abstraction which stems from a breakdown in the smooth process of performing an assignment and a subsequent disregard of Da-sein's first understanding of Being in the mode of familiarity and intimacy. This disregard yields the so-called psychophysical problem (ibid., pp. 59–62).

According to Heidegger, the original access to entities in their state of Being is not intellectual, as in Descartes's philosophy, but rather through use (*Umgang*) (Heidegger, 1967, p. 67). In introducing 'use' as the first encounter with entities in their state of Being, Heidegger has in mind the Aristotelian φρόνησις (phronesis) or 'practical knowledge'. These entities are first of all regarded as tools to accomplish assignments, and their Being, their meaning, is their function as tools. Intellectual perception can never have access to the 'essential' being of the tools (ibid., p. 68). Tools are never isolated substances but are related to each other, point (*verweist*) to each other, in a context of assignment within which their specific use is allocated. The tool has a structure of pointing, of signing, of referencing (*Zeichen*). The Being of things at hand (*vorhandensein*), as Heidegger argues, is reference, that is to say, they are revealed in their reference to other things at hand (ibid., pp. 83–4).

Da-sein projects this meaningful context, this 'relevance' (*Bewandtnis*) in which entities are discovered as tools. Intellectual perception can never disclose meaning and relevance. Dealing with tools is however not blind. Heidegger discerns in it a special kind of seeing which he calls 'circumspection' (*Umsicht*) (Heidegger, 1967, p. 69). In other words, he points at the role played by insight, understood as the Aristotelian νοῦς (nous, intuition), within 'use' understood as φρόνησις. As Heidegger contends, function is not an attribute of the *res extensa* [extended thing] but rather the first appearance of the entities in their Being. The kind of Being of the things at hand, their handiness (*Zuhandenheit*) is not a mere product of interpretation, aspects forced upon them. Handiness is rather their ontological determination as they are in themselves (ibid., p. 71).

Epistemologically seen, it is not a developed doctrine and cannot serve as a substantial alternative to Descartes's epistemology. Yet, Heidegger's main goal is to raise again the question concerning the meaning of Being and not to offer an alternative epistemology. His theory of Da-sein contains social and political assessments of modern society as it emerged out of Descartes's philosophy. Descartes's *cogito* leads to alienation between man and his body, his surroundings, and his mates, and the emerging society is pervaded with alienation. Contrary to this Cartesian alienation, Heidegger defines the Being of Da-sein as 'care' (*Sorge*). Thus, its attitude towards humans is 'concern' (*Fürsorge*) and towards entities is 'heedfulness' (*Besorgen*). Entities are never discovered as bare substance to which attributes and values are attached. They are rather discovered in their meaning. Likewise, Da-sein is not a bare subject that enters a world with bare entities. Da-sein rather always exists in a world familiar to it in which entities are already permeated with meaning. Da-sein enables the disclosure of things in their relevance. A network of interrelated things, which Heidegger calls 'world', is always given with the Being of Da-sein (Heidegger, 1967, p. 87).

Breakdown or interruption in carrying out the assignment brings about the alienated worldview of Descartes. Da-sein can try to overcome the alienation and retrieve the lost or partly lost intimacy. But it can also maximize this alienation and create a world in which it encounters entities deprived of meaning, split into bare subject and bare object, *res cogitans* vis-à-vis *res extensa*. According to Heidegger, it is only since the innerworldly things can be encountered at all, namely, as being in the world, that they can be merely perceived as a bare substance. In this mode of Being, they can be mathematically determined in 'functional concepts' (Heidegger, 1967, p. 88).

Descartes, according to Heidegger, thinks of Being only in terms of pure substance. For him, there are two kinds of created substances: *res cogitans* (thinking thing) and *res corporea* (corporeal thing), as well as God. Thought and expansion are the two essential characters of the created substance. The substantiality of substance, the source of its meaning, is in Descartes's view inaccessible. Hence, he never raises the question concerning the meaning of Being (Heidegger, 1967, p. 94). Descartes, as Heidegger contends, not only completely avoids the question regarding the Being of substance, its substantiality, but also stresses that it is inaccessible: *Verumtamen non potest substantia primum animadverti ex hoc solo, quod sit res existens, quia hoc solum per se nos non afficit.* ['Yet substance cannot be first discovered merely from the fact that it is an existing thing, for that fact alone does not affect us.'] That is to say, since 'Being' itself does not affect us, it cannot be conceived.

When Kant says that 'Being is not a real predicate' he is merely restating Descartes's claim (ibid.).

The sole concept of Being, which Descartes has in mind, is a constant objective presence (*Vorhandenheit*). Hence, he could never study Da-sein as being-in-the-world. Heidegger writes that Descartes's view of Being as a constant objective presence leads to the extreme definition of the Being of the innerworldly things as *res extensa*, as substance. It likewise bars the way to appropriate the ontological study of Da-sein (Heidegger, 1967, p. 98).

According to Heidegger, entities are first encountered with meaning. Starting from *res cogitans* and *res extensa* would never enable Descartes to reconstruct that first encounter, to 'fix' (*haften*) meaning to those stripped entities (Heidegger, 1967, p. 68).

Contrary to Descartes, intellectual perception, *cogitare*, is not the primary access to entities in their Being. We have mentioned care (*Besorgen*) and use (*Umgang*). *Res extensa* is only a late derived mode of existence of entities. Primarily, spatiality is understood in terms of meaning and not of empty space, Heidegger claims. According to him, the things at hand which we encounter through use have the character of proximity (*Nähe*). Being at hand has various ways of proximity which cannot be mathematically measured. Their proximity is determined by their usability, by their function in the network of things at hand, and as projects to be completed. This means that their 'spatiality' is not determined by the place they occupy in space (Heidegger, 1967, p. 102).

Things 'occupy' space because Da-sein projects spatial meaning upon them. Heidegger calls this projection of spatiality 'de-distancing' (*Ent-fernung*). He calls the projected spatial meaning 'region' (*Gegend*). It means that Da-sein draws entities closer to itself by putting them to use in its assignments.

De-distancing, as Heidegger explains, brings things closer by means of providing (*beschaffen*), appropriating (*bereitstellen*), and making them available (*zur Hand haben*). The essential tendency to proximity is given with Da-sein's way of Being (Heidegger, 1967, p. 105).

Thus, something that *physically* is very close to me may be located at a 'great distance' from me, since it is less important in the network of my occupation and assignment. Thus, nothing can be nearer to me than the eyeglasses on my nose, Heidegger says. Yet, they are more remote from me than the picture on the wall on the other side of the room on which I am now focused. In the same way, the street upon which I am now walking is more remote from me than my acquaintance who is now twenty steps away from me (Heidegger, 1967, p. 107). Bringing near, Heidegger concludes, is not understood in terms of distance from I-thing but rather in terms of heedful Being-in-the-world (ibid.).

The existence of space is explained by intimacy and familiarity. Three-dimensional space is an abstraction of the existence of space as it is disclosed in this mode of intimacy (Heidegger, 1967, p. 110). There is no encapsulated ego which should reach out to the external spatial world but rather Da-sein that exists intimately amidst the familiar context of assignments and works which it accomplishes. Heidegger thus concludes that space is neither within the subject nor outside it. It is rather disclosed along with Da-sein's Being (ibid., p. 111).

In its daily life, Da-sein's mode of Being is ruled by public opinion and judgement. Heidegger calls this mode of Being 'they'. In German it is *Das Man*. 'Man', a pronoun, refers to the anonymous person, as 'one' does in English: 'one thinks ...', 'one is fond of ...', 'one judges that ...'. In this mode of Being, Da-sein evades its 'being always my own' (*Jemeinigkeit*) and lives according to the dictation of public opinion. Also this mode of Being is characterized by intimacy and familiarity, otherwise Da-sein would not be able to immerse in it. Heidegger, however, strives to reach a higher level of intimacy – an intimacy in which Da-sein does not evade but rather takes upon itself its Being as 'being always my own'. As we have seen, Da-sein never exists as a pure ego, but rather as Being-in-the-world. In this way, Da-sein always exists with other people. Heidegger calls this co-existence 'Being-with' (*Mitsein*) and Being-with-other-Da-sein or *MitDa-sein*. The clarification of Being-in-the-world, Heidegger writes, demonstrates that a mere subject without a world is never originally given. Hence, an isolated I without other people is also never originally given (Heidegger, 1967, p. 116).

The world is always given along with other people (Heidegger, 1967, p. 118). The others are not given as objects which exist next to me. We rather co-exist in a mode of intimacy and familiarity. When we talk about Being with other people, Heidegger writes, we do not mean isolated subjects set apart from me. The others are rather those from whom I am usually not set apart. They are always given along with Da-sein's Being (ibid.).

Da-sein always exists *with* other Da-sein, even when it is alone, because co-existence is a way in which it understands Being. Thus, even when Da-sein is alone, it understands Being in the mode of co-existence (Heidegger, 1967, pp. 120–1). Da-sein can co-exist in a mode of indifference towards the others. The pure ego in Descartes's philosophy emerged out of this mode of indifference towards the others. The indifferent modes of co-existence, Heidegger says, lead us to the false ontological interpretation of co-existence as the purely objective presence of discrete subjects (Heidegger, 1996, p. 114). He calls the indifferent modes of co-existence 'they' (*das Man*). Heidegger uses this term 'they' to point out the neutral character of this kind of co-existence, its lack of a 'self' (ibid., p. 121).

'They' dictates the ways in which Da-sein understands most of the time its Being. It is always comfortable to live in this mode, since it releases Da-sein from all responsibilities. Although alienating Da-sein from its own self, this mode of Being creates a feeling of intimacy and tranquillity. This makes Da-sein 'fall prey' to the dictatorship of the crowd. This kind of co-existence completely melts one's own Da-sein to the extent that it enables the 'they' to unfold its dictatorship over the Da-sein and dictates its way of Being (Heidegger, 1996, pp. 126–7).

In this public inauthentic way of Being, 'they' constitutes the self of the Da-sein, its 'constancy' (*Ständigkeit*) (Heidegger, 1967, p. 128). This is not a developed epistemology or ontology of the 'other'. It is rather a cultural critique of Western civilization which exists as an alienated mass society and which has lost its authentic self and the meaning of Being.

'Da' stands for the 'spot' in which Being is enlightened. Heidegger compares it with *lumen naturale* (Heidegger, 1967, p. 133). Heidegger's next task is to explore the *Da*. In the statement *cogito ergo sum*, the thinking thing, the *res cogitans*, is identified with existence in the mode of present and actuality, the ego actually exists in the instance it says 'I think, therefore I exist'. In studying the *Da*, Heidegger also starts with the mode of the present and actuality. But this mode, as it will turn out later, is secondary to the mode of future and potentiality.

The first component of the *Da* which Heidegger discusses is attunement (*Befindlichkeit*). Heidegger characterizes it as a mood (*Stimmung*). Through attunement Da-sein finds itself thrown (*geworfen*) into a state of affairs which it did not choose or create but which has rather been forced upon it. Through mood Da-sein understands its Being as actual or what Heidegger designates as facticity (*Faktizität*). Mood, as Heidegger explains, brings Da-sein to face its Being to which it was born and which it must live (Heidegger, 1967, p. 134). And yet, the actuality of the Da-sein is not the same as the actuality of an object as *factum brutum*. The fact (das *Dass*) of Being can never be discerned by looking (Heidegger, 1967, p. 135).

Attunement makes Being matter to Da-sein and causes it to react. Attunement makes Da-sein care for its Being. Without it, the intimacy with its Being would be impossible. The *Da* is equiprimordially lit by understanding (*Verstehen*) which is a projection of possibility. Contrary to Descartes's ego, Da-sein always equally exists as potentiality. Da-sein, Heidegger emphasizes, is not a present object with possibilities or potentialities. It is rather defined as Being possible (*Möglichsein*). Being possible should not be understood as the modality of actuality. It is rather, as Heidegger claims, a basic way of Da-sein to relate to its Being (Heidegger, 1967, p. 143).

The potentiality of the Da-sein should never be seen in light of actuality, as the potentiality of the acorn is seen in light of the actual oak. On the contrary, it is rather the potentiality of Da-sein's own Being about which it cares. In order to distinguish this potentiality from the potentiality of an object, Heidegger refers to it as 'possibility qua possibility' (*Möglichkeit als Möglichkeit*) (Heidegger, 1967, p. 145). It is, in other words, the possibility of my own Being which is not defined, as the possibility of an entity, in light of its actuality.

Being ahead of or 'hovering above' actuality, understanding (*Verstehen*) provides Da-sein with the sight (*Sicht*) which is the condition of any seeing and reasoning, of any relation to entities (ibid., p. 146). Heidegger takes pains to distinguish it from the pure intellectual perception as well as from physical seeing (ibid., p. 147). By demonstrating that all kinds of sight are based upon understanding, Heidegger deprives intuition of the priority traditionally ascribed to it in accessing things. Intuition and thought, Heidegger contends, are remote derivatives of understanding (ibid., p. 147).

Understanding, the projection of possibilities, enables Da-sein to grasp something *as* something (*etwas als etwas*), for example, this entity as a tool to accomplish that assignment (Heidegger, 1967, p. 149). Thus, it enables Da-sein to insert and integrate that entity into its vicinity. Contrary to intellectual perception, understanding strives to create intimacy and familiarity. It follows that the bare ego, which relates to bare object, 'lacks' understanding. As Heidegger puts it, when we just look at something lying before us, we fail to understand it (ibid., p. 149).

Da-sein does not 'create' the possibilities of Being which it projects. It rather projects those possibilities into which it has been thrown. Thus, it projects the possibilities with which it is most intimately bound.

The third component, next to attunement and understanding, which makes up the *Da*, is discourse (*Rede*). Through discourse Da-sein is always confronted with articulated meaning. Discourse is the foundation of language, although articulated meaning does not always have to be verbally expressed (Heidegger, 1967, p. 161).

We are required to give up the Cartesian notion of an encapsulated ego which has to communicate its inner world to other egos in order to understand what Heidegger means by 'discourse'. Discourse is a way to disclose Being, which is primarily seen from the perspective of co-existence in the world. Communication, Heidegger goes on to explain, is never initially a verbal conveyance of inner content such as the opinions and wishes of one person to the inner experience of another person. Our Being-with (*Mitsein*) is shared in discourse (Heidegger, 1967, p. 162).

Hearing (*Hören*) is inherently bound up with discourse and it enables Da-sein to attend to its own Being (Heidegger, 1967, p. 163). Yet, it is not the *spoken* discourse and the hearing of the spoken words that provides Da-sein with access to its Being, but it is rather reticence (*Verschwiegenheit*). Reticence, Heidegger says, makes manifest and shuts up 'idle talk'. As a means of discourse, it articulates the Being of Da-sein in such an original way that it enables genuine hearing and Being-with (ibid., p. 165).

Most of the time, however, discourse (*Rede*) wears the form of idle talk (*Gerede*) that points Da-sein away from genuine disclosure of Being. Idle talk characterizes Da-sein's daily Being with other people. Idle talk, Heidegger says, loses genuine access to the disclosure of things and is focused instead on disclosed things. It communicates through the mode of spreading unfounded gossip and rumours (Heidegger, 1967, pp. 168–9).

More than anything else, this is a caricature of an alienated society, lost in endless and meaningless chatter which covers up and blocks the access to the original disclosure of Being. To idle talk Heidegger adds curiosity (*Neugier*) as a mode of discourse (§36) and ambiguity (*Zweideutigkeit*) (§37) which points Da-sein further away from the disclosure of Being. Idle talk, curiosity, and ambiguity make up what Heidegger calls 'falling-prey' (*Verfallen*). Falling-prey, Heidegger says, does not imply any negative assessment of this way of Being. It rather designates the way in which Da-sein exists most of the time, lost in the public way of Being ('they') which is directed by idle talk, curiosity, and ambiguity. This is an inauthentic (*uneigentlich*) way of Being (Heidegger, 1967, pp. 175–6).

'Falling-prey' constitutes the intimacy and familiarity of the public sphere in which Da-sein discloses Being in its average daily life. This public intimacy and familiarity mark alienation from one's own Being. Da-sein falls away from its own existence which is 'always mine' (*je meines*). It relates to and interprets its Being in line with the current public trends. Publicity utilizes tranquillization (*Beruhigung*) to prevent Da-sein from making the attempt to overcome that public alienation and return to its own self. In the 'they' mode of Being, Heidegger says, one feels that there is no need of authentic understanding, since one lives a full and genuine life in which everything is in its best order. Thus, this way of Being provides Da-sein with tranquillity (Heidegger, 1967, p. 177).

By means of tranquillization, falling-prey points Da-sein away from Being as *je meines*, from facing its own Being. Angst is the mood in which Da-sein obtains access to its authentic self. Heidegger writes, 'As a possibility of being (*Seinsmöglichkeit*) of Da-sein, together with the Da-sein itself disclosed in it, *Angst* provides the phenomenal basis for explicitly grasping the primordial totality of being (*Seinsganzheit*) of Da-sein' (Heidegger, 1996 , p. 171). As Heidegger tells us, the fleeing (*Flucht*) which we discerned in falling-prey – a fleeing into the hands of the crowd – is the fleeing in the face of the disclosure of Angst (Heidegger, 1967, p. 186). If the true self is disclosed in Angst, why does Da-sein flee in face of its true Being which should also mean the highest point of intimacy and familiarity?

As we have seen, Da-sein feels at home in its average daily life. The familiarity and intimacy in its vicinity enable it to immerse itself in its assignments and make it interpret Being in terms of the entities it encounters in its vicinity. This familiarity and intimacy is accompanied by alienation. Da-sein flees its own Being and interprets it in terms of the public opinion, of the 'they' (*Das Man*). This is what Heidegger calls 'falling-prey' (*Verfallen*). Angst shuts down the familiarity and intimacy of daily life. By that means, Angst brings about alienation. Consequently, Da-sein understands its Being in the mode of 'not being at home' (*Unzuhause*) (ibid., p. 189). At the same time, Angst points Da-sein back to its own Being (*je meines*). In Angst, everything occupying Da-sein in its daily life becomes irrelevant. Contrary to fear, Angst is about nothing. In Angst, Heidegger says, Da-sein is disclosed as a sheer possibility or potentiality of Being (*Seinkönnen*) (ibid., p. 186).

In Angst, everything dissolves into meaninglessness, and Da-sein is confronted with its own Being as a sheer potentiality. As Heidegger puts it in the lecture *What is Metaphysics?* 'Angst takes away our world. Since everything (*das Seiende im Ganzen*) slips away and consequently *Nothing* overwhelms, every use of "to-be" (*Ist-Sagen*) mutes in its face' (Heidegger, 1955, p. 32).[5]

In Descartes, Being is synonymous with actuality. Upon this assumption the ontological proof of God's existence is carried out. Likewise, the *ego cogito sum* is founded upon this identity of Being and actuality. Potentiality, referring ahead to the future, cannot guarantee clear and distinct validity. Contrary to the *ego cogito sum*, which has meaning only as a present actuality, Da-sein, once returned to itself in Angst, is revealed as sheer potentiality. In Angst, since the world fades away, Da-sein is no longer able to understand and interpret its Being in terms of the falling-prey, of the public way of Being. Angst individuates Da-sein and impels Da-sein to face its own Being as possibility (*Möglichsein*) (Heidegger, 1967, pp. 187–8).

With Angst, Heidegger achieves phenomenological access to the *Da* of Da-sein as a sheer potentiality or possibility to be. Da-sein is not an actual thing, *res cogitans*, but rather potentiality to be. Likewise, this is the highest point of intimacy: Being is no longer interpreted in terms of a substance and covered up by idle talk. Da-sein is rather seen now as its own possibility to be. This is a sweeping destruction, no less radical than Descartes's *Meditations*. Also in Heidegger it is bound with the question about truth and falsity. Heidegger writes, 'Being free *for* its ownmost potentiality-for-being, and thus for the possibility of authenticity and inauthenticity, shows itself in a primordial, elemental concretion in Angst' (Heidegger, 1996 , p. 179, italics in original). In Angst, Da-sein is brought to face its true Being as possibility.

In the *Fourth Meditation*, Descartes pursues the question where error comes from. By definition, Descartes claims, it cannot come directly from God; God would not deceive me. Likewise, it cannot come indirectly from Him; God would never create me with defective faculties. Descartes finds in himself two faculties whose relationship makes us err: intellect and will. Descartes sees that the human intellect is finite, that is, we can easily imagine an intellect with a greater capacity than ours. Our will, on the contrary, is infinite in its range of willing. The intellect presents the mind with ideas upon which it judges. As such, the mind cannot be the source of error, for error implies judgement. Likewise, the will as such cannot be the source of my errors, because it is perfect. It is rather, Descartes says, the relationship between both that makes us err.

> The scope of the will is wider than that of the intellect; but instead of restricting it within the same limits, I extend its use to matters which I do not understand. Since the will is indifferent in such cases, it easily turns aside from what is true and good, and this is the source of my error and sin. (Descartes, 1996, pp. 40–1)

Right application of the will within the scope of the intellect, of our understanding, will avoid errors and sins, according to Descartes. With Heidegger, on the contrary, we are on a different footing. Being is revealed in Angst as a sheer possibility. As we saw above, since Da-sein is defined as Being-in-the-world and the intellect is not the prime access to Being, truth can no longer primarily mean correspondence between the object and the intellect (*adaequatio rei et intellectus*) as in Descartes. As Heidegger notes, 'The question of whether there is a world at all and whether its being (*Sein*) can be demonstrated, makes no sense at all if it is raised by Da-sein as being-in-the-world – and who else should ask it?' (Heidegger, 1996, p. 188). A bit later he adds, 'The "scandal of philosophy" does not consist in the fact that this proof (of independent external world) is still lacking up to now, but *in the fact* that *such* proofs *are expected and attempted again and again*' (ibid., p. 190, italics in original). Contrary to Descartes, Da-sein's freedom is not defined as a free choice. It is rather the free or clear view of its Being as sheer possibility.[6] Da-sein does not create this possibility but it is rather delivered to it (*überantwortet sein*). Angst reveals to Da-sein its innermost potentiality to be (*Seinkönnen*). In Angst, Da-sein is free to choose its own Being as a possibility which it already is (ibid., p. 188).

Truth receives a new meaning in Heidegger's analysis of Da-sein. Heidegger claims that Being is given (*es gibt Sein*) only insofar as Da-sein is given. Da-sein lets entities emerge in light of their Being. 'However, only as long as Da-sein *is*, that is, as long as there is the ontic possibility of an understanding of being (*Seinsverständnis*), "is there" (*gibt es*) being (*Sein*). If Da-sein does not exist, then there "is" no "independence" either, nor "is" there an "in itself"' (ibid., p. 196, italics in original). And then Heidegger adds, 'Only if an understanding of being *is* (*Seinsverständnis*), are beings accessible as beings (*Seiendes als Seiendes*, i.e. entities); only if beings of the kind of being of Da-sein are, is an understanding of being possible as beings (*Seinsverständnis als Seiendes*)' (ibid.; italics in original).

The original meaning of 'truth', according to Heidegger, is discovery of entities in their Being: '*"There is" ("es gibt") truth only insofar as Da-sein is and as long as it is.* Beings are discovered only *when* Da-sein *is*, and only *as long as* Da-sein *is* are they disclosed' (ibid., p. 208, italics in original). This discovery takes place as Being-in-the-world. 'Being-true as discovering is in turn ontologically possible only on the basis of being-in-the-world. This phenomenon, in which we recognize a basic constitution of Da-sein, is the foundation of the primordial phenomenon of truth' (ibid., p. 201).

Descartes's notion of truth as correspondence is preceded by a more original experience of truth – discovering. This experience of truth is captured in the Greek term ἀλήθεια (aletheia, truth) which Heidegger hyphenates (i.e. ἀ-λήθεια) in order to stress the original meaning of 'truth' – tearing out of oblivion (Heidegger, 1967, p. 219). Discovering (*Entdecken*) things in their Being is a mode of Being in the world. The discovered things are 'true' in a secondary sense. In the primary sense, it refers to discovering as Da-sein's way of Being (ibid., p. 220).

Now, to truth as discovering belongs untruth as covering which is caused by Da-sein being in the state of falling-prey (*Verfallen*), ruled by the crowd and detached from the original disclosure of Being. Since falling-prey is Da-sein's way of Being, Da-sein is equiprimordially in truth and untruth, Heidegger says (Heidegger, 1967, p. 222).

This phenomenological description of truth as disclosure lies far away from any pragmatic theory of judgement and truth. Since it does not provide us with any practicable criterion to distinguish between true and false and since truth and untruth are 'equiprimordial' (*gleichursprünglich*), it cannot provide any foundation of pragmatic or scientific theory. It however sheds light on the constant interplay between intimacy and alienation, between authenticity and inauthenticity. Since Da-sein exists as 'always my own' (*je meines*) and its Being is sheer possibility, to exist truly or falsely cannot be a matter of indifference. It thus must involve will and choice. Heidegger defines Da-sein as 'Being-toward-death' (*Sein-zum-Tode*). By 'death' Heidegger does not mean the biological termination of Da-sein (Heidegger, 1967, p. 247). Being-toward-death is rather the way in which Da-sein exists in its ownmost possibility to be which nobody can take away from it. Death is a possibility of Being which Da-sein must assume. It cannot be bypassed or handed to somebody else. Thus, death brings Da-sein to face its innermost, non-relational possibility to be (*eigenste, unbezügliche Möglichkeit*) (ibid., p. 250).

This ownmost possibility to be is revealed to Da-sein through *Angst*. '*Angst* in the face of death is *Angst* "in the face of" the ownmost nonrelational potentiality-of-being not to be bypassed' (Heidegger, 1996, p. 232). Most of the time, 'they' (*das Man*) points Da-sein away from its ownmost possibility to be. '*The they does not permit the courage to have* Angst *about death*' (ibid., p. 235, italics in original). This does not say that Da-sein is not occupied with death in its daily life. It is, but in an inauthentic way. The entangled flight from death, Heidegger writes, shows that the 'they' itself is always determined as Being towards death. In other words, Da-sein is always preoccupied with death, even in an evasive, inauthentic, indifferent way (ibid., pp. 254–5).

Death as the ownmost possibility of Da-sein to be is not the same as the potentiality of an object which can become actual. The attitude towards the realization of the potentiality of an object Heidegger calls 'expecting' (*Erwarten*) (Heidegger, 1967, p. 262).[7] The attitude towards death as the ownmost possibility of Da-sein is different and cannot be understood in terms of realization. Heidegger calls 'anticipation' (*Vorlaufen*) Da-sein's attitude towards death, as its ownmost possibility to be. Death is related to as possibility. Heidegger calls the proper Being towards possibility, which never turns it into actuality or mode of actuality, 'anticipation of possibility' (*Vorlaufen in die Möglichkeit*). '*The nearest nearness of being-toward-death as possibility is as far removed as possible from anything real*' (ibid., p. 262, italics in original).

In order to make this claim clearer, we should go back, six to seven years before the publication of *Being and Time*. In a seminar dedicated to Paul's letters, Heidegger discusses the experience of the time of the revelation or eschatology among the early Christians – the καιρός. Revelation is potential – it lies ahead in the future – yet it cannot be regarded as a potentiality to be actualized in the future, for its occurrence is the end (ἔσχατον) of time. As Heidegger says:

> We never achieve the relational meaning of the παρουσία [parousia, presence, arrival] through bare analysis of the mental content (*Bewußtsein*) of a future event. The structure of the Christian hope (*Hoffnung*), which is in truth the relational meaning of parousia, is radically other than any expectation (*Erwartung*). 'Time and instant' (περὶ τῶν χρόνων καὶ τῶν καιρῶν 'always used together') provide a unique problem for the explication.[8] (Heidegger, 1995, p. 102)

In this early Christian sense, Da-sein's attitude towards death as its ownmost possibility to be should be understood. As possibility, Heidegger writes, death provides Da-sein with nothing to be realized. It is rather the possibility of the impossibility (Heidegger, 1967, p. 262).

In anticipating its innermost possibility of Being, Da-sein becomes free and can for the first time authentically understand and choose the factual possibilities (Heidegger, 1967, p. 264).

This attitude towards death as Da-sein's ownmost possibility is evident (*gewiss*) and it is accompanied by certainty (*Gewissheit*) (Heidegger, 1967, pp. 264–5). Contrary to Descartes, this certainty is not intuited by the intellect, but it is rather disclosed in a mood – Angst (ibid., p. 266). As we have earlier noted, possibility implies choosing (*Wählen*). This choosing follows a call of conscience to abandon the possibilities with which the 'they' (*das Man*) provides Da-sein and to turn to one's ownmost possibility to be. Contrary to the 'they' that is characterized by noise, the call of conscience is characterized by silence (*Schweigen*) (ibid., pp. 271, 273, 277). The call says nothing, conveys no information about events in the world; it is not even a conversation with itself (*Selbstgespräch*). It rather summons the self to itself, to its innermost potentiality to be (ibid., p. 273).

The call of conscience discloses Being as finite, as null, and permeated with guilt (*Schuld*). Da-sein is always guilty, since it has to live an actual life into which it has been thrown (*geworfen*). This life is one actualized possibility, the one which is provided by the 'they' (*Das Man*) in a mode of falling-prey (*Verfallen*). The call of conscience makes Da-sein take responsibility over its Being. The reaction to the call of conscience, the decision to live one's ownmost possibility, Heidegger calls 'resoluteness' (*Entschlossenheit*).

In resoluteness Da-sein chooses its ownmost possibility to be. In resoluteness Da-sein does not become an isolated subject, but it is rather brought to face its ownmost possibility to be as Being-in-the-world with other people in the mode of falling-prey (*Verfallen*). Resoluteness does not detach Da-sein from its world and turn it into isolated ego. It rather turns Da-sein into authentic Being in the world with other people (Heidegger, 1967, p. 298).

Facing this ownmost possibility to be Heidegger calls 'situation' (*Situation*): 'Situation is the there (*Da*) disclosed in resoluteness as which the existing being is there' (Heidegger, 1996, p. 276). Although this is the highest point of intimacy, the analysis cannot conclude here. As Heidegger notes right in the beginning of *Being and Time,* time is the horizon of any understanding of Being.[9] Thus, the intimacy which Da-sein achieves in choosing its ownmost possibility to be should be formulated in terms of time in order to account for Da-sein's constancy (*Ständigkeit*) as well as to attain positive access to history in terms of which Being is understood and interpreted (Heidegger, 1967, p. 322).

As it turned out, the highest point of intimacy is achieved in Da-sein facing its ownmost possibility to be which it chooses in resoluteness. The projection of one's ownmost possibility to be is first of all understood as futural. Future should not be understood here, Heidegger says, as a 'now' which has not yet become actual. Future rather means the coming (*Kunft*) of Da-sein to its innermost possibility of Being (Heidegger, 1967, p. 299).

In resoluteness Da-sein projects its ownmost possibility to be upon which it has been thrown (*geworfen*). Thus, Da-sein is likewise characterized by past, by having-been (*Gewesen*). In anticipatory resoluteness (*vorlaufende Entschlossenheit*), Da-sein understands itself as essentially guilty, since it is always the possibility into which it has been thrown (*geworfen*), which it has to choose (Heidegger, 1967, pp. 325–6).

The projection of possibility must always refer to the present in which Da-sein as Being-in-the-world acts. Thus, Da-sein is likewise characterized by present (Heidegger, 1967, pp. 299–300).

Contrary to Descartes who sees in time a chain of isolated nows, future, past (having-been), and present are not modes of a nows, but rather what Heidegger calls 'ecstasies' (*Ekstasen*); each ecstasy stretches into and contains within itself the two others. And although the ecstasies are equiprimordial, Heidegger gives primacy to the future, for it enables the disclosure of Being as my own possibility (Heidegger, 1967, 329). The time in which Da-sein faces its ownmost possibility to be Heidegger calls 'Moment' (*Augenblick*). In resoluteness, Heidegger explains, the present is not only retrieved from its dispersion in the world, in the activities in which Da-sein engaged. It is rather also held together with the future and past. This is the authentic present, the Moment (ibid., p. 338).

Taking upon itself the possibility into which Da-sein has been thrown, Da-sein's past, Heidegger calls 'retrieve' (*Wiederholung*). This structure of original time should account for Da-sein's consistency and historical Being. In Descartes, on the contrary, time consists of autonomous nows which are indifferent to each other. Descartes's main problem is to account for their co-existence and thus to the consistency of the self. Descartes resorts to God in order to solve this problem:

> For a lifespan can be divided into countless parts, each completely independent of the others, so that it does not follow from the fact that I existed a little while ago that I must exist now, unless there is some cause which as it were creates me afresh at this moment that is, which preserves me. For it is quite clear to anyone who attentively considers the nature of time that the same power and action are needed to preserve anything at each individual moment of its duration as would be required to create that thing anew if it were not yet in existence. Hence the distinction between

preservation and creation is only a conceptual one and this is or of the things that are evident by the natural light. (Descartes, 1996, p. 33)

The discussion on the history of Da-sein (*Geschichtlichkeit*), Heidegger claims, is an expansion of the discussion on its temporality (*Zeitlichkeit*) (Heidegger, 1967, p. 282). As we have already seen, Da-sein takes upon itself possibilities to which it has been thrown – historical possibilities. In resoluteness, Da-sein understands its authentic possibilities to be in terms of heritage (*Erbe*) which it takes upon itself as its own heritage (ibid., p. 382).

To be resolute means to expose one's ownmost possibility as fate (*Schicksal*). The finitude of Being thus grasped brings Da-sein to face its fate (*Schicksal*) (Heidegger, 1967, p. 384).

Since Da-sein always exists with other people, its destiny (*Schicksal*) is the common fate of its people (*Geschick*) (Heidegger, 1967, p. 384). Taking upon itself the historical possibilities to be, 'retrieve' (*Wiederholung*) is by no means a blind repetition of tradition and history. It rather exposes Da-sein's ownmost possibility to be as historical. History, as Da-sein's way of Being, emerges neither out of the past nor out of the connection between the past and the present. It rather emerges out of the future as the mode of time in which Da-sein exists as its innermost possibility (ibid., p. 386). '*Authentic being-toward-death, that is, the finitude of temporality, is the concealed ground of the historicity of Da-sein*' (Heidegger, 1996, p. 353, italics in original).

At this point, Heidegger completes his undertaking to overcome the alienation which emerged out of Descartes's philosophy and his view of the ego. In resoluteness Da-sein achieves the intimacy with its Being as historical possibility. It overcomes its dispersion over indifferent nows and retrieves its self as historical possibility to be.

In resoluteness, Da-sein achieves loyalty (*Treue*) to its Being which is now seen as its ownmost possibility to be (Heidegger, 1967, p. 391). It overcomes the situation of mistrust and doubt which characterizes the ego in Descartes's *Meditations*. Only in resoluteness Da-sein is truly *free* and not subservient to history and physical determinism, which is implied by time as an endless chain of nows, as in Descartes's philosophy.

Resoluteness constitutes the *loyalty* of existence to its own self. As resoluteness ready for *Angst*, loyalty is at the same time a possible reverence for the sole authority that a free existence can have, for the possibilities of existence that can be retrieved. (Heidegger, 1996, p. 357, italics in original)

So far, Heidegger has delivered a cultural criticism of modern mass society whose origin lies in the failure to raise the question concerning the meaning of Being and the notion of self as *ego cogito*, as *res cogitans*. In the background of his critique we saw the ancient Greek experience of Being, truth understood as ἀλήθεια, and reference to the early Christian experience of time as καιρός – introduced by Heidegger as antithetical to modern society and culture which emerged out of Descartes's philosophy. Once Heidegger proceeds from the study of the Da-sein to the study of Being as it has been conceived in Western thought, his critique becomes politically charged.

In 2014, the first volume of Martin Heidegger's *Überlegungen* [Reflections] came out, followed by two more volumes of *Überlegungen* and one volume of *Anmerkungen* [Remarks]. Together they form the 'notorious' *Black Notebooks*. Until their publication, scholars disposed mainly of smoking guns and rumours pointing to Heidegger's liaison with the Nazi regime. The awaited publication of the *Black Notebooks* was supposed to provide the final evidence to indict Heidegger as a rabid Nazi and anti-Semite. Once published, many conferences took place all over the world discussing the Nazi thinker. Beside statements regarding Judaism (but by no means a developed anti-Semitic doctrine), the *Black Notebooks* seem to reveal nothing new as far as Heidegger's philosophy is concerned; nothing which cannot be found in the *Beiträge* (Heidegger, 2003) and his lectures on Nietzsche (Heidegger, 1961, 1997). In these texts, Descartes occupies a central position. As Joseph Simon explains:

> Heidegger saw in Descartes's philosophy the paradigmatic expression of 'presenting thinking' (*vorstellendes Denken*), in which 'Being' is reduced to its presentation in consciousness. This thinking is for Heidegger an example that in the history of thought, only 'definite, distinguished realms of Being always came to the fore', and they then determined 'primarily the set of problems', '(the ego cogito of Descartes, subject, I, reason, mind, person)'; those 'realms of Being' themselves – 'in accordance with the general failure to pose the question concerning the meaning of Being' – remained unquestioned.[10] (Simon, 2000, pp. 77–8)

The failure to raise the question concerning the meaning of Being and the subsequent reduction of Being to perception are, in Heidegger's eyes, the cause of all modern maladies. Descartes occupies a central position in this history of thought. Through the introduction of the *ego cogito*, the method, *clara et distincta percepio* (clear and distinct perception) as the only criterion of truth, the reduction of Being to human perception, Descartes laid the ground to unrestrained technological expansion, nationalism, racism, overuse of power, arms race, and barbarism. Thus, in the 'notorious' *Black Notebooks* Heidegger writes:

> The 'rationalism' of Descartes means that the meaning (*Wesen*) of Being is determined in terms of certainty (*Gewißheit*) of thought, of self-confidence (*Selbstsicherheit*) in the object of thought (*Denkbarkeit*). Being receives now clearly the character (which has been up to that point repressed or only roughly conceived) of calculability (*Berechenbarkeit*) – of feasibility – in the broadest sense. This interpretation of Being becomes the fundamental condition of modern times and modern man.[11] (Heidegger, 2014, pp. 172–3).

According to Heidegger, the meaning of Being is determined, since Descartes, exclusively in mathematical terms and standards to promote production. This is in line with Descartes's ideal of scientific progress as he formulates it at the end of his *Discourse*: to become *le maître et possesseur de la nature* (the master and lord of nature). The history of Being, out of which this concept of man and nature emerged, is overlooked, as Joseph Simon explains. We should, according to Heidegger, approach history out of the way in which Being is conceived and interpreted, but not vice versa – the meaning of Being cannot be reconstructed out of the specific ways in which it is conceived and interpreted in a given historical period. This would lead to the assumption that the way to interpret and conceive Being in modern times, as Descartes represents them, is the only way to interpret Being. Heidegger writes in the *Black Notebooks*:

> Thus, it is almost an insane misjudgment of the current era and of its special ideologies, if one, starting from the current era (on the ground of the Nazi fake philosophy, for example) tries to attack Descartes's 'rationalism', apparently because Descartes is French and 'Western'. – Furthermore, it is the special greatness of the current ideologies and their 'claim to totality' that

they make valid the metaphysically conceived 'rationalism' as the innermost power of their will to power and reject all artificial 'mystical' and 'mythical'. Descartes's rationalism is neither 'French' nor Western (*westlich*) – it is rather occidental (*abendländisch*) and, 'French' – if one already wants to know – consists in that it brought into play for the first time the ability to make knowable that interpretation of Being. The 'knowable' itself is neither French nor German nor Italian nor English and nor American – it is rather the ground of this nation![12] (Ibid., p. 173)

Heidegger wants to approach modern times, nationalism, through the way in which Being is interpreted in modern times: human is conceived as a rational animal, Being is reduced to clear and distinct perception, and so forth, but never vice versa. Heidegger's statement is, politically seen, highly charged and passes judgement on current political ideologies and views. Yet it by no means indicates unreserved support of Nazi ideology, as scholars argue against him. On the contrary, no supporter of the Nazi ideology would ever refer to it as 'fake philosophy'. Heidegger traces politics back to the modern concept of man, as it is firmly formed in Descartes's philosophy, as *res cogitans*, as subject, to the reduction of Being to perception, as well as to method and the mathematical standard of truth as the only legitimate ways to conceive Being and truth. Let us turn to the following statement from the *Black Notebooks*:

Nietzsche tries to overcome Descartes's *subjectivism;* however, he conceives man even rougher than subjectum in that he interprets it as a 'body' instead of consciousness. The 'subjectivism' of the animality in the sense of social [animality] – is the 'most extreme' 'subjectivism' in regard to which the 'subjective' conduct of the 'private' 'life' (*Existenz*) remains a formless game and mostly even very 'objective'.

The 'Mythos of the 20th Century' is the utmost *realization* of the a-mythical subjectivism and liberalism of the 16th century. Therefore, the complete and unified unfolding of the essence (*die vollständige und geschlossene Wesenentfaltung*) of modernity begins firstly in the 20th century – the innermost outcome is '*world wars*' – as the race of the 'subjects' (which became free) of the bare will to 'life'.[13] (Ibid., p. 412, italics in original)

For Descartes, Being means being perceived by the ego. In Nietzsche's workbook W I 7 we find the following statement dated 1885:

> We modern are all enemies of Descartes and defend ourselves against his dogmatic recklessness. Certainty! We find everywhere, where there are profounder people, the opposite, the countermovement against the absolute authority of the goddess 'reason'.[14] (Nietzsche, 2004, p. 64)

And yet, as Heidegger shows, Nietzsche took Descartes's view of Being and man to the farthest extreme by reducing man to his body, to his animality, as he says.[15] Man now is nothing but a will to power – the will to extend his bodily rule. Alfred Rosenberg (1893–1946), one of the most important Nazi ideologues, the author of *The Myth of the 20th Century*, realized fully Nietzsche's concept of Being and man, as Heidegger points out. Finally, Heidegger traces back the world wars to that emergence of the corporeal subject. This is a charged political statement with overt critique of the Nazi movement. Heidegger draws a complex line between philosophy and politics, tracing back the catastrophes of the twentieth century to rationalism, its disregard of man and view of Being. The common attempt to dub this philosophy 'Nazi' and to reduce it to Nazi ideology misses the whole point. We will now turn to Heidegger's lectures on Nietzsche in which he explains more clearly the connection between Descartes's philosophy, the modern concept of man, and Being and politics.

In his lectures on Nietzsche from the early and mid-1940s, Heidegger portrays the way in which humans become dominant and the sole measure of everything which exists. In order to show the way in which the notion of Being has changed in modern times, Heidegger compares Protagoras with Descartes. Since Descartes, he argues, man is conceived exclusively as a subject (Heidegger, 1997, pp. 141–2). What is meant by 'subject'?

> The question: what entity is (*Seindes*)? becomes a question regarding the *fundamentum absolutum inconcussum veritatis*, regarding the unconditional, unshakeable foundation of truth. This change is the beginning of a new way of thinking, through which the era becomes new and the subsequent period (*Folgezeit*) becomes modern times.[16] (Ibid., p. 142)

Heidegger is talking here about a revolution in the way in which man understands and interprets Being and consequently himself. Man has released himself from the constraints of the Bible and the church. Man is now the only criterion of truth.

When we are claiming pointedly that the new notion of freedom consists in that man posits himself as a law and chooses what is binding by which he abides, then we are speaking in the language of Kant and hit upon the essence of the beginning of modern times.[17] (Ibid., p. 143)

For Heidegger, this complete release of the subject from any external binding – be it the Bible, church or the revelation of Being as in Protagoras – leads to the unrestrained will to power in the sense of striving for expansion and conquest as the sole way to regard and interpret Being.

It is therefore not true that in early times there was also power, and that only since Machiavelli it became one-sided and exaggerated, but 'power' in the correctly understood modern sense, that is to say, as the will to power, becomes metaphysically possible only as modern history.[18] (Ibid., p. 144)

The liberated Cartesian ego, to whose clear and distinct perception Being is reduced, gave birth to the will to power that strives to rule over the entire earth.[19] This attitude towards Being and man lies at the foundation of the modern ways to conceive man such as nation, the call to proletarians of all nations to unite, and the concept of *Volk* and race, according to Heidegger (ibid.). Man is now seen as a type. Nietzsche's *Übermensch*, Heidegger contends, whose model is the Prussian soldier and the Jesuit order, is the realization of that type of man who rules over the earth (ibid., p. 146). Nietzsche, and following him Alfred Rosenberg, is the most extreme development of that view of man. All this leads back to Descartes's view of Being and man (ibid., p. 147).

Descartes's *cogito ergo sum* is the foundation of that view of man and Being in modern times. The innovation which comes forth along with the statement *cogito ergo sum*, Heidegger argues, is that truth is now understood as certainty. Descartes, according to him, identifies at some point *cogitare* with *percipere*, to capture, take hold of something. *Cogitare* for Descartes means perceiving in the sense of presenting something in front of, *vor-stellen* (ibid., p. 151). Being is reduced to clear perception and is seen through the lens of calculating possession (*berechnende Verfügung*) (ibid., p. 152). All human attitudes towards Being Descartes identifies with *cogitare*: to comprehend (*intelligere*), to will (*velle*), to imagine (*imaginari*), and to sense (*sentire*) (ibid., p. 156). Man is a perceiving entity. Thus, Descartes says: '*sum res cogitans*' (ibid., p. 163). Something exists only in so far as it is perceived by man. Man is thus the *subjectum* of whatever exists which now becomes his object.[20] *Cogito sum*, Heidegger argues, implies that I exist (*sum*) as a thinking or perceiving thing (ibid., p. 162). C*ogito sum* means that 'perception (*Vor-stellen*), which is present to itself (*sich vor-gestellt*), relates to Being as being perceived (*Vor-gestelltheit*) and to truth as certainty' (ibid., p. 164).[21] The ascertained Being of the perceiver, his *cogito sum*, becomes the sole standard for the existence of the perceived entities. Truth, in turn, is now conceived as *adaequatio intellectus et rei* (correspondence between the intellect and the object) (ibid., p. 169).

> That to which everything is reduced as an unshakable ground is the full essence of perception itself in so far as out of it the essence of Being and truth and also the essence of man as perceiver and the mode of that condition are determined.[22] (Ibid., p. 162)

This according to Heidegger is the foundation of the unrestrained technological expansion, the 'mechanical economy' (*machinale Ökonomie*), and the arms race. This signifies the birth of a new type of man, Nietzsche's *Übermensch*, who is the only one who can measure up with this 'mechanical economy' and unrestrained technological expansion (ibid., p. 166). With the *cogito sum*, Descartes enabled and facilitated that transition to the new kind of man who strives without limit to rule over all the earth (ibid.).

Method is now conceived as the way to get hold of entities, Heidegger claims, referring to Descartes's statement: 'method is necessary to investigate the truth of things' ('*Necessaria est methodus ad rerum veritatem investigandam*') (ibid., p. 169). 'The attitude to entities is the mastering methodical pro-cedure (*das meisternde Vor-gehen*) towards conquest of the world and global domination of the world' (ibid., p. 171).[23] In order to demonstrate that emergence of the violent modern man, Heidegger compares Descartes to Protagoras. For Descartes, 'self' means representation, whereas for Protagoras it means belonging to the region in which entities as a whole get disclosed (*Umkreis des Unverborgenen*). For Descartes, the human subject is the essence of entities, whereas for Protagoras the essence of entities is unconcealedness. For Descartes, truth means certainty, whereas for Protagoras it is unconcealedness. Finally, and most important, for Descartes, man is the measure of everything in the sense of presumptuousness and expansion (*Entschränkung*) of perception, whereas for Protagoras it means aligning oneself in proportion with the unconcealedness and concealment of Being (ibid., pp. 172–3).

Descartes, according to Heidegger, marks the birth of that view of man and Being. With his *cogito sum*, he started that revolution and paved the way to the complete conquering and exploiting of the earth by means of technology. It was however Nietzsche in whose philosophy that attitude reached its apex. Descartes and Nietzsche, he says, share the same view of Being: Being is being perceived and truth means certainty (ibid., p. 182). For both, thinking is a means to promote economic use and exploitation of entities (ibid., p. 183). Nietzsche took it one step further, since for him everything is a will to power, to expansion. Nietzsche achieved that point by turning the I into body along with all its drives and urges. As Nietzsche states, 'the belief in the body is more fundamental than the belief in the soul' (ibid., p. 186).[24] Thus, Heidegger sums up, 'Nietzsche's metaphysics and along with it the ground of existence (*Wesensgrund*) of the "classic nihilism" can now be more clearly defined as the *metaphysics of the unconditioned (unbedingt) subjectivity of the will to power*' (ibid., p. 200, italics in original).[25] Heidegger concludes this discussion with a poignant evaluation of modern society as it emerged out of Descartes's *cogito* and reached its apex with Nietzsche's philosophy:

> The unconditioned essence of the subjectivity developed as the *brutalitas* [brutality] of the *bestialitas* [bestiality]. At the end of the era of metaphysics, we find the sentence: *homo est brutum bestiale* [man is bestial brute]. Nietzsche's term 'blond beast' is not an arbitrary exaggeration, but rather the characterization and reference to the context in which he knowingly stood without comprehending its essential historical characteristics.[26] (Ibid., pp. 200–1)

This is a scathing critical assessment of modern Western society, culture, politics, economy, and technology. The loss of access to the revelation of Being, as in Protagoras, and the view of the human subject as the sole starting point of any inquiry are the root of that problem. The Cartesian view of man and Being lies at the ground of unrestrained technological progress, the technological exploitation of the earth, as well as of the entire moral and cultural regression of the West. As the opening sentence of Adorno's and Horkheimer's *Dialektik der Aufklärung* (*Dialectic of Enlightenment*) reads:

Enlightenment in the most encompassing sense of progressing thinking has always pursued the task of releasing humans from fear and positing them as rulers. Yet, the altogether enlightened earth radiates with triumphal disaster.[27] (Horkheimer and Adorno, 1988, p. 15; cited in Frank, 1987, p. 101)

Or in the words of Michel Foucault: '*La torture, c'est la raison* [the torture, this is reason]' (ibid., p. 101).

***

As we shall see in Chapter 5, according to Franz Borkenau, an important and nowadays forgotten thinker who was affiliated with the Institute for Social Research while he was composing his work on the transition from feudalism to industrial society, Cartesian philosophy is not only the theoretical foundation of modern science and technology but is also the ideological and political foundation of industrialism, capitalism, and the exploitation of the worker and nature, which gave birth to a new type of man and nature, stripped of any unique characteristics. Borkenau looks at the transition from feudalism to capitalism, whose basis he discerns in Cartesian philosophy, through Marxist lens.

Notes

1   In the lecture text of the late 1930s or the early 1940s called *Descartes'*
    metaphysische Grundstellung Heidegger distances himself from the tendency to
    reject Descartes's philosophy entirely, as well as from the Neo-Kantian tendency to
    accept Descartes wholly as the beginner of true philosophy: 'Daß man jetzt ehenso
    blindlings Descartes *ablehnt*, wie ihn der Neukantianismus aller Richtungen vor
    wenigen Jahrzehnten als *den* Beginn des echten Philosophierens *gepriesen*; diese
    beiden Ahnungslosigkeiten gehören zusammen – beide sind gleich unwert einer
    Erörterung' (Heidegger, 2008, p. 71).
2   'So finden wir uns mit Descartes in einer trostlos gespaltenen Welt, konzeptuell
    entfremdet von der aüßeren Natur und von unserem eigenen Körper.'
3   'Human Da-sein' is not a tautology, since human can also be understood
    biologically, psychologically, sociologically, etc. In *Being and Time*, Heidegger
    transcribes it as 'Dasein'. Only in his handwritten remarks in his own copy of
    Being and Time do we find it written as 'Da-sein'. Joan Stambaugh, throughout her
    translation of *Being and Time*, uses 'Da-sein'.

4 Joan Stambaugh translates the noun '*Sein*' (being, existence) with 'being.' It may
be misleading, since '*Seiendes*' (entity) can also be translated with 'being.' Both
nouns stem from the verb 'to be' (*sein*) and each has its distinct use in *Being and
Time*. In quotations from Stambaugh's translation, we maintain 'being' for '*Sein*.'
Otherwise, we write 'Being.'

5 'Die Angst verschlägt uns das Wort. Weil das Seiende im Ganzen entgleitet und
so gerade das Nichts andrängt, schweigt im Angesicht seiner jedes „Ist"-Sagen.'

6 See Figal (2000).

7 'Alles Erwarten versteht und "hat" sein Mögliches daraufhin, ob und wann und
wie es wohl wirklich vorhanden sein wird.'

8 'Wir kommen niemals durch die bloße Analyse des Bewußtseins von einem
zukünftigen Ereignis auf den Bezugssinn der παρουσία. Die Struktur der
christlichen Hoffnung, die in Wahrheit der Bezugssinn zur Parusie ist, ist radikal
anders als alle Erwartung. "Zeit und Augenblick" (5, 1: "περὶ τῶν χρόνων καὶ
τῶν καιρῶν" immer in eins gebraucht) bieten ein besonderes Problem für die
Explikation.'

9 See also 'Andeutungsweise wurde gezeigt: zum Dasein gehört als ontische
Verfassung ein vorontologisches Sein. Dasein *ist* in der Weise, seiend so etwas
wie Sein zu verstehen. Unter Festhaltung dieses Zusammenhangs soll gezeigt
werden, daß das, von wo aus Dasein überhaupt so etwas wie Sein unausdrücklich
versteht und auslegt, *die Zeit* ist' (Heidegger, 1967, p. 17).

10 'So sah z. B. Heidegger in Descartes' Philosophie die paradigmatische
Ausprägung eines "vorstellenden" Denkens, in dem "das Sein" auf seine
Präsentation im Bewußtsein reduziert sei. Dieses Denken ist für Heidegger
ein Beispiel dafür, daß in der Geschichte des Denkens immer nur "bestimmte
ausgezeichnete Seinsbezirke in den Blick" kamen, die dann "primär die
Problematik" leiteten "(das ego *cogito Descartes*, Subjekt, Ich, Vernunft, Geist,
Person)"; daß aber diese "Seinsbezirke" selbst, "entsprechend dem durchgängigen
Versäumnis der Seinsfrage", "unbefragt" blieben.'

11 'Der "Rationalismus" des Descartes bedeutet, daß sich das Wesen des Seins aus
der Gewißheit des Denkens, aus der Selbstsicherheit der Denkbarkeit bestimmt.
Das Sein erhält jetzt ausdrücklich den bis dahin zurückgehaltenen oder erst
grob gefaßten Character der Berechenbarkeit – der Machbarkeit – im weitesten
Sinne. Diese Auslegung des Seins wird zur Grundbedingung der Neuzeit und des
neuzeitlichen Menschen.'

12 'Daher ist es eine fast irrsinnige Verkennung des jetzigen Zeitalters und
seiner nur ihm eigenen Weltanschauungen,wenn man von diesem her (auf
Grund einer "nationalsozialistischen" Scheinphilosophie z.B.) versucht, gegen
den "Rationalismus" Descartes' anzugehen, vermutlich weil Descartes ein
Französe und "Westler" ist.–Vielmehr ist es die eigene Größe der jetzigen

Weltanschauungen und ihres "Totalitätsanspruches", daß *sie den metaphysisch begriffenen "Rationalismus" als die innerste Macht ihres Machtwillens zur Geltung bringen und alle künstliche "Mystik" und "Mythik" ablehnen.* Descartes' Rationalismus *(vgl. oben)* ist weder "französisch", noch westlich – sondern abendländisch und das Französische, wenn man es schon wissen will, besteht darin, daß es das Vermögen ins Spiel brachte, zum erstenmal jene Auslegung des Seins wißbar zu machen. Das Wißbare selbst ist weder französisch, noch deutsch, noch italienisch, noch englisch, noch amerikanisch–wohl aber der Grund dieser Nation!'

13 '*Nietzsche* versucht den *Subjektivismus* Descartes' zu überwinden; aber er denkt den Menschen nur noch gröber als subjectum, indem er dieses statt als Bewußtsein als "Leib" auslegt. Der "Subjektivismus" der Tierheit im Sinne der gemeinschaftlichen– ist der "extremste" "Subjektivismus," dem gegenüber das "subjektive" Gebahren der "privaten" "Existenz" ein formloses Spiel und meist sogar sehr "objektiv" bleibt (Vgl. Oben S. 8f.). "Der Mythos des zwangzisten Jahrhunderts" ist die höchste *Vollendung* des a-mythischen Subjektivismus und Liberalismus des 16 Jahrhunderts. *Deshalb* beginnt im 20 Jahrhundert erst die vollständige und geschlossene Wesenentfaltung der Neuzeit– die innerste Folge sind die "*Welt-kriege*"– als der Wettlauf der "*frei*" gewordenen "Subjekte" des bloßen "Lebens" wollens.'

14 'Wir Neueren sind Alle Gegner des Descartes u wehren uns gegen seine dogmatische Leichtfertigkeit. Gewißheit! Wir finden das Umgekehrte, die Gegenbewegung gegen die absolute Autorität der Göttin "Vernunft" überall, wo es tiefere Menschen giebt.'

15 See also 'Ausgangspunkt vom Leibe u der Physiologie: warum? – Wir gewinnen die richtige Vorstellung von der Art unserer Subjekt-Einheit, nämlich als Regenten an der Spitze eines Gemeinwesens, nicht als "Seelen" oder "Lebenskräfte"' (Nietzsche, 2004, p. 66).

16 'Die Frage: Was ist das Seiende? wandelt sich zur Frage nach dem fundamentum absolutum inconcussum veritatis, nach dem unbedingten, unerschütterlichen Grund der Wahrheit. Dieser Wandel ist der Beginn eines neuen Denkens, wodurch das Zeitalter zu einem neuen und die Folgezeit zur Neuzeit wird.'

17 'Wenn wir zugespitzt sagen, die neue Freiheit bestehe darin, daß der Mensch sich selbst das Gesetz gibt und das Verbindliche wählt und darein sich bindet, dann sprechen wir in der Sprache Kants und treffen doch das Wesentliche des Beginns der Neuzeit.'

18 'Es ist also nicht so, daß es in früheren Zeitaltern auch schon die Macht gab und daß sie dann etwa seit Machiavelli – einseitig und übertrieben zur Geltung gebracht wurde, sondern "Macht" im recht verstandenen neuzeitlichen Sinne, d. h. als Wille zur Macht, wird metaphysisch erst als neuzeitliche Geschichte möglich.'

19 See 'Die Sicherung der höchsten und unbedingten Selbstentfaltung aller
    Vermögen des Menschentums zur unbedingten Herrschaft über die ganze Erde
    ist der geheime Stachel, der den neuzeitlichen Menschen zu immer neueren und
    neuesten Aufbrüchen antreibt und zu Bindungen nötigt, die ihm die Sicherung
    seines Vorgehens und die Sicherheit seiner Ziele sicherstellen' (Heidegger, 1997,
    p. 145).

20 See also 'Hier kündigt sich an, was das zum Grunde Liegende, das subiectum,
    ist – nämlich das Vorstellen – und *wofür* das Subjekt das subiectum ist –
    nämlich für das Wesen der Wahrheit' (Heidegger, 1997, p. 157). 'Das "Ich
    bin" wird aus dem "Ich stelle vor" nicht erst gefolgert, sondern das "Ich stelle
    vor" ist seinem *Wesen* nach jenes, was mir das "Ich bin" – nämlich der Vor-
    stellende – schon zugestellt hat. Wir lassen jetzt mit Grund aus der Formel
    des Descartesschen Satzes das verfängliche "ergo" beiseite' (Heidegger, 1997,
    p. 161).

21 'Das Vor-stellen, das sich selbst wesenhaft vor-gestellt ist, setzt das Sein als Vor-
    gestelltheit und dieWahrheit als Gewißheit.' See also 'Sum *res cogitans* besagt
    also nicht: ich bin ein Ding, das mit der Eigenschaft des Denkens ausgestattet ist,
    sondern: ich bin ein Seiendes, dessen Art zu *sein* im Vorstellen besteht dergestalt,
    daß dieses Vor-stellen den Vor-stellenden selbst mit in die Vorgestelltheit stellt.
    Das Sein des Seienden, das ich selbst bin, und das je der Mensch als er selbst ist,
    hat sein Wesen in der Vor-gestelltheit und in der dieser zugehörigen Gewißheit'
    (Heidegger, 1997, p. 164).

22 'Das, worauf alles als auf den unerschütterlichen Grund zurückverlegt wird, ist
    das volle Wesen der Vorstellung selbst, sofern sich aus ihm das Wesen des Seins
    und der Wahrheit, aber auch das Wesen des Menschen als des Vorstellenden und
    die Art dieser Maßgabe bestimmen.'

23 'Das Verhältnis zum Seienden ist das meisternde Vor-gehen in die Welteroberung
    und Weltherrschaft.'

24 'Der Glaube an den Leib ist fundamentaler, als der Glaube an die *Seele.*'

25 'Nietzsches Metaphysik und damit der Wesensgrund des "klassischen
    Nihilismus" lassen sich jetzt deutlicher umgrenzen als *Metaphysik der
    unbedingten Subjektivität des Willens zur Macht.*'

26 'Das unbedingte Wesen der Subjektivität entfaltet sich daher notwendig als
    die brutalitas der bestialitas. Am Ende der Metaphysik steht der Satz: Homo
    est brutum bestiale. Nietzsches Wort von der "blonden Bestie" ist nicht eine
    gelegentliche Übertreibung, sondern das Kennzeichen und Kennwort für einen
    Zusammenhang, in dem er wissend stand, ohne seine wesensgeschichtlichen
    Bezüge zu durchschauen.'

27 'Seit je hat Aufklärung im umfassendsten Sinn fortschreitenden Denkens das Ziel verfolgt, von den Menschen die Furcht zu nehmen und sie als Herren einzusetzen. Aber die vollends aufgeklärte Erde strahlt im Zeichen triumphalen Unheils.'

5

Franz Borkenau: Cartesianism and the exploitation of man and nature

In his book *Der Übergang vom feudalen zum bürgerlichen Weltbild; Studien zur Geschichte der Philosophie der Manufakturperiode* (The Transition from the Feudal to the Bourgeois Worldview: Studies on the History of the Manufacture Period), Franz Borkenau, a forgotten thinker who was associated with the Frankfurt School (The Institute for Social Research commissioned that work, and Max Horkheimer wrote the introduction to the book), describes the interplay between philosophy, science, religion, technology, economy, and society in the transition from a feudal to a bourgeois society. In order to understand that transition, we should first of all understand the change in the nature of production. According to Borkenau, production is no longer carried out by individual artisans or craftsmen. Borkenau claims that the process of production consists now in many routine simple assignments, each performed by unskilled workers. This process of production resembles mechanized work in which the worker is a cog in a huge machine, devoid of all human traits, subordinate to bourgeois materialism and the industrialist who directs this process. This is the bourgeois worldview. Descartes's philosophy, according to Borkenau, reflects that worldview and develops it further to the full mechanization and industrialization of nature. The *ego* in the Cartesian philosophy is the abstracted subject of the bourgeois worldview and the process of production. It develops that worldview, the mechanical notion of nature, to give further improvement and sophistication to the machinery by which man controls and exploits nature and thus consolidates the status of the bourgeoisie. The interplay between economy, social order, politics, philosophy, and technology, which Borkenau describes, seems at first sight to be unproblematic. We read, for example, in Ernst Cassirer the following description:

> Hobbes and Hugo Grotius are the two opposite poles of the seventeenth century's political thought. They disagree in their theoretical presuppositions and in their political demands. Nevertheless they follow the same way of thinking and arguing. Their method is not historical and psychological, but analytical and deductive. They derive their political principles from the nature of man and the nature of the state. And in this they follow the same great historical example of Galileo. We have a letter written by Hugo Grotius in which he expresses the greatest admiration for Galileo's work. The same holds for Hobbes. From the first beginning of his philosophy it was his great ambition to create a theory of the body politic equal to the Galilean theory of physical bodies – equal in clarity, in scientific method, and in certainty. In the introduction to his work *De jure belli et pacis* [*On the Law of War and Peace*], Hugo Grotius expressed the same conviction. According to him it is by no means impossible to find a 'mathematics of politics'. (Cassirer, 1946, p. 165)

An unproblematic picture emerges also from Carl Schmitt's description:

> The tolerant conservatism of Descartes should not make us overlook that through this philosopher all human issues have already undergone a revolutionary change in their essence, because he conceived the human body as a mechanism. That was the beginning of the future technical-industrial revolution.... As such it is possible to conceive the mechanism of the state without analogy to the human body. And yet, the mechanization of the state can also be conceived as a magnified reflection of the human body. Thus, it has a clearer and a more frightening effect than in Hobbes.[1] (Schmitt, 1936/7, p. 622)

Schmitt sums up, 'The mechanization of our notion of the state completed the anthropological notion of the human being' (ibid., p. 631).

In Borkenau, that relationship turns out to be much more complicated and intricate, and his account takes into consideration far more factors. This account is what Borkenau sets himself to provide. In his essay 'The Sociology of the Mechanistic World-Picture' (Borkenau, 1987), he describes the birth of a new worldview and notion of man. This new kind of thought he calls a 'mathematical-mechanistic world-picture' which evolves directly from the emergence of manufacture at the beginning of modern times. This emergence is what marks the transition from feudalism to the bourgeoisie. Thus, 'manufacture' is the key term here. Borkenau borrowed it from Karl Marx. Marx's usage of this term as a noun (*Manufaktur*) is unfamiliar to the English reader. We need first to dwell on it and explain its use by Marx in order to understand the connection which Borkenau tries to establish between philosophy, science, religion, technology, economy, and society as seen in the transition from feudalism to the bourgeoisie and the beginning of industrialization.

According to Marx, manufacture is the classical form of cooperation which is based on a division of labour. As a characteristic form of the capitalistic process of production, it prevailed during the period of manufacture which, he estimates, began in the middle of the sixteenth century and continued until the last third of the eighteenth century (Marx, 1883, p. 335). As Marx goes on to explain, out of the individual product of an independent artisan, who accomplishes many different assignments, the commodity changes into a corporative product (*gesellschaftliches Produkt*) made by a combination of workers, each of whom continually accomplishes only one and the same assignment (ibid., p. 337). During the course of the manufacture period, the working tools were facilitated, improved, and multiplied, and as Marx says, they were adapted to the specific functions of various workers and their specific routine assignment. Thus, manufacture is one of the material conditions of the machinery which is made up of a combination of simple instruments (ibid., pp. 341–2). As Karl Kautzky explains, it is 'that industry which is not yet the modern large industry with its machines, but it is already no longer the industry of the Middle Ages, nor the domestic industry' (Kautzky, 1894).[2] The product in the manufacture period is an outcome of that combination of various workers, each accomplishing a routine job (Marx, 1883, p. 357). Only the product of joint work becomes a commodity (*Ware*). Finally, Marx notes that this manifold of various handworkers working together is concentrated in the hand of the capitalist. Thus, it deprives the workers of their freedom, their bodies and souls, and the fruit of their labour. He writes:

> The manufacturing (*manufakturmäßig*) division of labor ... develops the corporative productive force not only for the sake of the capitalist rather

than for the sake of the worker, but [it does so] also through crippling the individual worker. It produces a new condition for the domination of the capital over labor. Thus, if on the one hand it appears as historical progress and a necessary component of the development in the economic formation process, it is, on the other hand, a civilized and sly means of exploitation.[3] (Ibid., p. 368)

As Karl Kautzky later puts it, 'The worker is physically and mentally crippled, his work loses for him any content, and he becomes an accessory of the capital' (Kautzky, 1894).[4] We can already sense the connection which Borkenau wants to establish between society, economy, and technology to which he will also add science and religion and imbeds Descartes's philosophy in that picture.

Marx serves as an important point of reference in Borkenau's account to which we will have to return later. As we shall see, Henryk Grossmann, an economist and historian who was also associated with the Frankfurt School, delivered a scathing critique of Borkenau's study of Descartes. According to Grossmann, Borkenau's study demonstrates an obtuse ignorance of historical sources and facts. Hence, his analysis of Descartes is noticeably missing. As a result, the connection which Borkemau tries to establish between philosophy, society, economy, and technology falls apart (Grossmann, 2009a, 2009b). As we shall see, everything seems to come down to Borkenau's and Grossmann's attitude towards Marx.

Borkenau's study on Descartes occupies most of *Der Übergang vom feudalen zum bürgerlichen Weltbild; Studien zur Geschichte der Philosophie der Manufakturperiode*. Since it was intended to explain the intricate relationship between philosophy, science, religion, technology, economy, and society, it is a voluminous and complicated study with numerous details and references taken from many fields of knowledge. There are a few motifs which make up his reading of Descartes. They can serve as a key to this complicated study. The first motif is God and the world. As Eric Voegelin puts it in a letter to Alfred Schütz:

Hence I would formulate the element of novelty in Descartes in terms of the sentiment of the *contemptus mundi* [contempt towards the world] giving way to the sentiment of interest in the world. Therefore, due to his concern for *episteme* [knowledge] the experience of transcendence becomes in this meditation an instrument of assurance of the world's objectivity. (Voegelin, 2002)

The *Discourse* and the *Meditations* are composed as an autobiographical monologue, a prevalent style in the Christian tradition. Yet, Descartes's attitude towards the world is completely different; it is a positive attitude, as Voegelin says. Belief in God and a positive attitude towards the world are parts of Descartes's worldview.

The second motif in Borkenau's reading of Descartes is Neo-Stoicism. Neo-Stoicism stands for, above all, the approval of and submission to reality, to the unchangeable laws of nature. Change can never be made in reality but only in our thought of reality, in our attitude to it. Cassirer surveys the prevalence of this doctrine in the time of Descartes:

> The political rationalism of the seventeenth century was a rejuvenation of Stoic ideas. This process began in Italy, but after a short time it spread over the whole of European culture. In rapid progress Neo-Stoicism passed from Italy to France; from France to the Netherlands; to England, to the American colonies. The best-known political books of this period show the clear and unmistakable imprint of the Stoic mind. These books were not only studied by scholars or philosophers. Works like Pierre Charron's *De la sagesse* [Of Wisdom], du Vair's treatise *De la constance* et *consolation ès* calamités *publiques* [On Constancy and Consolation of Public Calamities], Justus Lipsius' *De constantia* [On Constancy] or *Philosophia et physiologia Stoica* [Philosophy and Stoic Physiology] became a sort of lay breviary in ethical wisdom. The influence of these books was so strong that it made itself felt even in the field of practical political problems. In the education of princes and princesses the medieval treatises *De rege et regimine* [On King and Governance], or *De institutione principum* [On the Institution of the Leaders] were replaced by these modern treatises. We know from the example of Queen Christina of Sweden that her first teachers knew no better way to introduce her to the problems of politics than through the study of Lipsius and of the classic Stoic writers. (Cassirer, 1946, pp. 166–7)

The importance of Neo-Stoicism to Descartes is fully captured in Cassirer's treatment of the relationship between Descartes and Christina. The reform which Descartes craved and referred to in the *Discourse*, according to Cassirer, was meant only as internal reform, reform of his own mind. He refers to the following passage from the *Discourse* to demonstrate what he means by Neo-Stoicism in Descartes (Cassirer, 1995, p. 196). Descartes writes:

> That is why I cannot by any means approve of those meddlesome and restless characters who, called neither by birth nor by fortune to the management of public affairs, are yet forever thinking up some new reform. And if I thought this book contained the slightest ground for suspecting me of such folly, I would be very reluctant to permit its publication. My plan has never gone beyond trying to reform my own thoughts and construct them upon a foundation which is all my own. (Descartes, 1985a, p. 118)

This is a moral stance towards life. Cassirer refers to Pascal's basic statement of morality:

> *Toute notre dignité consiste donc en la pensée. C'est de là qu'il faut nous relever, et non de l'espace et de la durée, que nous ne saurions remplir. – Travaillons donc à bien penser: voilà le principe de la morale.* [All our dignity consists therefore of thought. It is from there that we must be lifted up and not from space and time, which we could never fill. So let us work on thinking well. That is the principle of morality.] (Pascal, 1999, p. 73)

Then he adds, 'Descartes was in the 17th century the great teacher of that morality which even somebody like Pascal could not evade' (Cassirer, 1995, p. 214).[5] The *cogito ergo sum*, according to Cassirer, reflects this Neo-Stoic worldview (ibid., p. 217). 'It means that man cannot acquire his happiness and value from an external source, but he rather has to create them by himself' (ibid., p. 218).[6] As Christina notes in regard to Cyrus, Alexander, and Scipio, '*leurs ames étaient encore plus grandes que leur fortune* [there souls were greater than their fortune]' (ibid., p. 220). Since the Renaissance, Cassirer writes, this Stoic state of mind was always advanced (ibid., pp. 223–4). As Montaigne says, '*De l'experience que j'ay de moy, je trouve assez de quoy me faire sage* [from the experience which I make of myself, I find enough to make me wise]' (ibid., p. 225).

Religion or religious institution is another motif in Borkenau's reading of Descartes. Of course, we cannot detach it from belief in God and from Neo-Stoicism. Its addition to the whole picture makes Borkenau's treatment much more complicated. Cassirer underlines Descartes's refusal to cast in doubt anything which pertains to religion (ibid., p. 206). In *Beyond Good and*

Evil, §54, Nietzsche discerns in Descartes and the entire subsequent modern philosophy a disguised attack on Christianity: the postulate of the eternal soul and thus of God. Nietzsche writes:

> Since Descartes (and, in fact, in spite of him more than because of him) all the philosophers have been out to assassinate the old concept of the soul, under the guise of critiquing the concepts of subject and predicate. In other words, they have been out to assassinate the fundamental presupposition of the Christian doctrine. As a sort of epistemological skepticism, modern philosophy is, covertly or overtly, *anti-Christian* (although, to state the point for more subtle ears, by no means anti-religious). (Nietzsche, 2002, p. 42)

Borkenau's attitude to Descartes is more complex than Nietzsche's and Cassirer's. In his interpretation of Descartes's dreams, he sees an indication of his bad conscience for doubting religious matters as well as divine revelation which Descartes receives as assurance that he is on the right path to truth. Borkenau writes:

> His doubting of the traditional conception of nature and the human world and vision of a systematic reformulation of the whole of human knowledge on metaphysical presuppositions requires that he question religious truths. This accounts for the deep crisis of conscience which was loosed in three dreams on November 11, 1619, and which he took as God's direct revelation. He believes he received in them God's permission to follow the path of doubt, and the assurance that this path would not lead him to destruction, but rather to the restoration of God-given religious and moral truths. (Borkenau, 1987, p. 120)

We will later see how belief in God is indispensable to make Descartes's system adequate, according to Borkenau. The process of industrialization and the related development of modern technology are another important motifs in Borkenau's reading of Descartes. The question is how all these motifs can make up an adequate reading of Descartes. How, in other words, belief in God, positive attitude towards the world, Neo-Stoicism and modern technology can exist side by side. Arpad Szakolczai suggests the following explanation:

> The world is not chaos, rather a perfectly functioning mechanical whole. Only the human world is chaotic, whose order however can be assured and restored by imposing on it a conformity with the mechanisms governing

nature. Human and social life can also return to normality and order if such natural order, with its mechanical regularities, is taken as the model of human existence. The implication of Cartesian pure science and pure rationality is an effective and in a way optimistic mass morality: one simply must take as model for life the mechanical laws of nature, which are equal for all. In this way Cartesian meditations replace the *Imitatio Christi* [Imitation of Christ] with the imitation of nature, prescribing a similar way for the social and human sciences, which they are indeed increasingly following. (Szakolczai, 2011, p. 116)

This explanation is obviously far from being a sufficient and precise reading of Borkenau. Szakolczai sees the problem in adapting one's self to the laws of nature. The matter, as Borkenau discerns it, is more complicated and it also refers to politics, society, and the role of manufacture in that time. In the following passage, we can see how intricate is the relationship between economy, society, and philosophy in Borkenau's reading of Descartes. Borkenau writes:

> The extreme decomposition of labor creates on the one hand an abstract, general substrate that is worked on, whose chemical and other qualities are ignored as much as possible, and which is to be considered only as raw material, as pure matter, and on the other hand, the completely unqualified laborer, who is considered only as labor power in itself, whose activity is abstract labor, pure physical movement. (Borkenau, 1987, p. 110)

After this abstracted substrate has emerged out of the new conception of manufacture, Neo-Stoicism requires a correspondence between the human mind on the one hand and the laws of nature on the other. This correspondence is much more complicated than Szakolczai's description, since it refers to social, psychological, and economic components as well. Regarding this correspondence, Borkenau writes:

> Here Descartes formulates the fundamental problem of bourgeois philosophy as it was posed again and again from himself until Hegel. This basic philosophical problem is supposed to overcome the tension that exists between the undeniable mechanistic fatality of bourgeois fate and the effort to interpret it optimistically.
>
> The contemplative attitude is conditioned only secondarily by the French gentry's acceptance of the basic characteristics of the social relations of power of its time. *All* bourgeois philosophy has this contemplative attitude,

which arises from the subjection of human beings to the fatality of events in capitalism. The specific contribution of the gentry to the formulation of Descartes's question lies in his effort to conceive this fatality optimistically. (Borkenau, 1987, p. 120)

The addition of religion to that picture makes it even more complicated. Descartes, Borkenau claims, never criticized Christianity. He only criticized paganism which he understood alternatively as Stoicism (Borkenau, 1934, p. 275). As Descartes writes in the *Discourse*:

> They [i.e. the Stoics] extol the virtues, and make them appear more estimable than anything else in the world; but they do not adequately explain how to recognize a virtue, and often what they call by this fine name is nothing but a case of callousness, or vanity, or desperation, or parricide. (Descartes, 1985a, p. 114)

The Stoic moral, as Descartes sees it, is a natural moral: nothing exists except the mechanism of nature. We do not have access to that mechanism, according to the Stoics. It is a fatalist and pessimistic worldview. Descartes is not opposed to the Stoic notion of natural morality, but he rather wishes to found it on a secure and valid understanding of nature. This will turn the pessimistic Stoic worldview into an optimistic worldview. Descartes's principal task, Borkenau claims, is to achieve a unity between morality and nature by means of a universal science (Borkenau, 1934, p. 276). As Descartes writes in the *Discourse*:

> Above all I delighted in mathematics, because of the certainty and self-evidence of its reasonings. But I did not yet notice its real use; and since I thought it was of service only in the mechanical arts, I was surprised that nothing more exalted had been built upon such firm and solid foundations. (Descartes, 1985a, p. 114)

Nothing in Descartes's philosophy can be understood, according to Borkenau, if we overlook that connection between morality and nature (Borkenau, 1934, pp. 276–7). As Descartes writes in the *Principles of Philosophy*:

> Thus the whole of philosophy is like a tree. The roots are metaphysics, the trunk is physics, and the branches emerging from the trunk are all the other sciences, which may be reduced to three principal ones, namely medicine,

mechanics and morals. By 'morals' I understand the highest and most perfect moral system, which presupposes a complete knowledge of the other sciences and is the ultimate level of wisdom. (Descartes, 1985b, p. 186)

This is Neo-Stoicism. It does not imply a simple submission to nature, as classical Stoicism does. According to the Neo-Stoicism, to change the world means to change one's own thought about the world or its interpretation by means of the new science. This new understanding and interpretation of nature is based on the new science. This is the source of the optimism in the Neo-Stoicism. In the *Discourse*, in what Descartes calls his provisory moral code, he writes:

My third maxim was to try always to master myself rather than fortune, and change my desires rather than the order of the world. In general I would become accustomed to believing that nothing lies entirely within our power except our thoughts, so that after doing our best in dealing with matters external to us, whatever we fail to achieve is absolutely impossible so far as we are concerned. This alone, I thought, would be sufficient to prevent me from desiring in future something I could not get, and so to make me content. (Descartes, 1985a, pp. 123–4)

Borkenau adds that the change from Stoicism to Neo-Stoicism, from pessimism to optimism, is founded on Descartes's conviction that the rules of nature are also the rules of man (Borkenau, 1934, p. 307). As we know from the *Meditations*, this requires a union of body and mind which only God can produce. Thus, belief in God becomes an indispensable motif in Borkenau's reading of Descartes. Descartes writes:

Now there is in me a passive faculty of sensory perception, that is, a faculty for receiving and recognizing the ideas of sensible objects; but I could not make use of it unless there was also an active faculty, either in me or in something else, which produced or brought about these ideas. But this faculty cannot be in me, since clearly it presupposes no intellectual act on my part, and the ideas in question are without my cooperation and often even against my will. So the only alternative is that it is in another substance distinct from me – a substance which contains either formally or eminently all the reality which exists objectively in the ideas produced by this faculty (as I have just noted). This substance is either a body, that is, a corporeal nature, in which case it will contain formally (and in fact) everything which is to be found objectively (or representatively) in the ideas; or else it is God or some creature more noble than a body, in which case it will contain eminently whatever is to be found in the ideas. But since God is not a deceiver, it is quite clear that he does not transmit the ideas to me either directly from himself, or indirectly, via some creature which contains the objective reality of the ideas not formally but only eminently. For God has given me no faculty at all for recognizing any such source for these ideas; on the contrary, he has given me a great propensity to believe that they are produced by corporeal things.[7] (Descartes, 1995, p. 55)

In other words, as Borkenau puts it, 'God is the ultimate good, because He is what we always try in vain to become. Without that God, Descartes's optimistic worldview would be impossible' (Borkenau, 1934, p. 327).[8] Yet, a complete adequacy between the mind and reality is something we can only strive to achieve in an endless approximation. This implies the notion of endless progress which would have been inconceivable without the notion of eternity, of God. At this point, Borkenau argues, belief in God and capitalism converges. And he writes:

Optimism can be granted in the bourgeois world either, as in Spinoza, through abstraction of the whole concrete 'modal' existence (*Dasein*) or, as in Descartes, through projection of an infinitely remote point of time at which the contradiction resolves, [that is] through the idea of an infinite progress. [This idea of infinite progress] is in accord with the limitless striving of the capitalistic man; or – the same seen from a different perspective – the lack of immediate identity between desire and social reality. The bourgeois optimism is pure 'idealistic'; it does not refer to a real social situation, but rather to a pure ideal resolution of its contradictions.[9] (Ibid.)

We now see the connection which Borkenau tries to establish between all the motifs in his reading of Descartes. He sums it up as follows:

The goals of the bourgeois philosophy – mastering nature through insight into natural occurrence and, on the other side, insight into social occurrence merely in order to accept it – are contained in Descartes's questioning (*Fragestellung*). This is the meaning of changing the world by means of pure thought, this [is] the way in which the contradiction between theory and practice should be resolved; this [is] the theoretical inference [which Descartes draws] from the mystical revelation [i.e. God's revelation to him in his dreams] which promised to bind theoretical doubts with practical obedience.[10] (Ibid., pp. 301–2)

At the beginning of his extensive and intricate study, *Der Übergang vom feudalen zum bürgerlichen Weltbild; Studien zur Geschichte der Philosophie der Manufakturperiode*, Borkenau contends that it is easy to demonstrate the dependency of the new worldview, the mechanistic worldview, on manufacture (Borkenau, 1934, p. 7). He goes on to specify the nature of this dependency (ibid., pp. 7–8). Production in the Middle Ages, he claims, was focused on quality and was thus limited to a specific branch of production, which was carried out by a highly skilled craftsman. Its highest achievement was an individually artistic refinement of the final product. Manufacture, on the contrary, consists of speed and accuracy. Everyone is supposed to be able to accomplish it, even a child and an imbecile (*Schwachsinniger*). It is founded on a routine. Quality is replaced with quantity, division of labour leads to a higher quantity of production, and unqualified workers are cheap labour. Thus, the profit is higher. The reduction of everything to quantity is the realization of the main principle of capitalism, Borkenau claims, since only pure quantity is completely commensurable. We can see how this new process of manufacture yields the notion of pure subject, bereft of any specific qualities, as well as of pure material which is defined in sheer mathematical terms. 'Hence, manufacture is the precondition of modern mechanics', he sums up (ibid., p. 8).[11] To this Borkenau adds an interesting remark: manufacture creates the realm of true metaphysics, of true transcendence, the transcendental realm beyond the realm of the sensual materiality. Plato's ideas as well as the Renaissance's secrets of nature, he claims, were only duplications of reality but not a real metaphysics.

> Only manufacture made it possible to actually transcend in thought the realm of the phenomena (*Erscheinung*), because manufacture was the first to abstract from the realm of the phenomena, which is determined qualitatively, as much as possible. Only manufacture strives in principle to achieve the utmost elimination of organic processes, [to achieve] the utmost dealing with material as pure substrate bereft of any spontaneity, [to achieve] mechanization of the work process.[12] (Ibid., pp. 11–12)

Manufacture turns out to be not only the precondition of modern mechanics but also of true metaphysics, of Descartes's philosophy. Manufacture, according to him, reduced any kind of spontaneity, of movement, to abstract material, in order to enable a purely mechanical system. 'The mechanical worldview is an application of manufacturing processes to the whole cosmos' (ibid., p. 12).[13] Regarding the content of this mechanical worldview Borkenau writes, 'Manufacture was a necessary precondition for the large mechanics, in so far as it created for the first time abstract material and abstract labor' (ibid., p. 13).[14] We now have a clearer notion of the connection which he attempts to establish between economy, technology, society, and philosophy. He writes:

> In the manufacturing work process, man becomes, for the first time, the bearer of a work per se in his relationship to nature which consequently becomes mechanized. But exactly in that, man himself becomes mechanized, [he becomes] an organ in a society which is created neither traditionally nor consciously. In this society, the social (*gesellschaftlich*) processes establish themselves above man's head. The mechanization of labor (of the productive forces) and of social (*gesellschaftlich*) life (of the relations of production) are one and the same process of the capitalistic penetration.[15] (Ibid., p. 14)

Borkenau goes on to explain the connection between this worldview and Descartes:

> The rejection of qualitative philosophy, the creation of mechanistic worldview, is a radical change which began around 1615 and culminated in Descartes's *Discourse* (1637), Galilei's *Discoursi* (1638), and Hobbes's *Elements* (1640). Manufacture developed gradually since the beginning of the 16th century.[16] (Ibid.)

Manufacture, according to this account, emerged at the beginning of the sixteenth century. What is then its relationship to Descartes, Galilei, and Hobbes, who worked about hundred years later? There cannot be a simple answer to this question. They should have been influenced by the worldview which developed along with the manufacture period. They may have contributed to this worldview and developed it further. Yet, they were individual men and the attempt to identify them with a general worldview and social trends is problematic. For Borkenau, however, there is a simple answer, 'Descartes was the first who attempted to create a coherent worldview out of the categories which determine the life of the capitalistic individual' (ibid., p. 268).

Borkenau takes upon himself a difficult task, to describe the interaction between theory and socio-economic factors. On the one hand, Descartes's philosophy and the mechanical worldview stemmed from manufacture and the division of labour. On the other hand, this philosophy formulated everything in quantitative terms and formed a rigorous mathematical perspective of man, society, and nature. Thus, it furthers the alienation of man and helps to found industrialism and capitalism. History is made up of innumerable factors. Chances, mistakes, unintended actions, coincidence, and spontaneity play a role in its formation. The *terminus ad quo* and the *terminus ad quem* in any historical account are arbitrarily determined by the historian. Likewise, the selection of details and references are preceded by an arbitrary decision of the historian. In order to corroborate his theory on the relationship between theory and socio-economic reality, Borkenau provides examples which are supposed to demonstrate an obvious connection between the two. For instance, he tries to show how the epistemological problem to account for our access to reality emerges out of socio-economic circumstances:

> The mode of thinking which conceives the mind (*Denken*) as a passive mirroring (*wiederspiegeln*) of the objectively fixed reality (*Außenwelt*) and the human act as a passive accomplishment of natural automatisms – [this mode of thinking] is a product of the 'self-alienation' of man in capitalism. Therefore, only within this mode of thinking the problem can emerge, [that is], how the human mind (*Denken*) can perceive the alien reality from which it is substantially different. Consequently, the ability to 'mirror' reality must be ascribed to the mind; the essence of this mirroring is determined by the current form – which is socially determined – of projecting the problems of the capitalistic individual upon reality.[17] (Borkenau, 1934, p. 317)

The separation of mind and reality is not something which is primarily given in thought, Borkenau claims. Its source is rather the isolated subject in capitalistic society (ibid., p. 318). Next, he refers to Descartes's observation of the human will as infinite. Descartes writes:

> It is only the will or freedom of choice which I experience within me to be so great that the idea of any greater faculty is beyond my grasp; so much so that

it is above all in virtue of the will that I understand myself to bear in some way the image and likeness of God. (Descartes, 1985a, p. 40)

Borkenau identifies the infinity of the will in Descartes's philosophy with capitalism. It reflects the birth of a new type of man. Borkenau writes:

> For the scholastics, the question regarding the freedom of the will (*Willensfreiheit*) was not bound with the question regarding its scope (*Willensbreite*). For Thomas, man is a limited and fixed creature with natural purposes who constantly changes. They determine in advance the scope of his will. Man is free to choose the means to achieve these purposes. But the bourgeois 'I' in Descartes's philosophy is abstract and infinite, since it has no longer concretely determined 'natural' instinctual purposes (*Triebziele*) that can limit it. On the contrary, it has the need to always set itself new purposes. The infinity of the bourgeois will is admittedly – to put it in a Cartesian terminology – not 'infinite', it does not refer to infinitely many objects, it is rather 'indefinite'. It is limitless, it always will and must have more. Descartes presents, in the possibly deepest formulation, the problem of the free will of the bourgeois individual.[18] (Borkenau, 1934, p. 322)

Next, Borkenau claims that in the four rules of the method which Descartes set up in the *Discourse* we find the principles of any manufactural thinking (Descartes, 1985a , p. 120). The first rule concerns the criterion for any true perception – it should be *clara et distincta perceptio* (clear and distinct perception). Borkenau discerns here the principle of graphicality or vividness (*Anschaulichkeit*) which, according to him, is one of the main demands of manufactural production (ibid., pp. 347–8). The second rule stipulates the division of any problem into simple parts. This, Borkenau claims, reflects the division of labour in the manufacture period, and eventually, the two first rules demand that we reduce all quality to quantity. The third rule stipulates the systematic building of the complex from simple parts. And the fourth rule stipulates the completeness of induction. As Borkenau sums it up: 'The four rules are, therefore, the classical program of manufactural thinking. Descartes strived to introduce this program into reality in any respect' (ibid., p. 348).[19]

In 1935, Henryk Grossmann published an essay entitled *Die gesellschaftlichen Grundlagen der mechanistischen Philosophie und die Manufaktur* (*The Social Foundation of Mechanistic Philosophy and Manufacture*) in the *Zeitschrift für Sozialforschung* (Journal for Social Research). The essay was conceived as a critique and a correction of Borkenau's *Der Übergang vom feudalen zum bürgerlichen Weltbild; Studien zur Geschichte der Philosophie der Manufakturperiode*. Like Borkenau's study, Grossman's essay was commissioned by the Institute of Social Research. Borkenau's book was regarded by the members of the Institute as superficial, and Grossmann was called upon to save the face of the Institute. Grossmann's essay remained mainly unnoticed. Alexandre Koyré, who knew Grossmann's work, wrote that Grossmann's critique was 'far more instructive than this work [i.e. Borkenau's] itself' (cited in Freudental and McLoughlin, 2009, p. 26). When Borkenau's book was reprinted in 1971 by a scholarly publisher in Germany, a pirate edition followed with Grossmann's text as appendix (ibid., p. 27). Grossmann first tries to show that Borkenau's historical study is completely fallacious. This enables him, consequently, to demonstrate that the connection which Borkenau tries to establish between economy, society, mechanism, technology, and religion is wrong. If Grossmann is right, then Borkenau's study on Descartes turns out to be nothing but an obsession with Descartes. The first claim which Grossmann makes concerns the entire framework of Borkenau's study.

> The historian has methodological doubts from the very beginning: Does history really take so rectilinear a course as Borkenau would have it? Do the single stages of the process really follow each other in such a sequence that one can speak of *the* world-picture of Scholasticism, of *the* Renaissance and of modern times as clearly distinct concepts? And are there never any regressions – often lasting for centuries – which also should be taken into account and explained? Yet doubts arise not only with regard to the succession in time but also to the proximity in space: do not different world-pictures coexist in every period, e.g. in the Scholastic, hence rendering the scholar's work even more complicated; does he not also have to explain this particular coexistence? (Grossmann, 2009a, p. 106)

This claim concerns not only Borkenau but any historical study. As we mentioned earlier, any historical study involves many arbitrary decisions. Borkenau may have even been more selective than a historian, since he referred only to the events and picked out only those details which could back up his philosophical theory and framework. This problem is, however, not specific to Borkenau but to anyone who embarks on an undertaking of this kind. Grossmann, who tries to correct Borkenau's study, risks falling into the same trap of manipulative historical readings.

Grossmann divides his critique of Borkenau into several points. In what follows I will discuss only those points which are most relevant to our discussion.

> The assumption seems to suggest itself that mechanistic philosophy and scientific mechanics derived their basic mechanical concepts from the observation of mechanisms, of *machines*. Borkenau however deduces the rise of mechanical conceptions not from the machines but from the division of human labor in the crafts. (Ibid., p. 107, italics in original)

This point is the bone of contention between Grossmann and Borkenau. As we saw, Borkenau traces back the emergence of the machine and mechanical worldview to economic change, that is, manufacture and the division of labour. On the contrary, Grossmann claims that the mechanical worldview evolves out of a reflection on machines and mechanical processes as observed in nature. He shows that the development of the machine and of the mechanical worldview can already be found in Leonardo da Vinci, that is to say, about 150 years before Descartes. Grossman's point is to show that the beginning of the scientific revolution preceded both Descartes and the period of manufacture. Hence, there is no real connection between them, according to him. In other words, the development of machines refers back to machines or mechanical processes observed in nature and not to economic change; 'Mechanistic thinking and the progress of scientific mechanics show no trace of a closer relationship to the manufactural division of labor, but are always and everywhere closely related to the use of machines!' (ibid., p. 127). Grossmann writes further:

> Leonardo's pioneering work in the field of comparative anatomy is based on the realization that the functions of the animal body and the motion of its limbs are governed by the laws of mechanics. 'The whole world, including living things, is subject to the laws of mechanics; the earth is a machine, and so is man. He regards the eye as a camera obscura, ... he determines the crossing point of the reflected rays.' (Ibid., p. 108)

Grossmann sums up as follows:

> According to Borkenau, the concept of mechanical work has its origins at the beginning of the seventeenth century only, in connection with the division of industrial labor and with highly skilled work being replaced by 'general

human' work. In fact, the concept of mechanical work was already well known to Leonardo by the end of the fifteenth century and he developed it from observing the effect of machines which replace human performance. (Ibid.)

Next, Grossmann goes on to show that Borkenau is also wrong regarding the beginning of capitalism.

> In contrast to Marx's view, that in Italy 'we meet the first beginnings of capitalist production as early as the fourteenth or fifteenth century, sporadically, in certain towns of the Mediterranean', Borkenau says that not before the turn of the seventeenth century did the introduction of monetary capital into the sphere of production 'have its first decisive success'. (Ibid., p. 112)

Grossmann's main argument against Borkenau is that 'since in Descartes there is no reference to division of crafts labor, the question arises: What do his texts reveal regarding the sources of his mechanistic inspiration?' (ibid., p. 133). This argument seems to be weak. Critical Theory is like psychoanalysis: it strives to expose the socio-economic subconscious of philosophies, theories, and ideologies. Thus, the fact that Descartes never mentioned manufacture and division of labour does not undermine Borkenau's theory. It rather calls upon the utilization of Critical Theory. Hence, Grossmann should find other sources to back up his argument against Borkenau. According to him, Descartes's motivation to develop machines is to ease human labour. The source of his motivation is other machines which he observed.

> The source which provided the initiative for working out the mechanical concept of work is in the machines, and not connected with the division of labor in manufacture, as Borkenau claims. The practical aim of easing human labor through the work of machinery presupposes the comparison between both types of work, their reduction to general mechanical concepts of work and the quantification of the work done. Only thus can it be ascertained whether the machine really does reduce human labor. (Ibid., pp. 134–5)

Next, Grossmann writes:

> Only in the fifth part [of the *Discourse*], and referring to the description of the heart's and blood's movements, does Descartes say: 'que ce mouvement que je viens d'expliquer suit aussi nécessairement de la seule disposition des

organes [that the movement which I have just explained follows from the mere arrangement of the organs] … qu'on peut connaître par expérience, que fait celui d'une horloge, de la force, de la situation et de la figur de ces contrepoids et de ses roues' [as one can know from experience that in the same way the movement of the clock follows from force, the position and shape of its counterweights and wheels]. There is no allusion to the division of labor in manufacture, but there is a comparison with a machine, with the clock; the movements of the heart and blood are just as much conditioned by the disposition of the bodily organs as the movement of a clock is conditioned by the disposition of its weights and wheels! (Ibid., p. 137)

As we saw, Borkenau traces the emergence of the technological worldview back to manufacture. Grossmann shows that 'this presentation of the character of manufactorial work at the turn of the sixteenth and seventeenth centuries is sheer fantasy' (ibid., p. 120). The question is whether the reason for such a mediocre outcome, as he assesses Borkenau's study, is the outcome of slack historical work on Borkenau's part or whether there is rather something else which impeded him. It seems that according to Grossmann, the reason lies in Borkenau's method. Instead of conducting historical research, Borkenau subsumes history under a fixed theoretical construction. According to Grossmann:

> Borkenau's generalized conception of manufacture is evidently based on the description in the first chapter of [Adam Smith's] *Wealth of Nations*, illustrated by the far-reaching division of labor and dissection of the work process into simple manipulations of the production of metal pins. He transfers the situation and conceptions described by A. Smith which apply to the conditions of the second half of the eighteenth century to those prevailing in the sixteenth century, without giving a thought to the question as to whether the 'manufacture' of the sixteenth century can be identified with that of the eighteenth century. (Ibid.)

In his conclusion, Grossmann says:

> We now want to demonstrate that Borkenau's failure is due to his method. In contrast to the isolating way of viewing history, such as Max Weber's, who 'only knows separate factors in historical events which determine the course of history', Borkenau acknowledges 'the dialectic materialism which is based on the categories of totality and objective tendency'. He strongly

emphasizes that 'two inseparably linked determinants, forces and relations of production, determine the whole ideology'. However, in his work he neglects to explain the mechanistic world picture via the forces and relations of production at the time of its emergence. (Ibid., p. 145)

In other words, according to Grossmann, historical study should start with a description of the forces and the relations of production and then ascend to generalization, theory, and ideology. Borkenau does the contrary, according to Grossmann: he applies theoretical construction to historical events. The framework of Borkenau's study is extremely complicated. It professes to bind together many different components: technology, theology, economy, and processes of production. This requires in turn a highly selective approach to a huge number of details which must be fitted into that complicated scheme. The outcome is so complicated that it is perhaps impossible to say at what point Borkenau is right or wrong as far as his historical research is concerned. Grossmann seems to be right in claiming that Borkenau imposes theoretical construction upon history. This theoretical construction seems, however, to be not Adam Smith's *Wealth of Nations*, as Grossmann argues against Borkenau, but rather Karl Marx's *Das Kapital* (Capital) to which Borkenau relates as an authority. Like Borkenau, Grossmann also relates to Marx's *Das Kapital* as an authority in analysing historical processes. Borkenau's study on Descartes may be historically flawed, but in many cases it seems to be in complete accord with Marx's analysis.

As we saw, Grossmann argues against Borkenau that the mechanical worldview did not stem from manufacture but rather from reflection on machines and mechanical processes in nature. To substantiate his claim that the mechanical worldview emerged out of reflection on machines or mechanical processes in nature, Grossmann refers to the example from the fifth part of the *Discourse* in which Descartes compares the human body to a clock (*horloge*) (Descartes, 1985a, p. 136). Grossmann may be right as far as history and Descartes are concerned. Borkenau, however, seems to follow Marx's analysis of historical process. As Marx writes in *Das Kapital*:

> The period of manufacture simplifies, improves, and multiplies the tools through their adjustment to the exclusively specific functions of each worker. Thus, it creates at the same time one of the material conditions

for the machinery which consists of combination of simple instruments.[20] (Marx, 1883, pp. 341–2)

As we saw, Grossmann argues against Borkenau that the use of machinery began long before Descartes, with Leonardo da Vinci. Marx says that we can discern examples of machines in use already in the Roman Empire, that is, water mills. Yet, machinery played only a minor role by that time (ibid., p. 349). At least according to Marx, Grossmann is right that the mechanical worldview stemmed from reflection on machines and not on economy. Marx writes: 'The sporadic use of machinery in the 17th century was very important, since it provided the great mathematicians of that time with practical grounds and a stimulant to create modern mechanics' (ibid.).[21] Yet, this machinery emerged out of the division of labour as embodied in manufacture. Marx writes:

> We observe here, that is, in manufacture, the immediate technical foundation of the heavy industry. The former [i.e. manufacture] produced the machinery with which the other [i.e. heavy industry] superseded (*aufhob*) the handwork and manufacturing activity in the realms of production which it first seized (Ibid., p. 386)[22]

Marx describes this transition from manufacture to the complete mechanization of production as a transition from subjectivity to objectivity. The worker is consumed in this mechanical process and loses all the characteristics that make him an individual person. He writes:

> In the mechanical system, the heavy industry embodies a complete objective organism of production which the worker encounters as a completed material condition for production. In the simple cooperation as well as in the cooperation which is specified through the division of labor, the suppression of the individual worker in the associated (*vergesellschaftet*) labor is still, more or less, accidental. The machinery, with some exception to be mentioned later, functions only under the control of a direct associated or common labor. The machinery functions under the control of a socialized or collective labor. Thus, the cooperative character of the work process becomes now, through the nature of the means of production itself, a technically dictated necessity.[23] (Ibid., p. 390)

Marx describes here the disappearance of the worker as a human being in the capitalistic machinery of production. The worker is deprived of his body and soul, the fruit of his labour and his human traits are taken away from him. If we look at Borkenau's work from a distance and let the numerous details and citations fade away, we see that this is exactly what he finds in Descartes's philosophy: man is reduced to an abstract thinking substance, and the material world is reduced to an abstract expanding substance which can be rendered only by means of mathematics. Borkenau perhaps conducts a bad historical study, as Grossmann argues. In dealing with Descartes, Borkenau seems to refer more to Marx's analysis than to history, which Grossmann also conceives as an authority.

***

In the eyes of Franz Böhm, a forgotten thinker of the *völkisch* philosophy, the abstraction of man and nature, and the separation of body and mind, which derived from Cartesian philosophy, led man to abandon his *Volk*, culture, and soil, which are the ethnic foundation of real human community and the only meaning of human existence. Chapter 6 deals with all the detrimental effects of Cartesianism, according to Böhm.

Notes

1 'Der tolerante Konservatismus des Descartes darf aber nicht darüber hinwegtäuschen, daß gerade durch diesen Philosophen alle menschlichen Dinge im Kern bereits revolutionär verändert waren, weil er den menschlichen Körper als Mechanismus begriffen hatte. Das war der Anfang der kommenden technisch-industriellen Revolution.... An sich ist es möglich, den Staat als künstlichen Mechanismus aufzufassen, ohne den menschlichen Körper in analoger Weise zu mechanisieren. Doch kann die Mechanisierung des Staates auch ein vergrößerndes Spiegelbild der mechanistischen Auffassung des menschlichen Körpers sein, und dann wirkt sie um so deutlicher und schreckhafter, wie das bei Hobbes der Fall ist.'

2 'Jene Industrie, die noch nicht die modern große Industrie mit ihren Maschinen ist, die aber bereits weder die Industrie des Mittelalters noch die Hausindustrie mehr ist.'

3 'Die manufakturmäßige Teilung der Arbeit ... entwickelt die gesellschaftliche Produktivkraft der Arbeit nicht nur für den Kapitalisten, statt für den Arbeiter, sondern durch die Verkrüppelung des individuellen Arbeiters. Sie produziert neue Bedingungen der Herrschaft des Kapitals über die Arbeit. Wenn sie daher

einerseits als historischer Fortschritt und nothwendiges Entwicklungsmoment im ökonomischen Bildungsprocess der Gesellschaft erscheint, so anderseits als ein Mittel civilisirter und raffinirter Exploitation.'

4 'Der Arbeiter aber wird körperlich und geistig verkrüppelt, seine Arbeit verliert für ihn jeden Inhalt, jedes Interesse, er selbst wird ein Zubehör des Kapitals.'

5 'Descartes war im 17. Jahrhundert der große Lehrer dieser Moral, der sich selbst eine Natur wie Pascal nicht entziehen konnte.'

6 'Es besagt, daß dem Menschen sein Glück und sein Wert nicht von außen zufallen kann, sondern nur daß er selbst beides hervorzubringen hat.'

7 See also Borkenau (1934, pp. 318–19).

8 'Gott ist das höchste Gut, weil er das ist, was wir stets vergeblich zu werden streben. Ohne diesen Gott wäre Descartes' optimistische Weltanschauung nicht möglich.'

9 'Der Optimismus kann in der bürgerlichen Welt nur entweder, wie bei Spinoza, durch Abstraktion von dem ganzen konkreten "modalen" Dasein, oder, wie bei Descartes, durch Hinausschiebung in einen unendlich entfernten Zeitpunkt, wo das Widersprechende sich deckt, durch den Gedanken eines unendlichen Progresses, gewahrt werden. Letzteres ist in Übereinstimmung mit dem ins Unbegrenzte gehenden Streben des kapitalistischen Menschen; oder – dasselbe von einer anderen Seite gesehen – dem Fehlen der unmittelbaren Identität von Trieb und gesellschaftlicher Wirklichkeit. Der bürgerliche Optimismus ist rein "idealistisch", der bezieht sich nicht auf die reale gesellschaftliche Situation, sondern auf rein gedankliche Aufhebung ihrer Widersprüche.'

10 'Die Ziele der bürgerlichen Philosophie: Naturbeherrschung durch Einsicht in das Naturgeschehen, dagegen Einsicht in das gesellschaftliche Geschehen, bloß um es hinzunehmen, sind in der Fragestellung Descartes' enthalten. Das ist der Sinn der Änderung der Welt durch das bloße Denken, das [ist] die Richtung, in der der Widerspruch zwischen Theorie und Praxis überwunden werden soll; das [ist] die theoretische Folgerung aus der mystischen Offenbarung, die theoretische Zweifel mit praktischem Gehorsam zu verbinden versprach.'

11 'So ist die Manufaktur die Voraussetzung der modernen Mechanik.'

12 'Erst die Manifaktur hat es möglich gemacht, im Denken über die Erscheinung wirklich hinauszukommen, weil sie als erste im Produktionsprozeß von der qualitativ bestimmten Erscheinung, soweit wie möglich, abstrahiert.... Erst die Manifakturperiode strebt grundsätzlich nach möglichster Ausschaltung der organischen Prozesse, nach möglichster Behandlung des Stoffes als jeder Spontanität bares bloßes Substrat, nach Mechanisierung des Arbeitsprozesses.'

13 'Das mechanistische Weltbild ist eine Übertragung der Vorgänge in der Manufaktur auf den gesamten Kosmos.'

14 'Die Manufaktur war eine notwendige Voraussetzung der modernen Mechanik, insofern sie zum ersten Mal abstrakte Arbeit und abstrakte Materie schuf.'

15 'Im manufakturellen Arbeitsprozeß wird der Mensch zum erstenmal Träger von Arbeit schlechthin in seinem Verhältnis zur Natur, das dadurch mechanisiert wird. Eben dadurch aber wird er selbst mechanisiert, zum Glied einer nicht mehr traditionell noch bewußt geleiteten Gesellschaft, in der sich die gesellschaftlichen Prozesse über seinen Kopf hinweg durchsetzen. Die Mechanisierung der Arbeit (der Produktivkräfte) und des gesellschaftlichen Lebens (der Produktionsverhältnisse) sind ein und derselbe Prozeß des Durschdringens des Kapitalismus.'

16 'Die Verwerfung der qualitativen Philosophie, die Schöpfung des mechanistischen Weltbilds ist ein scharfer Umbruch, der um 1615 beginnt und in Descartes' "Discours" (1637), Galilei's "Discorsi" (1638), Hobbes' "Elements" (1640) gipfelt. Die Manufaktur entwickelt sich schrittweise seit dem Beginn des 16. Jahrhunderts.'

17 'Die Denkform, die das Denken als eine passive Wiederspiegelung einer objektiv feststehenden Außenwelt, das menschliche Handeln als einen passiven Volzug natürlicher Automatismen faßt, ist ein Resultat der "Selbstentfremdung" des Menschen im Kapitalismus. Nur innerhalb dieser Denkform kann dann das Problem entstehen, wie das menschliche Denken die fremde Außenwelt, von der es substantiell verschieden ist, erfassen kann. Dann muß dem Denken in dieser oder jener Art die Fähigkeit zugeschrieben werden, die Außenwelt "wiederzuspiegeln"; worin diese Wiederspiegelung besteht, bestimmt die jeweilige, gesellschaftlich bestimmte Form der Projektion der Probleme des kapitalistischen Individuums in die Außenwelt.'

18 'Für die Scholastik war die Frage der Willensfreiheit überhaupt nicht mit der der Willensbreite verbunden gewesen. Der Mensch ist für Thomas ein begrenztes und bestimmtes Wesen, mit natürlichen, ständig verschiedenen Lebenszielen, die die Breite seines Wollens vorweg determinieren. Frei ist er in der Wahl der Mittel zu diesen Zwecken. Das bürgerliche Ich Descartes' aber ist abstrakt und unendlich: denn es hat keine konkret bestimmten "natürlichen" Triebziele mehr, die es begrenzen könnenten, dagegen die Notwendigkeit in sich, sich immer neue Ziele zu setzen. Die Unendlichkeit des bürgerlichen Willens ist freilich – um in der schönen cartesianischen Terminologie zu sprechen – kein "infinitum," sie bezieht sich nicht auf unendlich viele Gegenstände, sondern ein "indefinitum," sie ist schranklos, sie will und muß immer weiter. Descartes stellt, in der tiefsten möglichen Formulierung, das Willensfreiheitsproblem des bürgerlichen Individuums.'

19 'Die vier Regeln sind also ein klassisches Programm des manufakturellen
   Denkens. Dieses Program hat Descartes nach jeder Richtung zu verwirklichen
   gesterbt.'

20 'Die Manufakturperiode vereinfacht, verbessert und vermannigfacht
   die Arbeitswerkzeuge durch deren Anpassung an die ausschließlichen
   Sonderfunktionen der Teilarbeiter. Sie schafft damit zugleich eine der materiellen
   Bedingungen der Maschinerie, die aus einer Kombination einfacher Instrumente
   besteht.'

21 'Sehr wichtig wurde die sporadische Anwendnng der Machinerie im 17.
   Jahrhundert, weil sie den grossen Mathematikern jener Zeit praktische
   Anhaltspunkte und Reizmittel zur Schöpfung der modemen Mechanik darbot.'

22 'Wir erblicken hier also in der Manufaktur die unmittelbare technische
   Grundlage der grossen Industrie. Jene produzierte die Maschinerie, womit
   diese in den Produktionssphären, die sie zunächstt ergriff, den handwerks- und
   manufakturmäßigen Betrieb aufhob.'

23 'Im Maschinensystem besitzt die große Industrie einen ganz objektiven
   Produktionsorganismus, den der Arbeiter als fertige materielle
   Produktionsbedingung vorfindet. In der einfachen und selbst in der durch
   Teilung der Arbeit spezifizierten Kooperation erscheint die Verdrängung
   des vereinzelten Arbeiters durch den vergesellschafteten immer noch mehr
   oder minder zufällig. Die Maschinerie, mit einigen später zu erwähnenden
   Ausnahmen, funktioniert nur in der Hand unmittelbar vergesellschafteter oder
   gemeinsamer Arbeit. Der kooperative Charakter des Arbeitsprozesses wird jetzt
   also durch die Natur des Arbeitsmittels selbst diktierte technische Notwendigkeit.'

6

Franz Böhm: German philosophy
at war with Cartesianism

Franz Böhm's forgotten voluminous work *Anticartesianismus: Deutsche Philosophie im Widerstand* (Anti-Cartesianism: German Philosophy in Resistance) is a massive attack on Cartesian philosophy which he defines as an ideology and the ideology of progress (Böhm, 1938, pp. 46, 86, 258–61). The jargon, concepts, and worldview which are used in his attack on Cartesianism, liberalism, democracy, and ideology of progress are borrowed from the *völkisch* arsenal of ideas. Böhm defines this war on Cartesianism as a *völkisch* German war (ibid., p. 238). He calls upon his readership, that is the German people, to return to their *Volk*, to their genuine and deep roots, and to abandon the Cartesian *ratio*. But what is *Volk*? What makes it up: A set of beliefs? Ideas or ideals? Race? Citizenship? Language? Geography? The answer to this question is much more complicated than the one which Hitler provides in *Mein Kampf* (*My Struggle*), a trivial reduction of everything to race. As Julian Köck writes in the introduction to his study on the *völkisch* thought, 'It is not without a certain irony that the *völkisch* [thinkers] themselves also devoted a rather significant portion of their avid journalistic energy to the discussion about what should actually be understood under the heading "*völkisch*"' (Köck, 2015, p. 9).[1] As a solution to this methodical problem, Köck suggests that the *völkisch* movement is a collective movement (*Sammelbewegung*) which was formed with the foundation of the German empire or, at the latest, during the 1890s, in reaction to the distortions of the time (ibid., p. 11). But what are these main distortions of the time? Reiner Hering says:

> The *völkisch* movement emerged as a reaction to modernity, to rapid industrialization, and social mobilization which brought along a loss of

meaning in the traditional understanding of education (*Bildungsverständnis*), the decline of the artisan middle class, and the emergence of mass parties.[2] (Cited in ibid., pp. 11–12)

To this, Köck adds the disappointment of the hope for a spiritual unification of the nation which stemmed from the Romantic ideal (ibid., p. 12). According to Moshe Zimmermann, after 1918 there were about four hundred *völkisch* associations with seven hundred associated newspapers (ibid., p. 15). Thus, even with that generalization, we are still far away from capturing the entire phenomenon.

In the *Reden an die deutsche Nation* (Addresses to the German Nation), the lecture series addressed to the German nation by Fichte in 1807, the *Volk* consists of language, *reine Sprache* (pure language). Pure German language is supposed to link all the descendants of the German *Volk*. Since 'German' does not designate one language but rather a group of Germanic languages, this answer cannot be satisfying. Later on, in his article *Was ist Deutsch?* (What is German?) (1865–78), Richard Wagner identifies the *Volk*, inter alia, with language and geographical boundaries. Both attributions are problematic. Boundaries change hands, while *Volk* remains the same. Wagner then identifies *Volk* with heroism (*Heldenthum*). Houston Stewart Chamberlain, whose *Die Grundlagen des neunzehnten Jahrhundrets* (*The Foundations of the Nineteenth Century*) counts for many as the 'Bible' of racial truth, racial thinking, and racial victory, identifies it once with race (Mosse, 1979, p. 109).[3] Chamberlain refers back to Darwin and his son-in-law, Francis Galton (Chamberlain, 1904, pp. xxii, xxxviii, xlvi). Later, in the *Arische Weltanschauung* (Aryan Worldview), he no longer traces *Volk* exclusively back to race but also to ideas. The main problem in defining *Volk* as race is to demarcate the 'outline' of a specific race and to determine exactly who are the members that fall within those outlines. The criterion of 'three generations back' was a Nazi political device to approve Aryanism. As Horst Junginger asserts, the Nazi attempt to determine the race of a person *biologically* turns out mainly to rely on Church registers (Junginger, 2011, p. 13).

As far as religion is concerned, the question becomes even harder, for it requires us to draw a 'non-congregational' line within the Christian religion which is a very complicated undertaking to accomplish, as we know from

Dietrich Bonhoeffer's reaction to the Aryan Paragraph (Arnold and Lenhard, 2015, pp. 21–2). We will later see an attempt to combine Christianity with *Volk*. As George Mosse shows, various people of the *völkisch* movement tried either to find a way to come to terms with Christianity or to establish a new heliocentric religion specifically for Germans (Mosse, 1979, pp. 69–98).

In his essay *Was heißt völkisch?* (What is völkisch?) dated 1924, the German philosopher Max Wundt (1879–1963) complains that there is almost no reflection on the question what is *völkisch* (Wundt, 1924, p. 6). Likewise, Hedda Gramley points out the ambiguity in the definition of *Volk* as such and in connection with other terms such as *Vaterland* (fatherland), *Heimat* (homeland), and *Vaterlandliebe* (love for the fatherland) (Gramley, 2001, pp. 166–7). Anne Löchte, who writes on the use of *Volk* in Herder's writings, lists a great variety of meanings of *Volk*. If there is a common characteristic to all of them, it is so vague that we can hardly talk unequivocally about *Volk*. In Herder, the term *Volk* refers back to four semantic fields:

1. The collective name for a multitude of people.
2. State unity with no reference to the origin of the people.
3. The lower classes of society.
4. Tribe (*Völkerschaft*) or nation (Löchte, 2005, pp. 78–9).

Leafing through the studies by Mosse, Köck, and Rolf-Peter Sieferle, we find how diverse the *völkisch* movement is in its references to a huge variety of spheres in life and thought. Bringing up all these characteristics of the *völkisch* movement here would be impossible. This immense variety also makes it impossible to convey the meaning of *Volk* in a single English word. Thus, I will use the German noun *Volk*, the plural form *Völker*, and the adjective *völkisch*.

In what follows, I will first of all review those characteristics of the *völkisch* movement which are required in order to understand the context of Böhm's study.

We can easily derive the main characteristics of *völkisch* thought from the clear call to abandon reason and return to the *Volk*. It must mean giving up the claim to equality among all humans. From here we can derive the dominance of nation and culture as determining factors. Democracy is also a product of reason which dictates equality among people. Thus, we can already assume a rejection of democracy. In his article *Was ist Deutsch?* (What is German?) (1865–78), Richard Wagner claims that *deutsch* (German) refers to those people who remained on the German side of the Rhine, that is, the eastern side, and did not give up their language.

> The notion '*deutsch*' is, thus, tightly bound up with the language and the original fatherland (*Urheimat*) and the time has come in which those '*deutsch*' people will become aware of the advantage of the loyalty to their fatherland and language; for out of the bosom of this fatherland emerged, throughout the centuries, the inexhaustible renewal and recreation of the tribes living overseas which almost fell into ruins.[4] (Wagner, 1911, p. 38)

Obvious characteristics of the *Volk* in this quotation are *loyalty* (*Treue*) to the fatherland and language. *Volk*, according to Wagner, is not an essential definition of man without which he could not live. It is rather man's worthiest way of living, morally seen: he can have it or he can lose it. Thus, Wagner's worst fear is the Jew, that man who lives with no *Volk*, infects and corrupts other people with that immoral malady (ibid., pp. 43–4).[5] In the same vein, Chamberlain writes in *Arische Weltanschauung* (Aryan Worldview): 'The issue is not whether we are "Aryan" but rather that we become "Aryan". In this regard, we all have an enormous task to accomplish: the inner release from Semitism which grasps and suffocates us' (Chamberlain, 1938, p. 10).[6] For the *völkisch* thinkers, the 'Jew' stands for urbanism, industrialism, and materialism, as Mosse shows (Mosse, 1979, pp. 36–7).[7]

But how can one become something which one is actually not? That is, can one exist as a German only *potentially*? And if the answer is positive, then how one can become *actually* what one is already *potentially*? What prompts that transition? Max Wundt tries to resolve this difficulty. *Volk*, he says, is a natural, innate trait with which the members of a group of people are born and yet are unaware (*unbewußt*) of it. *Volkstum* is the activity by which these members realize this innate trait. At this stage, the members of the group are already aware of their *Volk*. Lastly, *Volksheit* is the idea, the τέλος (telos, end), the ideal which the members of the group strive to realize. This is the higher level of awareness, of self-awareness (*Selbstbewußtsein*), in which the *Volk*-identity is fully realized (Wundt, 1924, pp. 7–8). In order to make the story clearer, Wundt adds 'blood' and 'soil' as the preconditions of the *Volk*. Blood is the *inner* and soil is the *outer* condition (ibid.). Wundt qualifies the racial element, the blood, and says that it is not sufficient to make up a *Volk* (ibid., pp. 9–11). Through work, the essence of the people, the blood, is embodied in the soil. Working the soil (*Arbeit am Boden*) gathers the people together. Thus, the physical area becomes imbued with meaning, with the blood of the *Volk*, and forms part of its essence (ibid., pp. 14–15). As Mosse writes, working the land means rootedness (*ländliche Verwurzelung*), which is opposed to urban rootlessness (*Entwurzelung*) (Mosse, 1979, pp. 23–36). *Soil* (*Boden*), permeated with historical meaning, is used to emphasize the antagonism towards the Enlightenment, the industrial and technological revolution for which there is only abstracted *nature* (Sieferle, 1984, p. 194).

History (*Geschichte*) plays an important role in *völkisch* thinking, for the essence of the *Volk* is realized above all in history, in the stories about heroic events and deeds. As the *völkisch* thinker Heinrich Claß (1868–1953) writes, 'One who thus wants to seriously collaborate in reviving our *Volk* must endeavor to show and to open the way for our *Volk* to its great past, to the meaning of its history, to its historical vocation' (cited in Köck, 2015, p. 56).[8] In *Reines Deutschtum* (Pure Germanness), one of the main pillars of *völkisch* thought, Friedrich Lange (1852–1917) says that we should regard history as the book of the revelation of God's will (ibid., p. 58). He says further that the knowledge of one's essence lies within every German person. It can, however, be evoked only through immersing (*Versinken*) in history (ibid., p. 59). Max Wundt argues that in '[history] the *Volk* reaches clarity of itself and understands its own essence in contrast to the essence of other *Völker*' (cited in ibid., 2015, p. 59).[9] *Geschichte* is the term used in all these writings on the *Volk*, and not *Historie*. In the view of *völkisch* thinkers, *Geschichte* refers to the process which determines the present and the future of the *Volk*, whereas *Historie* refers to the study of a concluded event or series of events which is carried out objectively and from an academic perspective. Returning to history as a way of renewing the *Volk* and combating degeneration was the *credo* of the *völkisch* movement (ibid., p. 67).

Working as the means to realize the potential essence of the *Volk* is a duty (*Pflicht*), according to Wundt (Wundt, 1924, pp. 15–16). By realizing its innate essence, the *Volk* distinguishes itself from other *Völker* and becomes a military community (*Wehrgemeinschaft*) (ibid., p. 22). So far, Wundt did not make any exceptional claim. It seems that his theory of the emergence and the formation of the *Volk* could be applied to any people whatsoever. Yet there is something unique in his theory which we should notice. It is the direct transition from the *Volk* to the state. There seems to be no intermediate steps in the state's evolution out of the *Volk*. On the contrary, there is a call to dismantle state institutions and return to the *Volk*. 'The state possesses its most secure foundation in the military community (*Wehrgemeinde*) of the *Volk*' (ibid., p. 26).[10] As George Mosse says with regard to Ludwig Langbehn, another 'prophet' of the *völkisch* movement, 'Not the state but rather the *Volk* is the genuine place (*Stätte*) for creating a German nation with the highest significance' (Mosse, 1979, p. 55).[11] Noteworthy in this regard is the hierarchy between different peoples. The idea of equality among all peoples comes from the Enlightenment and should be rejected: 'The tyranny of the abstraction', as Karl Berg puts it (cited in Köck, 2015, pp. 50–1).

'Fatherland' (*Heimat*) is mentioned very often in *völkisch* writings. It means being at home, among your people, the opposite of alienation. 'Hence, he [i.e. the German] returns [from his travels overseas] to the fatherland, since he knows that only there he is *understood*', as Wagner puts it (Wagner, 1911, p. 44).[12] Fatherland is firstly not a physical entity but rather a spiritual entity, a moral concept and not a land. According to Wagner, 'The *Volk* has been annihilated [in the Thirty Years War] but the German spirit survived. This is the essence of the spirit which one calls "Genius" in some highly-talented people' (ibid., pp. 45–6).[13] What makes up the German *Volk*, Wagner contends, is not the body of laws, as with the *French* people, but rather the German spirit (ibid., pp. 45–6). As Nietzsche puts it, 'Meistersinger: contrast with civilization, German contra French' (Nietzsche, 1922, p. 365).[14] There is a statement by Lagarde which recurs in all the main *völkisch* writings, 'Germanness does not consist in blood but rather in spirit' (cited in Mosse, 1979, pp. 41–2).[15] These views have changed, and in 1910 we read in the work of Ernst Graf zu Reventlow (1869–1943) *Welt, Volk und Ich* (World, Volk, and Me) the following statement: '[The] nation, the *Volk*, the race [are] not an accidental formation ... but rather an organic form of nature' (cited in Köck, 2015, p. 52).[16]

The contrast with Descartes's view of a human being is immense. Man is free not as pure, rational thought, but rather as part of the *Volk*. As L. Külz says in an essay published in *Hammer*: 'The German man has a distinctive predisposition to recognize the most capable person as the Führer. Only in his fellowship (*Gefolgschaft*) does he lose the feeling of insecurity and obtains a real freedom' (cited in Köck, 2015, p. 53).[17]

This leads directly to the *völkisch* detestation of parliamentarism and democracy (which are both identified with the *French* spirit and the 'achievements' of the *French Revolution*). As Paul de Lagarde notes, 'Only the great, firm, pure will of one man can help us, neither parliaments, nor laws, nor the striving of powerless individuals' (Lagarde, 1933, p. 10).[18] In contrast with the cohesive *Volk*, democracy is an aggregate of nucleus individuals. Democracy is thus an enemy of the German spirit which is spiritual and non-political. *In Betrachtungen eines Unpolitischen* (*Reflections of a Non-Political Man*), an early work by Thomas Mann (1918) from which he later dissociated himself, Mann writes: 'The political spirit, [which is] anti-German as a spirit, is, as politics, hostile towards [what is] German by logical necessity' (Mann, 1920, p. xxxii).[19] All this yields an authoritarian state. As Mann notes:

> The German *Volk* will never be able to like political democracy for the simple reason that it cannot like politics as such. [Thus,] the much notorious 'authoritarian state' is, and will remain, the only form of state which is appropriate and befitting it, and which is in principle willed by it.[20] (Ibid.)

From the sharp contrast between spirit and politics, Mann goes on to characterize the German *Volk* and to distinguish it from another *Volk* (obviously the French): culture instead of civilization, soul instead of society, freedom instead of suffrage, and art instead of literature (ibid., p. xxxiii). As Julian Köck argues, 'culture' is not the opposite of 'nature'. It is rather the outcome of an organic development of the *Volk* (Köck, 2015, p. 52). 'Civilization', on the other hand, is a hollow organization of people; it is focused on objects and not on humans (ibid., pp. 53–4).

Resorting to racism seems to be a later development of the *völkisch* movement. According to Wagner, for example, the essence of the *Volk* is rather spiritual. At the same time, he calls to bodily activity and heroism. In *Heldenthum und Christenthum* (Heroism and Christianity), Wagner argues that heroism is what distinguishes between low and high races (Wagner, 1881, p. 251). But also this heroism, although connected with heroic physical action, consists above all in spiritual accomplishment which cannot get lost even when the supreme nature, the heroic *Volk*, is subjugated by other *Völker* (ibid., pp. 251–3). Heroism as such is the core of any national mythos of birth and survival and not unique to the German people. The detestation of democracy, parliamentarism, and everything French is something else. As Eugen Diederichs (1867–1930) puts it: 'democracy is equal to civilization, aristocracy is equal to culture' (cited in Mosse, 1979, p. 71).[21]

Volk is not yet identified as a race in Wagner. Hence, it is interesting to notice how he attempts to connect Germanic heroism with a universal Christianity: 'Almost more unwavering than the pride of the hero is the humility of the holy person, and his truthfulness becomes a martyr-delight' (Wagner, 1881, p. 253).[22] Wagner's following statement is directed against racial distinction which Gobineau makes in *Essai sur l'inégalité des races humaines* (1853–5) (*Essay on the Inequality of Human Races*): 'The blood of the savior, running from his head, from his wounds at the cross – who wanted sinfully to ask whether it belongs to the white or to another race?' (Wagner, 1881, p. 254).[23] And yet, attempts had been made to combine the two. Thus, the German Protestant theologian Isaak August Dorner (1809–1884) argues – referring to Corinthians 1:17, 'Let him who boasts boast in the Lord' – that we should boast above all God, since He let the Reformation 'be born out of the spirit (*Gemüth*) of the German *Volk*'. Although other peoples are likewise Christian, the German *Volk* has been 'predestined', through nature and history, for a higher Christian stage of salvation (*Heilsstufe*) (cited in Gramley, 2001, p. 83).

As Rolf-Peter Sieferle argues, we can never really separate the idea of *Volk* from the idea of race. The question concerning people of different races was prevalent at the turn of the century within the conservative critique of civilization. The assumption in this critique was that there are different human races which demonstrate not only physiological differences but also cultural differences.

> Hence, a state (*Zustand*) of 'pure race' was also a state of cultural sovereignty, *völkisch* particularity, and solid foundation (*Bodenständigkeit*). The unity of a racially closed 'Volk' with a 'soil' (*Boden*) which it shaped is demonstrated then in a closed, consistent, and strong culture. The race theory then provided here a biological adaptation and foundation for the older concept 'Fatherland' (*Heimat*).[24] (Sieferle, 1984, p. 194)

Anti-Intellectualism is another characteristic which is directly derived from abandoning reason and returning to the *Volk*. In the foreword to the first edition of *Die Grundlagen des neunzehnten Jahrhunderts* (*The Foundations of the Nineteenth Century*), Houston Stewart Chamberlain writes, 'Who knows, maybe for dilettantism, which is today so disreputable, there is still an important task to accomplish lying ahead?' (Chamberlain, 1904, p. vii).[25] Chamberlain explains this as follows:

> Yet, he [the dilettante] may and must say to himself that there is something which is higher and holier than knowledge: this is life itself. What is written down hereby is experienced (*erlebt*). Some actual statements may turn out to be a traditional mistake, some judgment – a prejudice, and some inferences – a fallacy, a complete untrue is [however] nothing; for the orphaned reason often cheats [but] full life – never does.[26] (Ibid., p. x)

The animosity towards reason, urbanism, and the Jews is linked to the animosity towards progress (*Fortschritt*). As Mosse shows, all these maladies are embodied for many people in one person – Heinrich Heine. Mosse writes:

> Heine was accused of defending progress, whereas the *völkisch* movement strives to establish a society which is healed through history, rooted in nature, and exists in accordance with a cosmic vital spirit (*Lebensgeist*). These are no new forces or uncovered areas, but rather facts which are darkened only by a society for which Heine stood out as a symbol.[27] (Mosse, 1979, p. 39)

Returning to nature is conceived as the antidote to modernity and its alienation (ibid., p. 43). In the wake of the defeat in the First World War, the November Revolution, and the Weimar Republic, the accelerated rationalism and Americanism, the *völkisch* movement, whose essence has always been a critique of civilization, became much more radical, as Sieferle shows.

> The *völkisch* movements in the Republic stood in the tradition of the critique of civilization of 1890, yet they were more radical. Their resentment lived off the national humility, the accelerated rationalism, but also off the symbolic wretchedness of the Republic, the turbulent 'Americanized' cultural scene and the lack of prospects for the perishing educated middle class. Escapism, dropping-out (*Aussteigertum*), settlement movements, reform plans of all kind, but also militant activism were the answer.[28] (Sieferle, 1984, p. 209)

As Oswald Spengler (1880–1936) writes in his book *Der Mensch und die Technik: Beitrag zu einer Philosophie des Lebens*, 1931 (*Man and Technics: A Contribution to a Philosophy of Life*):

> Faustian thinking starts to get tired of technology. Tiredness spreads out, a sort of pacifism in the battle against nature. One turns to simpler forms of life, closer to nature, one engages in sport instead of conducting technical experiments, one hates the big cities, one wishes to escape the bondage of soulless activities, the slavery of the machine, of the clear and cold atmosphere of the technical organization. It is especially the creative faculties that move away from practical problems, and sciences and turn to pure speculation. Occultism and spiritualism, Indian philosophies, metaphysical meditations with Christian or pagan shades, which one despised in the time of Darwinism, surface again.[29] (Spengler, 1931, pp. 80–1)

In Böhm's attitude towards Descartes, we discern motives we have already encountered in Langbehn and Heidegger: the precedence of existence over thinking or essence. 'It is a common conviction of German philosophy that the Cartesian "Cogito ergo sum" should be reversed' (Böhm, 1938, p. 236).[30] Böhm begins his study by lamenting the negative stance towards the past; the past not as a subject of historical study but rather as what should define our stance towards the present and the future. Only through an active determined stance (*Entschlossenheit*) towards the future can we regain the meaning of the past (ibid., p. 2). History (*Geschichte*), he explains, can serve as our instructor only if we take the unswerving position towards the future from which we return to history (ibid., p. 3).

In other words, one should be ready to fight for the future of the *Volk* in order to rescue its past. Contrary to Descartes, one should have the courage not to get rid of his traditional and historical prejudices but rather to accept them as the foundation of one's own future over which one will at some point need to fight and sacrifice one's life. But what exactly are we supposed to retrieve and restore from the past? Böhm talks about forces (*Kräfte*) which create history but are not historical in themselves (Böhm, 1938, p. 3). They remain identical despite historical changes. And what are these forces which make up history? Böhm seems to say that they are ideals; not transcendental ideals, but rather ideals which are experienced within reality (ibid., pp. 5–6). Towards the end of the book, he calls these ideals 'mythical existence' (*Bestand*) (ibid., pp. 242–7).[31] Böhm goes further and says that this historical reality is our *völkisch*-political Dasein. By returning to it, we overcome all the dualistic schisms which Cartesianism introduced into philosophy. The reality which we mean here lies beyond all schisms and conceptualization, as he explains. Its claim to universality means that all questions become possible against its background. Likewise, transcendence has meaning for us only through it (ibid., p. 7).

The priority of reality as a whole over the parts reminds us of *Lebensphilosophie* (philosophy of life). Similar calls to return to reality, to the 'things themselves', *Lebenswelt* (life world), *Welt* (world) are found in the philosophies of Husserl and Heidegger.[32] Also in their philosophies, it is about returning to the source of meaning and overcoming dualism. Our alienated existence, Böhm argues, detaches us from that source of meaning; it is a broken, divided existence: Art, science, religion, state, and church are separated institutions with no inner connection (Böhm, 1938, p. 7). Likewise, politics, detached from that source of meaning, is only about organization of the state (ibid., p. 8). These parts of our existence can be understood but never experienced (*erlebt*), he says (ibid.). Böhm speaks out against academic philosophy, philosophy as an academic profession. According to him, philosophy is rather a *Weltanschauung*; it receives its meaning from reality (ibid., p. 13). Descartes's philosophy is the beginning of a radical rationalism and the end of *Weltanschauung* (ibid., p. 15). Irrational philosophy is the reaction to Descartes's philosophy, but it does not manage to reach the source of rationalism (ibid., pp. 15–16). This rational philosophy is the sworn enemy of *völkisch* thought, since it levels off everything which is unique, which is special (ibid., p. 93).[33] European philosophy, Böhm argues, is nothing but a continuous levelling of all peculiarities, of all authentic attempts to go behind dogmatic congealment and rational development. It is a tragic process, he says, which grinds down everything achieved by the *Volk* (ibid., p. 16).

The alternative philosophy, the philosophy of the *Weltanschauung*, which Böhm proposes, does not use concepts but rather symbols, since reality cannot be conceptualized. It lets reality show itself as a racial-*völkisch* existence (Böhm, 1938, p. 20). Philosophy as *Weltanschauung* does not strive for a universal truth but rather for a particular truth – the truth of the particular *Volk*. Böhm refers back to Henri Bergson's text *La philosophie française* (The French Philosophy) to demonstrate how serious is the misunderstanding of the difference between the *Völker* and the source of philosophy, '*Toute la philosophie moderne dérive de Descartes ... Tout l'idéalisme moderne est sorti de là, en particulier l'idéalisme allemand* ... toutes les tendances de la philosophie moderne coexistent chez Descartes' [All modern philosophy derives from Descartes ... All modern idealism has emerged out of it, especially German idealism ... all the trends of modern philosophy coexist in Descartes.] (ibid., p. 25). The *völkisch* battle to retrieve the German *Weltanschauung* is directed against Descartes but is also waged against Hegel who promulgates Descartes's philosophy and turns it into the new standard of German philosophy (ibid., p. 35).

> The liberation from Hegel implies more than historical correction. It would imply, if it succeeds, that we receive again our philosophical history – which has so far been controlled (*dosiert*) and arranged (*zurechtgestellt*) by Hegel – from first hand.[34] (Ibid., p. 35, italics in original)

And yet, the young Hegel was still able to see Cartesian dualism as the main problem of philosophy, as Böhm shows by referring to the text *Über das Wesen der philosophischen Kritik überhaupt und ihr Verhältnis zum gegenwärtigen Zustand der Philosophie insbesondere* (On the Essence of the Philosophical Critique in General and Its Attitude toward the Present State of Philosophy in Particular). Hegel and Schelling published this text together in the journal *Das kritische Journal der Philosophie* (Critical Journal of Philosophy) which they edited between 1802 and 1803.[35]

The war against Cartesianism, against the universalism which suffocates the *Volk,* is not over metaphysical or epistemological issues. Its cause is rather moral and political. The modern type of rationalism, Böhm writes, poses a historical problem for us, that is, the claim of rationalism to limitless domination over life (Böhm, 1938, p. 43).

This domination of rationalism is the lot (*Schicksal*) of the West, he says. Once it comes to its culmination, it will collapse and the *völkisch Weltanschauung* will emerge (Böhm, 1938, pp. 43–4). In this scheme, Descartes occupies the highest point. As Böhm explains, the historical place of Descartes is the beginning of the road into emptiness and unreality. At the end of this road, the neglected reality will be retrieved (ibid., p. 44).

At this final stage, rational philosophy is completely detached from reality, from anything which is experienced (*erlebt*), since it has cast it into doubt (Böhm, 1938, p. 45). Later, Böhm says that the most awkward thing for German philosophers is the claim that the Cartesian Archimedean point can really be experienced (*empfunden*) and can replace reality (ibid., p. 92). Thus, he demands, 'The historical reflection on Descartes must be able to steer away the furthest from that worship of the external success upon which at last the ideology of rationalism lies' (ibid., p. 46).[36] Cartesianism is the source of all European ideology, Böhm asserts.[37] For him, ideology or ideological perspective (*Weltanschauung*) is the foundation of everything, natural sciences included (ibid., p. 230–1). 'The all-encompassing *scope* of *Weltanschauung* makes it the *presupposition* of science' (ibid., p. 231).[38]

Böhm draws a clear distinction between the 'West' and 'Europe'. West is defined by reference to the *Volk* and its unique history. Europe, on the contrary, is defined by reference to geographical borders only. Europe is only a semantic definition, lacking any historical reference. Descartes embodies the demise of the old Western (*abendländisch*) man and the birth of the European (*europäisch*) man, the rationalist with no reference to history and tradition, according to him. Man now is an empty substance (Böhm, 1938, p. 55). Descartes carried out the turn from the Western consciousness to the European consciousness (ibid., p. 57). The deed of the European man 'lacks the true venture and the deeper insight into the constant exposure of the real acting man' (ibid., p. 56).[39] Böhm details the core of that turn. The most crucial point is that Descartes made rationalism pictorial (*weltbildlich*). With his latent sense of lost reality Descartes thought that he found new certainty in logic which is the foundation of that worldview (ibid., p. 83).

This is the construction of mechanical, mathematical, and geometrical reality. It is the source of the dualism which, in Böhm's eyes, embodies the detachment from the *Volk*. True reality gets entirely lost in the Cartesian dualism of the isolated subject on the one hand and the objective existence (*Gegenüber*) on the other hand. This leads to *nihilism*, according to him (1938, p. 93). Reality as objectivity, as *res extensa*, can be accounted for (*begründen lassen*), because it is a product of rational projection. On the contrary, true reality (*Wirklichkeit*), since it is all-encompassing, cannot be proved but only shown (*aufweisen lassen*) (ibid., p. 94). He rejects rationality altogether as a philosophical means to achieve truth.

> Reality allows no rational recourse *behind* itself, but only a rational approach to it along with the intention to tear off the disguises and coverings which 'culture', conceptuality, religiosity, etc., – which became traditional – have imposed upon it. This *liberation alone* can be the sense of philosophy which understands itself, and the moving force of all the philosophical reformations, with which the rationalism of Descartes is unjustly identified, stems from the passion [to return to] the undiscovered or again covered reality in its depth and wealth, which no rationality anticipates.[40] (Ibid., p. 94, italics in original)

As it is already clear, Böhm is not interested in solving epistemological and metaphysical problems. He speaks above all about a different stance towards reality. The philosophical protagonist is no longer the Stoic passive observer of reality as in Descartes but rather an active participant who shapes reality:

> By nature, man is originally an active agent (*Handelnder*) and not a 'pure' perceiver (*Erkennender*), a co-player, and not a passive spectator (*bloßer Zuschauer*), somebody who is surrounded (*Umgriffener*) and not an isolated free observer. This fundament of anthropology, which one attempts today to establish again out of a new and opened sense of reality, is radically destroyed in Descartes.[41] (Böhm, 1938, p. 97)

The immediate outcome of the passive stance towards reality is the loss of community (*Gemeinschaft*). Descartes's philosophy lacks any sense of community. And community cannot be built up later upon a collection of isolated egos.

> I only know of a community in so far as I myself am part of it and conceive its task as my task, its destiny as my destiny. Whenever this community is denied – and it is denied in Descartes through the methodical beginning with the isolated subject – there exists only a post hoc connection, a greater or smaller association, society as a substitute.[42] (Ibid., pp. 97–8)

Lack of community implies, in turn, a loss of the meaning of sacrifice. Descartes is the founder of the theories that are blind to community (*gemeinschaftsblinde Theorien*). They are in turn also the foundation of the social contract theories and the French revolution (ibid., p. 98). Lack of community means also a lack of history. 'World without nature and community has likewise no room for historical realities' (ibid.).[43]

The original time experience, according to Böhm, is the time of destiny, or what Mircea Eliade calls 'sacred time' (Eliade, 2001, pp. 68–113). Descartes turned time into a static dimension of space, and thus he destroyed community. He emptied history of its most important element – decision or reaction to destiny. In the infinity of space, which can be thought of only 'physically', no destiny is possible, but only anthropomorphous *coincidence* (ibid., p. 219).[44]

> In this [Cartesian view of] 'history', there is no decisive hour any more, since everything which has been missed in the present can be caught up later. It does not matter whether human 'progress' (*Fortschritt*) as an all-human certainty and whether unbounded domination over nature will achieve completion in hundred or thousand years. On the other hand, out of a genuine historical consciousness an hour can decide the destiny of a *Volk*, perhaps even the future of humanity.[45] (Ibid., p. 99)

This destruction of history and the *Volk* goes back to Descartes's beginning with the pure ego.

> The point (*Punktualität*) of the worldless subject – which has future only through rational reaching out (*Ausgriff*) of its I-loneliness or can only dream of it – empties history and turns it into a line of discrete events which are organized on the monotonous line of 'progress'.[46] (Ibid.)

As we saw, Böhm does not dispute with Descartes over epistemological or ontological problems but rather over the nature of philosophy. The question then is what is a philosophy according to Böhm? In his eyes, philosophy is the reaction to reality, response to destiny. Paracelsus, Luther, Hamann, and Fichte, all philosophized in reaction to reality, according to him (1938, p. 99). This mode of philosophical thinking he calls disclosing (*erschließend*) thinking. It destroys the layers of concepts with which rational philosophy covered reality. The disclosing thinking does not conceptualize reality (which would turn it into rational philosophy) but rather refers to it by means of symbols which do not destroy it, as rational thinking does (ibid., p. 126). Thus, disclosing thinking leads us back to the bond between philosophy and mythology which got lost in rational philosophy (ibid., p. 127).

Depth (*Tiefe*) is another characteristic of *völkisch* philosophy which distinguishes it from the Cartesian philosophy. Cartesian philosophy strives to achieve clarity and security, whereas German *völkisch* philosophy struggles against shallowness and platitudes. Method and clarity are important, but they are not the goal of German philosophy, Böhm claims (ibid., p. 129). Depth, as he asserts, means being seized by reality and delving into it, instead of shunning it by creating a philosophy which is detached from it. 'As a goal, depth is an essential dimension of German philosophy, even if no philosopher ever succeeded in actually elucidating that depth', since reality can never be fully elucidated (ibid., p. 132).[47]

Instead of abstracted substance, we see in Böhm the *Volk*. But what makes up this *Volk* in Böhm's eyes? So far, in this regard, Böhm has not mentioned race and the Jews, as commonly done among his contemporaries. But at some point he does mention race and blood: 'In that, we understand *Volk* as the natural *community*, founded upon blood and race, which, as a real acting unity, experiences and shapes *destiny*, that is, has *history*' (ibid., pp. 149–50).[48] It seems that race and blood are necessarily required in order to overcome Cartesian dualism, against which Böhm protests. '*Volk is the community in which nature and history are one. Nature works as history. There is no Volk as bare nature just as there is no history without nature (naturlose Geschichte)*' (ibid., p. 150, italics in original).[49] Cartesian radical doubt, he goes on to say, is entirely foreign to German philosophy:

> One of the characteristics of German philosophy is that it does not autonomously carry out that demolition of the house which became uninhabitable in order then to build a new one, so to speak, from scratch (*auf dem Nichts*), but it carries the new into that which can no longer contain it, and then demolishes it from within.[50] (Ibid., p. 169)

There is a war between rational philosophy and *völkisch* philosophy. Rational philosophy, Böhm argues, lives off killing (*Vernichtung*) *völkisch* philosophy (ibid., p. 177). *Völkisch* philosophy precedes rational philosophy, according to him, and it can never be replaced by rational philosophy. He claims that *völkisch* philosophy tolerates no 'other Gods' beside itself, let alone the false god of rationality (*Begriffsgötze*). It tolerates rationalism and mechanism, Böhm says, only in so far as they do not profess to replace reality as an ideological foundation (ibid., p. 234). On the contrary, rational philosophy cannot live without *völkisch* philosophy: 'Liberal philosophy, which stemmed from the Cartesian spirit, no longer understood its task and thus it became a non-philosophy in its unrealistic (*wirklichkeitsfremd*) hubris' (ibid., p. 178).[51] Even if the task of rational philosophy is progressive (*aufklärerisch*), it emerges out of the deep need of the *Volk* (ibid.).

In Böhm's eyes, the essence of man is *Volk* and not abstracted and static substance. Thus, according to him, Cartesianism neglects the inquiry into the essence of man. Descartes has never posed the question concerning the meaning of man, but only indirectly as related to other questions (Böhm, 1938, p. 193). *Volk* is not a different kind of inert substance, but rather it is a dynamic *activity* and *commitment*.

> 'Community' is not a sociological 'fact' which one has to account for, but it is real (*wirklich*) and active (*wirkend*) only as long as it is experienced as commitment (*Verpflichtung*) and realized through acting. 'Community' is the real actuality of man which he is always potentially.[52] (Ibid., p. 198)

In identifying humans with their *Volk* and community, Böhm must address the question regarding freedom, that is to say, to what extent humans are free agents once *Volk* is regarded as their 'essence'. As we have already seen, he opposes Cartesian passivity and submissiveness to *völkisch* activity. According to him, there can be no Cartesian ethics, since ethics must be tightly bound with activity. Spinoza, Descartes's follower, took this passivity and submissiveness to its extreme. His *Ethics*, Böhm says, 'teaches its disciple how one completely withdraws from acting through a putatively demonstrative insight into the necessity of all occurrence and becomes "wise" in the appeasement of a perfect theory' (ibid., p. 202).[53] Kant's ethics is deeper, he argues, since in it acting is determined by inner disposition. Yet, even Kant does not conceive the full nature of freedom, according to him (ibid., p. 214). Meaningful freedom is realized in sacrificing (*Opfern*), through the ability to sacrifice one's self for the *Volk*, Böhm says. 'We are free only in so far as we can sacrifice' (ibid., p. 216).[54]

Sacrifice cannot be carried out in a vacuum, it must refer to historical events and challenges, to what Böhm calls destiny (*Schicksal*). Böhm criticizes the French revolution, democracy, and liberalism, which are the products of Cartesianism (ibid., p. 217), as examples of a lack of real freedom.[55] He contrasts them with *National Socialism* which demonstrates true freedom.

> The appeal of the National Socialist Reich to the willingness of German man to sacrifice in any is not an external measure for the removal of a temporal state of emergency. [It is] rather the true calling to realization and effectiveness of the community. [Without this] constant scarifying, [the community] would become an ideological 'principle', and eventually, as all 'principles', [would become] unable to mold history as destiny.[56] (Ibid., p. 217)

National Socialism as ideology, as *Weltanschauung*, stems from the encounter of the *Volk* with its destiny and its decision to be a *Volk*, and as such to determine the order of existence.[57] Böhm's attitude towards history is *eschatological*. From this perspective, history is shaped by heroes in those moments of revelation (*Augenblick*) (ibid., pp. 254, 267). He contrasts this heroic attitude to history, to destiny, with the rationalistic, liberal attitude which lacks heroism (ibid., p. 267).

Böhm indeed leads philosophy back into reality, into the political struggle between Germany and the West, and above all Germany and France which he identifies with Descartes. Philosophy for him is part of that reality, part of the circumstances in which it is written down, and yet we expect a distance which creates room for reflection, for an objective perspective. Böhm's philosophy seems to stand 'too close' to reality. This leads him to demand an active reaction to events in reality instead of a passive reflection about reality as in Cartesian philosophy, to talk about heroism, and to call his philosophy 'ideology'. The close ties to reality make his philosophy look like ideology and propaganda. We can find many parallels between Böhm, Heidegger, and Husserl: the call to return to non-reflective experience, to the *Lebenswelt* (life-world), to *Alltäglichkeit* (everydayness), and to found a philosophy upon it. The eschatological view of history is known to us from Heidegger. Likewise, we can easily point at parallels between Böhm and Borkenau: technology and the 'ideology' of progress lead to alienation, to destruction of the true nature of human being, and to society. Borkenau and Böhm trace these maladies of Western civilization back to Descartes. Borkenau does not offer a solution, an antidote to these maladies. Being Marxist, we can guess what he may have had in mind. For Böhm, on the contrary, the solution is a return to the *Volk* and its myths of heroism.

Böhm's study provides no new insights into the philosophy of Descartes. It is, however, an important historical document. It shows how Cartesian philosophy was received at that time within a wide circle of intellectuals as representative of the French spirit, of France, with which Germany was in continuous conflict. It shows us how the outcome of the First World War was conceived and, although written before the Second World War burst out, how the tension between Germany and France was viewed and interpreted at that time as a tension between two opposing philosophies, two opposing worldviews, two opposing *Völker*.

Notes

1 'Es ist nicht ohne eine gewisse Ironie, dass auch die Völkischen selbst einen nicht unbeträchtlichen Teil ihrer regen publizistischen Energie auf die Diskussion verwendeten, was unter "völkisch" eigentlich zu verstehen sei.'

2 'Die völkische Bewegung war als Reaktion auf die Modernisierung, auf die rasante Industrialisierung und soziale Mobilisierung entstanden, die u.a. einen Bedeutungsverlust traditionellen Bildungsverständnisses, den Abstieg des handwerklichen Mittelstandes und die Entstehung von Massenparteien mit sich brachte.'

3 Julian Köck mentions two other books which along with Chamberlain's are the most important for the *völkisch* movement: Heinrich Claß's *Deutsche Geschichte* (1909) and the volumes by Heinrich Wolf in the series *Angewandte Geschichte*. See Köck (2015, p. 21).

4 'An der Sprache und der Urheimat haftet daher der Begriff "deutsch", und es trat die Zeit ein, wo diese "Deutschen" des Vorteils der Treue gegen ihre Heimat und ihre Sprache sich bewußt werden konnten; denn aus dem Schoße dieser Heimat ging Jahrhunderte hindurch die unversiegliche Erneuerung und Erfrischung der bald in Verfall geratenden ausländischen Stämme hervor.'

5 Paul de Lagarde distinguishes between 'Jews', a people lacking *Volk*, and 'Hebrews' who formed a *Volk*: 'Aus der historischen Perspektive bewunderte Lagarde die alten Hebräer, denn er sah in ihnen ein Volk, das in einem wahren, spontan eingegebenen, nicht-dogmatischen religiösen Geist zusammengeschweißt war' (Mosse, 1979, p. 47).

6 'Nicht darauf kommt es an, ob wir "Arier" sind, sondern darauf, daß wir "Arier" werden. In dieser Beziehung bleibt ein ungeheures Werk an uns allen zu vollbringen: die innere Befreiung aus dem uns umfassenden und erstickenden Semitismus.'

7 See also Mosse on Lagarde: 'Der Feind, die Modernität in allen ihren Spielarten, waren die Juden. Durch ihre eigene nationale Religion hatten sie eine bindende Kraft innerhalb der eigenen Gruppe geschaffen, die es ermöglichte, sie als ein separates Element der Bevölkerung zu identifizieren' (Mosse, 1979, p. 45).

8 'Wer darum an unseres Volks Erneuerung ernstlich mitarbeiten will, der muß bestrebt sein, unserem Volke den Weg zu seiner großen Vergangenheit, zum Sinn seiner Geschichte, zu seinem geschichtlichen Beruf zu weisen und zu eröffnen.'

9 'In ihr kommt das Volk zur Klarheit über sich selbst und versteht sein eigenes Wesen im Unterschiede zu dem Wesen anderer Völker.'

10 'In der Wehrgemeinde des Volks besizt der Staat seine sicherste Grundlage.'

11 'Nicht der Staat, sondern das Volk sei als die eigentliche Stätte für die Erschaffung einer deutschen Nation von größter Bedeutung.'

12 'Er kehrt deshalb in die Heimat zurück, weil er weiß, daß er nur hier verstanden wird.'

13 'Das Volk war vernichtet, aber der deutsche Geist hatte bestanden. Es ist das Wesen des Geistes, den man in einzelnen hochbegabten Menschen "Genie" nennt.'

14 'Meistersinger: Gegensatz zur Civilisation, das Deutsche gegen das Französe.'

15 'Das Deutschthum liegt nicht im Geblüthe sondern im Gemüthe.'

16 'Die Nation, das Volk, die Rasse [ist] kein zufälliges Gebilde … sondern eine organische Form der Natur.'

17 'Der Deutsche hat eine ausgesprochene Anlage, den Tüchtigsten als Führer anzuerkennen. Erst in seiner Gefolgschaft verliert er das Gefühl der Unsicherheit und erlangt eine wirkliche Freiheit.'

18 'Nur eines Mannes großer, fester, reiner Wille kann uns helfen, nicht Parlamente, nicht Gesetze, nicht das Streben machtloser Einzelner.'

19 'Der politische Geist, widerdeutsch als Geist, ist mit logischer Notwendigkeit deutschfeindlich als Politik.'

20 'Das deutsche Volk [wird] die politische Demokratie niemals lieben können, aus dem einfachen Grunde, weil es die Politik selbst nicht lieben kann, und daß der vielverschrieene "Obrigkeitstaat" die dem deutschen Volke angemessene, zukömmliche und von ihm im Grunde gewolte Staatsform ist und bleibt.'

21 'Demokratie gleicht Zivilisalion, Aristokralie gleicht Kultur.'

22 'Fast unersehütterlicher als der Stolz des Heiden ist die Demuth des Heiligen, und seine Wahrhaftigkeit wird zur Martyrer-Freude.'

23 'Das Blut des Heiland's, von seinem Haupte, aus seinen Wunden am Kreuze
   fliessend – wer wollte frevelnd fragen, ob es der weissen oder welcher Race sonst
   angehörte.'

24 'Ein Zustand "reiner Rasse" war daher auch einer kultureller Eigenständigkeit,
   völkischer Besonderheit und Bodenständigkeit. Die Einheit von rassisch
   geschlossenern "Volk" und des ihm eigenen, von ihm gestalteten "Bodens"
   manifestierte sich dann in einer widerspruchsfreien, geschlossenen und starken
   Kultur. Die Rassentheorie lieferte hier also eine biologische Umschreibung und
   Fundierung des älteren "Heimat"-Begriffs.'

25 'Wer weiss, ob dem heute so verrufenen Dilettantismus nicht eine wichtige
   Aufgabe bevorsteht?'

26 'Jedoch er durfte und er musste sich sagen, es etwas giebt, höher und heiliger
   als alles Wissen: das ist das Leben selbst. Was hier geschrieben steht, ist erlebt.
   Manche thatsächliche Angabe mag ein überkommener Irrtum, manches Urteil
   ein Vorurteil, manche Schlussfolgerung ein Denkfehler sein, ganz unwahr ist
   nichts; denn die verwaiste Vernunft lügt häufig, das volle Leben nie.'

27 'Heine wurde beschuldigt, den Fortschritt zu verteidigen, während die völkische
   Bewegung dahin strebe, eine Gesellschaft zu errichten, die durch die Geschichte
   geheiligt, in der Natur verwurzelt und in Einklang mit dem kosmischen
   Lebensgeist sei. Dieses seien keine neuen Mächte oder unentdeckte Gebiete,
   sondern Tatsachen, die nur von einer Gesellschaft verdunkelt würden, für die
   Heine als Symbol stand.'

28 'Die völkischen Bewegungen in der Republik standen in der Tradition der
   Zivilisationskritik von 1890, waren jedoch radikaler. Ihr Ressentiment nährte sich
   an der nationalen Demütigen, der beschleunigten Rationalisierung, aber auch an
   der symbolischer Dürftigkeit der Republik, der turbulenten "amerikanisierten"
   kulturellen Szene und der Perspektivlosigkeit des untergehenden
   Bildungsbürgertums. Eskapismus und Aussteigertum, Siedlungsbewegungen,
   Reformangebote aller Art, aber auch militanter Aktivismus waren die Antwort.'

29 'Das faustische Denken beginnt der Technik satt zu werden. Eine Müdigkeit
   verbreitet sich, eine Art Pazifismus im Kampfe gegen die Natur. Man wendet
   sich zu einfacheren, naturnäheren Lebensformen, man treibt Sport statt
   technischer Versuche, man haßt die großen Städte, man möchte aus dem
   Zwang seelenloser Tätigkeiten, aus der Sklaverei der Maschine, aus der klaren
   und kalten Atmosphäre technischer Organisation heraus. Gerade die starken
   und schöpferischen Begabungen wenden sich von praktischen Problemen und
   Wissenschaften ab und der reinen Spekulation zu. Okkultismus und Spiritismus,
   indische Philosophien, metaphysische Grübeleien christlicher oder heidnischer
   Färbung, die man zur Zeit des Darwinismus verachtete, tauchen wieder auf'
   (cited in Sieferle, 1984, pp. 209–10).

30 'Es ist die gemeinsame Überzeugung deutscher Philosophie, daß das cartesische
   "Cogito ergo sum" *umzukehren* sei.'

31 See also: 'Wir müssen heute den Mut haben, den Mythos als das schlechthin
   Ungeschichtliche, das sich in aller Geschichte offenbar macht, selbst wieder
   ungeschichtlich zu sehen und zu erleben' (Böhm, 1938, p. 247). 'Der Mythos
   ist die Ewigkeit eines Volkes; im Umgang mit seinem eigenen Ursprung ist ihm
   jederzeit die schaffende Tiefe seines Lebens erschlossen' (ibid., p. 253).

32 Later, Böhm criticizes Husserl for bracketing and suspending reality and thus
   turning it into a product of our thought. 'Wirklichkeit wird *gelebt* und als
   Aufgabe, Anspruch und Forderung *gehört* und verstanden. Wer glaubt, diese
   gelebte und fordernde Wirklichkeit "einklammern" und als "naïve Weltansicht"
   auch nur vorläufig "suspendieren" zu können, um sich einen schlechthin
   rationalen Weg zu ihr zu bahnen und dann auf dem rational gesicherten
   Ausgangpunkt die zunächst abgewiesene Fülle der Wirklichkeit wieder aufrichten
   zu können, verkennt dabei das Wesen der Wirklichkeit ebensosehr, wie er die
   Kraft und die Tragweite des Rationalen überschätzte' (Böhm, 1938, pp. 95–6).

33 'Er hat auf der Grundlage der allgemeinen und gleichen Rationalität die
   Menscheit geeint und die Schranken niedergelegt, die bis dahin die Völker aus
   dem großen allmänschlichen Verband ausgesondert haben' (Böhm, 1938, p. 93).

34 'Das Freiwerden von Hegel bedeutet mehr als eine geschichtliche Richtigstellung.
   Es würde, wenn es gelingt, bedeuten, daß wir unsere philosophische Geschichte
   wieder *aus erster Hand* empfangen, die uns bisher durch Hegel dosiert und
   zurechtgestellt war.'

35 See: 'Gegen die kartesische Philosophie, welche den allgemein um sich greifenden
   Dualismus in der Kultur der neueren Geschichte unserer nordwestlichen Welt
   ausgesprochen hat, mußte, wie gegen die allgemeine Kultur, die sie ausdrückt,
   jede Seite der lebendigen Natur, so auch die Philosophie, Rettungsmittel suchen'
   (Böhm, 1938, p. 36).

36 'Die geschichtliche Besinnung über Descartes muß am stärksten jener Anbetung
   des äußeren Erfolges steuern können, auf dem im Letzten die Ideologie des
   Rationalismus beruht.'

37 See: 'die gesamte Ideologie des modernen Europa entstammt dem cartesischen
   Ansatz' (Böhm, 1938, p. 93).

38 'Das *Umgreifende* der Weltanschauung macht sie zur *Voraussetzung* der
   Wissenschaft.'

39 'Seiner Tat fehlt das echte Wagnis und die tiefere Einsicht in die unaufhebbare
   Ausgesetztheit des wirklich Handelnden.'

40 'Wirklichkeit gestattet keinen rationalen Rückgriff *hinter* sie, sondern nur
   ein rationales Zugehen auf sie mit der Absicht, die Verkleidungen und
   Überlagerungen abzutragen, die eine herkömmlich gewordene 'Kultur',

Begrifflichkeit, Religiosität usw. auf ihr abgesetzt haben. Diese *Befreiung* *allein* kann der Sinn einer sich selbst verstehenden Philosophie sein, und die bewegende Kraft aller philosophischen "Reformationen", in die sich der Rationalismus Descartes' zu Unrecht eingereiht hat, entstammt der Leidenschaft für die unentdeckte oder wieder verhüllte Wirklichkeit in ihrer Tiefe und Fülle, die keine Rationalität vorwegnimmt.'

41 'Daß der Mensch von dieser Naturgrundlage her ein ursprünglich Handelnder, kein "rein" Erkennender, ein Mitspieler, kein bloßer Zuschauer, ein Umgriffener, kein isolierter freier Betrachter ist, dieses Fundament einer erst heute wieder versuchten und aus neu eröffnetem Wirklichkeitsgefühl unternommen Anthropologie, ist bei Descartes grundsätzlich zerstört.' See also Böhm (1938, pp. 201–2).

42 'Von Gemeinschaft weiß ich nur, insofern ich selbst in Gemeinschaft stehe, ihre Aufgabe als meine Aufgabe, ihr Schicksal als mein Schicksal venrehme. Wo solche Gemeinschaft geleugnet ist – und sie ist bei Descartes mit dem methodischen Ansatz im isolierten Subjekt geleugnet – bleibt nur noch die nachträgliche Verbindung, der größere oder kleinere Verein, die Gesellschaft als Ersatz bestehen.'

43 'Eine naturlose und gemeinschaftlose Welt hat auch keinen Raum für die geschichtlichen Wirklichkeiten.'

44 'In der Unendlichkeit des nur noch "physikalisch" gedachten Weltraums war kein Schicksal, sondern nur noch der anthropomorphe *Zufall* möglich.'

45 'In dieser "Geschichte" gibt es keine entscheidende Stunde mehr, weil alles nachzuholen ist, was eine jeweilige Gegenwart versäumt. Es ist gleichgültig, ob der menschliche "Fortschritt" als allmenschliche Sicherheit und schrankenlose Naturbeherrschung in hundert oder in tausend Jahren zur Vollendung kommt, während aus echtem Geschichtsbewußtsein heraus eine Stunde über das Schicksal eines Volkes, ja vielleicht über die Zukunft der Menschheit *entscheiden* kann.'

46 'Die Punktualität des weltlosen Subjekts, das nur noch durch den rationalen Ausgriff aus seiner Ich-Einsamkeit eine Zukunft hat oder wenigstens eine solche sich erträumt, entleert die Geschichte zur bloßen Reihe einzelner Ereignisse, die auf einförmige Schnur des "Fortschritts" aufgereiht werden.'

47 'Als *Zielrichtung* ist Tiefe die wesentliche Dimension deutscher Philosophie, auch wenn es keinem Philosophen noch gelungen wäre, diese Tiefe *wirklich* aufzuschließen.'

48 'Wir verstehen dabei unter Volk die naturgegebene, in Blut und Rasse gegründete *Gemeinschaft*, die als eigentlich handelnde Einheit ein *Schicksal* erfährt und gestaltet, d.h. *Geschichte* hat.'

49 '*Volk ist die Gemeinschaft, in der Natur und Geschichte eins sind, Natur als
    Geschichte handelt.* Es gibt kein Volk als bloße Natur, so wenig eine naturlose
    Geschichte gibt.'

50 'Es gehört zu den Kennzeichen deutscher Philosophie, daß sie jenes Abtragen
    des unbewohnbar gewordenen Hauses nicht selbstständig vollzieht, um dann
    gleichsam auf dem Nichts das Neue erstehen zu lassen, sondern daß sie das Neue
    in das, was ihr ungemäß ist, hineinträgt, und es von innen her sprengt.'

51 'Die liberale, aus cartesischem Geiste stammende Philosophie [verstand] ihre
    eigentliche Aufgabe nicht mehr, daß sie in wirklichkeitsfremder Überheblichkeit
    zur *Unphilosophie* geworden war.'

52 ' "Gemeinschaft" ist keine soziologische "Tatsache," der man Rechnung zu tragen
    hat, sondern sie ist nur wirklich und wirkend, insofern sie vom Menschen als
    Verpflichtung erfahren und durch Handeln vollzogen wird. "Gemeinschaft"
    ist die wahre "Aktualität" des Menschen, die er aus seiner Möglichkeit immer
    schon ist.'

53 'Sie [die *Ethik*] lehrt ihren Jünger, wie man sich durch angeblich demonstrative
    Einsicht in die Notwendigkeit alles Geschehens dem Handeln restlos entzieht
    und in der Beruhigung lückenloser Theorie zum "Weisen" wird.'

54 'Wir sind nur so weit frei, als wir opfern können.'

55 See: 'Der Zauber der "natürlichen Freiheit," das Pathos Rousseaus und
    der Französischen Revolution, der gleichheitlichen Demokratie und des
    staatsscheuen Liberalismus, hat die Jahrhunderte der Modernität geblendet,
    daß sie eine schicksallose und ungeschichtliche Verwirklichung der Freiheit im
    Idyll erstrebten. Sie verstanden nicht mehr, daß Freiheit nur in der Begegnung
    mit dem Schicksal *wird* und nur dort *konkrete* Freiheit sein kann, wo sich
    die natürlichen Einheiten völkischer Wirklichkeit in die Entscheidungen der
    geschichtlichen Existenz heraufheben' (Böhm, 1938, p. 216).

56 'Der Appel des nationalsozialistischen Reiches an die Opferbereitschaft des
    deutschen Menschen in jedem Ausmaß ist keine äußere Maßnahme zur
    Behebung eines vorübergehenden Notstandes, sondern der eigentliche Aufruf
    zur Verwirklichung und Wirksamkeit der Gemeinschaft, die ohne den ständigen
    Vollzug des Opfers ein ideologisches "Prinzip" und, wie alle "Prinzipien", im
    letzten ohnmächtig wäre, Geschichte als Schicksal zu gestalten.'

57 See: 'Es ist der weltanschauungsgeschichtliche Sinn der nationalsozialistischen
    Revolution, daß sie aus der Wirklichkeit eines einzigen Volkes heraus über die
    Möglichkeit gebundener und gestalthafter Daseinsordnung *entschieden* hat'
    (Böhm, 1938, p. 232).

Bibliography

Albistur, Maïté, and Armogathe, Daniel (1977). *Histoire du féminisme français: Du Moyen Age à nos jours*. Paris: De Femmes.

Arendt, Dieter (1970). *Nihilismus: Die Anfänge von Jacobi bis Nietzsche*. Köln: Jakob Hegner Verlag.

Arendt, Hannah (1978). *The Life of the Mind*. New York: A Harvest Book.

Arnold, Oliver, and Lenhard, Hartmut (2015). *Kirche ohne Juden: Christlicher Antisemitismus 1933–1945*. Göttingen: Vandenheock & Ruprecht.

Azouvi, François (1998). 'Descartes'. In *Realms of Memory: The Construction of the French Past*. Vol. 3. *Symbols*. Ed. Pierre Nora and Lawrence D. Kritzman. Trans. Arthur Goldhammer. New York: Columbia University Press, 483–522.

Baader, Franz Xaver von (1831). *Vierzig Sätze aus einer religiösen Erotik*. München: Georg Franz.

Baader, Franz Xaver von (1854). *Sämtliche Werke*. Vol. 7. Leipzig: Verlag von Herrmann Bethmann.

Baader, Franz Xaver von (1855a). *Sämmtliche Werke*. Vol. 8. Leipzig: Verlag von Herrmann Bethmann.

Baader, Franz Xaver von (1855b). *Sämmtliche Werke*. Vol. 9. Leipzig: Verlag von Herrmann Bethmann.

Baader, Franz Xaver von (1860). *Sämtliche Werke*. Vol. 12. Leipzig: Verlag von Herrmann Bethmann.

Baader, Franz Xaver von ([1824] 1970a). 'Baader A Windischmann'. In *Nihilismus: Die Anfänge von Jacobi bis Nietzsche*. Ed. Dieter Arendt. Köln: Jakob Hegner Verlag, 289–92.

Baader, Franz Xaver von ([1824] 1970b). 'Über Katolizismus und Protestantismus'. In *Nihilismus: Die Anfänge von Jacobi bis Nietzsche*. Ed. Dieter Arendt. Köln: Jakob Hegner Verlag, 265–74.

Baader, Franz Xaver von (1991). *Sätze aus der erotischen Philosophie und andere Schriften*. Ed. Gerd-Klaus Kaltenbrunner. Frankfurt am Main: Insel Verlag.

Barre, François Poullain de la (2002). *Three Cartesian Feminist Treatises*. Trans. Vivien Bosley. Chicago, IL: University of Chicago Press.

Benjamin, Walter ([1940] 1968). 'Theses on the Philosophy of History'. In *Illuminations*. Ed. Hannah Arendt. Trans. Harry Zohn. New York: Schocken Books.

Berlin, Isaiah (1980). *Vico and Herder: Two Studies in the History of Ideas*.
    London: Chatto and Windus.

Betanzos, Ramon (1992). 'Franz von Baaders Philosophie der Liebe'. In *Die
    Philosophie, Theologie und Gnosis Franz von Baaders: Spekulatives Denken
    zwischen Aufklärung, Restauration und Romantik*. Ed. Peter Koslowski.
    Wien: Passagen Verlag, 51–65.

Blumenberg, Hans (1983). *The Legitimacy of the Modern Age*. Trans. Robert M.
    Wallace. Boston: MIT Press.

Böhm, Franz (1938). *Anticartesianismus: Deutsche Philosophie im Widerstand*.
    Leipzig: Felix Meiner Verlag.

Borkenau, Franz (1934). *Der Übergang vom feudalen zum bürgerlichen
    Weltbild*. Paris.

Borkenau, Franz ([1932] 1987). 'The Sociology of the Mechanistic World-Picture'.
    Trans. Richard W. Hadden. *Science in Context*, 1 (1): 109–27.

Brandom, Robert B. (2002). *Tales of the Mighty Dead: Historical Essays in the
    Metaphysics of Intentionality*. Cambridge, MA: Harvard University Press.

Burke, Edmund ([1790] 1951). *Reflections on the French Revolution*. London: J.
    M. Dent.

Burrow, J. W. (2000). *The Crisis of Reason: European Thought, 1848–1914*. New
    Haven, CT: Yale University Press.

Cassirer, Ernst (1946). *The Myth of the State*. New Haven, CT: Yale University Press.

Cassirer, Ernst ([1939] 1995). *Descartes: Lehre, Persönlichkeit, Wirkung*.
    Hamburg: Felix Meiner Verlag.

Chamberlain, Houston Stewart ([1899] 1904). *Die Grundlagen des neunzehnten
    Jahrhunderts*. München: Verlagsanstalt F. Bruckmann.

Chamberlain, Houston Stewart ([1905] 1938). *Arische Weltanschauung*. München:
    F. Bruckmann.

Condorcet, Nicholas de (2013). *Political Writings*. Ed. Steven Lukes and Nadia
    Urbinati. Cambridge: Cambridge University Press.

Derrida, Jacques (1991). *Of Spirit: Heidegger and the Question*. Trans. Geoffrey
    Bennington and Rachel Bowlby. Chicago, IL: University of Chicago Press.

Descartes, René ([1637] 1985a). *Discourse on the Method*. In *The Philosophical
    Writings of Descartes*. Vol. 1. Trans. John Cottingham, Robert Stoothoff, and
    Dugald Murdoch. Cambridge: Cambridge University Press.

Descartes, René ([1644] 1985b). *The Principles of Philosophy*. In *The Philosophical
    Writings of Descartes*. Vol. 1. Trans. John Cottingham, Robert Stoothoff, and
    Dugald Murdoch. Cambridge: Cambridge University Press.

Descartes, René ([1641] 1995). *Meditations on First Philosophy. The Philosophical Writings of Descartes*. Vol. 2. Trans. John Cottingham, Robert Stoothoff, and Dugald Murdoch. Cambridge: Cambridge University Press.

Descartes, René ([1641] 1996). *Meditations on First Philosophy with Selections from the Objections and Replies*. Trans. John Cottingham. Cambridge: Cambridge University Press.

Descartes, René ([1641] 2004). *Meditations on First Philosophy*. Trans. John Cottingham. Cambridge: Cambridge University Press.

Descartes, René ([1641] 2013). *Meditations on First Philosophy with Selections from the Objections and Replies*. A Latin-English Edition. Ed. and trans. John Cottingham. Cambridge: Cambridge University Press.

Dilthey, Wilhelm (1921). *Weltanschauung und Analyse des Menschen seit Renaissance und Reformation*. Gesammelte Schriften. Vol. 7. Leipzig: Verlag von B. G. Teubner.

Dreyfus, Hubert L. (1990). *Being-in-the-World: A Commentary on Heidegger's Being and Time*. Boston: MIT University Press.

Eliade, Mircea (2001). *The Sacred and the Profane: The Nature of Religion*. New York: Houghton Mifflin Harcourt.

Feuerbach, Ludwig (1833). *Geschichte der neueren Philosophie von Bacon von Verulam bis Benedikt Spinoza*. Sämmtliche Werke. Vol. 3. Stuttgart: Fr. Frommanns Verlag.

Feuerbach, Ludwig ([1843] 1906). *Grundsätze der Philosophie der Zukunft. Sämtliche Werke*. Vol. 2. Stuttgart: Frommanns Verlag.

Figal, Günter (2000). *Martin Heidegger: Phänomenologie der Freiheit*. Weinheim: Beltz Athenäum.

Fink, Eugen ([1932, 1933–4] 1988). *VI. Cartesianische Meditation. Teil 1: Die Idee einer Transzendentalen Methodenlehre*. Ed. Hans Ebeling, Jann Holl, and Guy van Kerckhoven. Dordrecht: Kluwer.

Foucault, Michel ([1961] 2006). *History of Madness*. Trans. Jonathan Murphy and Jean Khalfa. London: Routledge.

Frank, Manfred (1987). 'Zwei Jahrhunderte Rationalitäts-Kritik und ihre "postmoderne" Überbietung'. In *Die Unvolendete Vernunft: Moderne versus Postmoderne*. Ed. Dietmar Kamper and Willem van Reijen. Frankfurt am Main: Suhrkamp, 99–121.

Freudental, Gideon, and McLaughlin, Peter (2009). *The Social and Economic Roots of the Scientific Revolution: Texts by Boris Hessen and Henryk Grossmann*. Dordrecht: Springer.

Funke, Gerhard (1960). 'Cogitor Ergo Sum: Sein und Bewusstsein'. In *Sinn und Sein: Ein philosophisches Symposium*. Ed. Richard Wisser. Tübingen: Max Niemeyer, 155–82.

Geldhof, Joris (2005). ' "Cogitor Ergo Sum": On the Meaning and Relevance of Baader's Theological Critique of Descartes'. *Modern Theology* 21 (2): 237–51.

Graeme, Garrard (2006). *Counter-Enlightenments: From the Eighteenth Century to the Present*. London: Routledge.

Gramley, Hedda (2001). *Propheten des deutschen Nationalismus: Theologen, Historiker und Nationalökonomen 1848–1880*. Frankfurt am Main: Campus Verlag.

Grassi, Ernesto (1976). *Macht des Bildes: Ohnmacht der rationalen Sprache: Zur Rettung des Rhetorischen*. München: Wilhelm Fink Verlag.

Grossmann, Henryk ([1935] 2009a). 'The Social Foundations of the Mechanistic Philosophy and Manufacture'. In *The Social and Economic Roots of the Scientific Revolution: Texts by Boris Hessen and Henryk Grossmann*. Ed. and trans. Gideon Freudental and Peter McLaughlin. Dordrecht: Springer, 103–56.

Grossmann, Henryk ([1946] 2009b). 'Descartes and the Social Origins of the Mechanistic Concept of the World'. In *The Social and Economic Roots of the Scientific Revolution: Texts by Boris Hessen and Henryk Grossmann*. Ed. and trans. Gideon Freudental and Peter McLaughlin. Dordrecht: Springer, 157–230.

Hazard, Paul ([1961] 2013). *The Crisis of the European Mind 1680–1715*. Trans. J. Lewis May. New York: New York Review Books.

Hegel, Georg Wilhelm Friedrich ([1807] 1990). *Phänomenologie des Geistes*. Berlin: Akademie Verlag.

Heidegger, Martin ([1929] 1955). 'Was ist Metaphysik?'. Siebte Auflage. Frankfurt am Main: Vittorio Klostermann.

Heidegger, Martin (1961). *Nietzsche*. Pfullingen: Günter Neske.

Heidegger, Martin ([1927] 1967). *Sein und Zeit*. Elfte, unveränderte Auflage. Tübingen: Max Niemeyer Verlag.

Heidegger, Martin ([1929] 1976). 'Was ist Metaphysik?'. *Wegmarken*. Frankfurt am Main: Vittorio Klosterman, 103–22.

Heidegger, Martin ([1938] 1977). 'Die Zeit des Weltbildes'. *Holzwege*. Frankfurt am Main, 75–113.

Heidegger, Marin ([1957] 1983). 'Wege zur Aussprache'. *Aus der Erfahrung des Denkens 1910–1976*. Gesamtausgabe. Vol. 13. Frankfurt am Main: Vittorio Klostermann, 15–21.

Heidegger, Martin ([1920–1] 1995). *Einleitung in die Phänomenologie der Religion*. Gesamtausgabe, Vol. 60. Frankfurt am Main: Vittorio Klostermann.

Heidegger, Martin ([1927] 1996). *Being and Time*. Trans. Joan Stambaugh.
Albany: State University of New York Press.

Heidegger, Martin ([1961] 1997). *Nietzsche*. Gesamtausgabe, Vol. 6.2. Frankfurt am
Main: Vottorio Klostermann.

Heidegger, Martin ([1938] 2001). 'The Age of the World Picture'. In *Off the Beaten
Track*. Ed. and trans. Julian Young and Kenneth Haynes. Cambridge: Cambridge
University Press, 57–85.

Heidegger, Martin ([1936–8] 2003). *Beiträge zur Philosophie (Vom Ereignis)*.
Gesamtausgabe, Vol. 65. Frankfurt am Main: Vittorio Klostermann.

Heidegger, Martin (2008). *Seminare (Übungen) 1937/38, 1941/42*. Gesamtausgabe,
Vol. 88. Frankfurt am Main: Vittorio Klostermann.

Heidegger, Martin (2014). *Überlegungen VII-XI (Schwarze Hefte 1938/39)*.
Gesamtausgabe, Vol. 95. Frankfurt am Main: Vittorio Klostermann.

Henry, Michel ([1965] 1975). *Philosophy and Phenomenology of the Body*. Trans.
Girard Etzkorn. The Hague: Martinus Nijhoff.

Horkheimer, Max (1987). 'Vico and Mythology'. Trans. Fred Dallmayr. *New Vico
Studies* 5: 63–76.

Horkheimer, Max, and Adorno, Theodor ([1947] 1988). *Dialektik der Aufklärung:
Philosophische Fragmente*. Frankfurt am Main: Fischer Verlag.

Howard, Thomas Albert (2017). *The Pope and the Professors: Pius IX, Ignaz
von Döllinger, and the Quandary of the Modern Age*. Oxford: Oxford
University Press.

Huet, Pierre-Daniel ([1723] 2003). *Against Cartesian Philosophy*. Trans. Thomas M.
Lennon. New York: Humanity Books.

Huizinga, Johan (1987). *The Waning of the Middle Ages*. Trans. F. Hopman.
London: Penguin Books.

Husserl, Edmund (1956). *Erste Philosophie (1923/1924). Erster Teil: Kritische
Ideengeschichte*. Gesammelte Werke, Vol. 7. Haag: Martinus Nijhoff.

Husserl, Edmund ([1935] 1970). *The Crisis of European Science and
Transcendental Phenomenology*. Trans. David Carr. Evanston: Northwestern
University Press.

Husserl, Edmund ([1929] 1973). *Cartesianische Meditationen und Pariser Vorträge*.
Husserliana, Vol. 1. Ed. S. Strasser. The Hague: Martinus Nijhoff.

Husserl, Edmund ([1935] 1976). *Die Krisis der Europäischen Wissenschaften und
die transzendentale Phänomenologie: Eine Einleitung in die phänomenologiesche
Philosophie*. Gesammelte Werke, Vol. 6. Hague: Martinus Nijhoff.

Husserl, Edmund ([1929] 1982). *Cartesian Meditations: An Introduction to
Phenomenology*. Trans. Dorion Cairns. The Hague: Martinus Nijhoff.

Husserl, Edmund (1993). *Die Krisis der Europäischen Wissenschaften und die transzendentale Phänomenologie: Ergänzungsband und Texte aus dem Nachlass 1934-1937. Husserliana*, Vol. 29. Ed. Reinhold N. Smid. Dordrecht: Springer.

Israel, Jonathan (2006). *Enlightenment Contested: Philosophy, Modernity, and the Emancipation of Man 1670-1752.* Oxford: Oxford University Press.

Jacobi, Friedrich Heinrich ([1799] 1970). 'An Fichte'. In *Nihilismus: Die Anfänge. Von Jacobi bis Nietzsche.* Ed. Dieter Arendt. Köln: Jakob Hegner Verlag, 107-33.

Jaeger, Michael (2004). *Fausts Kolonie: Goethes kritische Phänomenologie der Moderne.* Würzburg: Königshausen & Neumann.

Joisten, Karen (2014). *Philosophie der Heimat: Heimat der Philosophie.* Berlin: Walter de Gruyter.

Junginger, Horst (2011). *Die Verwissenschaftlichung der >Judenfrage< im Nationalsozialismus.* Darmstadt: WBG.

Kaltenbrunner, Gerd-Klaus (1991). 'Einleitung'. Franz Xaver von Baader. *Sätze aus der erotischen Philosophie und andere Schriften.* Frankfurt am Main: Insel Verlag, 9-57.

Kant, Immanuel ([1784] 1850). *Beantwortung der Frage: Was ist Aufklärung?.* Potsdam: Stuhr'sche Buchhandlung.

Kant, Immanuel ([1781] 1889). *Kritik der reinen Vernunft.* Ed. Erich Adikes. Berlin: Mayer & Müller.

Kautzky, Karl (1894). *Karl Marx' ökonomische Lehren.* Fünfte, unveränderte Auflage. Stuttgart: Verlag von I. H. W. Dietz (http://gutenberg.spiegel.de/buch/karl-marx-oekonomische-lehren-9243/12).

Kennington, Richard (2004). *On Modern Origins: Essays in Modern Philosophy.* New York: Lexington Books.

Kierkegaard, Søren (1849). *Die Krankheit zum Tode.* Jena: Eugen Diederichs Verlag.

Köck, Julian (2015). *'Die Geschichte hat immer Recht': Die völkische Bewegung im Spiegel ihrer Geschichtsbilder.* Frankfurt am Main: Campus Verlag.

Koops, Willem, Dorsman, Leen, and Verbeek, Theo, eds. (2005). *Née Cartesienne / Cartesiaansch Gebooren: Descartes en de Utrechtse Academie 1636-2005.* Assen: Van Gorcum.

Lagarde, Paul de (1933). *Bekenntnis zu Deutschland.* Jena: Eugen Diederichs Verlag.

Lampert, Laurence (2001). *Nietzsche's Task: An Interpretation of Beyond Good and Evil.* New Haven, CT: Yale University Press.

Langbehn, August Julius (1890). *Rembrandt als Erzieher.* Leipzig: C. L. Hirschfeld Verlag.

Landgrebe, Ludwig (1963). 'Husserls Abschied vom Cartesianismus'. In *Der Weg der Phänomenologie: Das Problem einer ursprünglichen Erfahrung.* Gütersloh: Gütersloher Verlagshaus, 162–203.

Lichtenberg, Georg Christoph (1994). *Sudelbücher II, Heft K. 1793–6. Schriften und Briefe.* Vol. 2. Frankfurt: Zweitausendeins.

Löchte, Anne (2005). *Johan Gotfried Herder: Kulturtheorie und Humanitätsidee der Ideen, Humanitätsbriefe und Adrastea.* Würzburg: Königshausen & Neumann.

Löwenthal, Leo (1923). *Die Sozietätsphilosophie Franz Baaders: Beispiel und Problem einer 'religiösen Soziologie'.* Inaugural Dissertation. Universität zu Frankfurt am Main.

Löwith, Karl (1957). 'Nietzsche's Revival of the Doctrine of Eternal Recurrence'. In *Meaning in History.* Chicago, IL: University of Chicago Press, 214–22.

Löwith, Karl (1964). 'Das Verhängnis des Fortschritts'. In *Die Philosophie und die Frage nach dem Fortschritt.* Ed. Helmut Kuhn and Franz Wiedmann. München: Verlag Anton Pustet, 15–29.

Luft, Sebastian (2002). *"Phänomenologie der Phänomenologie": Systematik und Methodologie der Phänomenologie in der Auseinandersetzung zwischen Husserl und Fink.* Dodrecht: Kluwer Academic.

Maistre, Joseph de ([1819] 1850). *The Pope: Considered in His Relations with the Church, Temporal Sovereignties, Separated Churches, and the Cause of Civilization.* Trans. Aeneas McD Dawson. London: C. Dolman.

Mann, Thomas ([1918] 1920). *Betrachtungen eines Unpolitischen.* Berlin: Fischer Verlag.

Marcuse, Herbert ([1968] 2009). *Negations: Essays in Critical Theory.* Trans. Jeremy J. Shapiro. UK: May Flay.

Maritain, Jacques (1944). *The Dream of Descartes.* Trans. Mabelle L. Adison. New York: Philosophical Library.

Marx, Karl ([1867–83] 1883). *Das Kapital: Kritik der politischen Ökonomie.* Dritte vermehrte Auflage. Vol. 1. Hamburg: Otto Meissner Verlag.

Mosse, George (1979). *Ein Volk, Ein Reich, Ein Führer: Die völkischen Ursprünge des Nationalsozialismus.* Königstein: Athenäum.

Müller, Sascha (2007). *René Descartes' Philosophie der Freiheit. Ad imaginem et similitudinem Dei: Philosophische Prolegomena zu einer Theorie der religiösen Inspiration.* München: Herbert Utz Verlag.

Nietzsche, Friedrich ([1884–8] 1906). *Der Wille zur Macht.* Taschen-Ausgabe. Vol. 9. Leipzig: Naumann Verlag.

Nietzsche, Friedrich (1922). 'Aus den Vorarbeitungen zu Richard Wagner in Bayreuth (1875–1876)'. *Gesammelte Werke.* Vol. 7. München: Musarion Verlag, 359–77.

Nietzsche, Friedrich ([1886] 2002). *Beyond Good and Evil: Prelude to a Philosophy of the Future*. Trans. Judith Norman. Cambridge: Cambridge University Press.

Nietzsche, Friedrich (2004). *Der handschriftliche Nachlass ab Frühjahr 1885. Arbeitshefte W I 3 – W I 7*. Kritische Gesamtausgabe, Vol. 9.4. Ed. Marie-Luise Haase and Martin Stingelin. Berlin: Walter de Gruyter.

Nietzsche, Friedrich ([1908] 2017). *Ecce Homo: Wie man wird, was man ist*. Berlin: Dearbooks Verlag.

Nizan, Paul ([1937] 2013). *The Tricentennial of a Manifesto*. Trans. Mitchell Abidor. Marxists Internet Archive (https://www.marxists.org/archive/nizan/1937/descartes.htm).

Orth, Ernst Wolfgang (2000). 'Die unerfüllte Rolle Descartes' in der Phänomenologie'. In *Descartes im Diskurs der Neuzeit*. Ed. Friedrich Wilhelm Niebel, Angelica Horn, and Herbert Schnädelbach. Frankfurt am Main: Suhrkamp, 286–302.

Pallandt, Elisabeth Simmern van, and Descartes, René (2007). *The Correspondence between Princess Elisabeth of Bohemia and René Descartes*. Ed. and trans. Lisa Shapiro. Chicago: Chicago University Press.

Pascal, Blaise ([1670] 1999). *Pensées and Other Writings*. Ed. Anthony Levi. Trans. Honor Levi. Oxford: Oxford University Press.

Proudhon, Pierre-Joseph ([1853] 2009). 'The Philosophy of Progress'. In *The New Proudhon Library*. Vol. 20, part 1. Trans. Shawn P. Wilbur and Jesse Cohn. Left Liberty, 1–72.

Rosenau, Hartmut (2000). 'Selbstgewißheit und Verzweiflung: Von der *theologia rationalis* Descartes' zur Existenztheologie Kierkegaards'. In *Descartes im Diskurs der Neuzeit*. Ed. Friedrich Wilhelm Niebel, Angelica Horn, and Herbert Schnädelbach. Frankfurt am Main: Suhrkamp, 125–42.

Rousseau, Jean-Jacques (1977). *'The Discourses' and Other Early Political Writings*. Ed. and trans. Victor Gourevitch. Cambridge: Cambridge University Press.

Rousseau, Jean-Jacques ([1762] 1979). *Emile or on Education*. Trans. Allan Bloom. New York: Basic Books.

Sanderson Haldane, Elizabeth (1905). *Descartes: His Life and Times*. London: John Murray.

Scheler, Max ([1915] 1963). 'Das Nationale im Denken Frankreichs'. In *Schriften zur Soziologie und Weltanschauungslehre*. Bern: Francke Verlag, 131–57.

Scheler, Max ([1927] 2016). *Die Stellung des Menschen im Kosmos*. Ed. Karl-Maria Guth. Berlin: Hofenberg.

Schelling, Friedrich Wilhelm Joseph ([1827] 1861). *Zur Geschichte der neueren Philosophie*. Sämmtliche Werke. Vol. 10. Stuttgart: Gotta'cher Verlag.

Schiller, Friedrich ([1796] 1893). 'Xenien aus dem Almanach'. In *Schriften der Goethe-Gesellschaft*. Vol. 8. Ed. Bernhard Suphan. Weimar: Verlag der Goethe-Gesellschaft, 89–106.

Schlegel, Friedrich (1798). 'Fragmente'. *Athenaeum*. Vol. 1, part 2. Ed. Wilhelm August Schlegel and Friedrich Schlegel. Berlin: Friedrich Vieweg, 2–146.

Schlickel, Ferdinand (1998). *Edith Stein. Die neue Heilige: Jüdin und Ordensfrau*. Regensburg: Schnell & Steiner.

Schmidt, Jochen (2001). *Goethes Faust: Erster und zweiter Teil. Grundlagen: Werk, Wirkung*. München: Verlag C. H. Beck.

Schmitt, Carl (1936/7). 'Der Staat als Mechanismus bei Hobbes und Descartes'. *Archiv für Rechts- und Sozialphilosophie*, 30: 622–32.

Schmitz, Stefan (1975). *Sprache, Sozietät und Geschichte bei Franz Baader*. Bern: Herbert Lang.

Schnädelbach, Herbert (2000). 'Descartes und das Projekt der Aufklärung'. In *Descartes im Diskurs der Neuzeit*. Ed. Friedrich Wilhelm Niebel, Angelica Horn, and Herbert Schnädelbach. Frankfurt am Main: Suhrkamp, 186–206.

Shorto, Russell (2008). *Descartes' Bones: A Skeletal History of the Conflict between Faith and Reason*. London: Doubleday.

Sieferle, Rolf-Peter (1984). *Fortschrittsfeinde?: Opposition gegen Technik und Industrie von der Romantik bis zur Gegenwart*. München: C. H. Beck.

Simon, Joseph (2000). 'Descartes' "cogito" unter zeichenphilosophischem Aspekt'. In *Descartes im Diskurs der* Neuzeit. Ed. Friedrich Wilhelm Niebel, Angelica Horn, and Herbert Schnädelbach. Frankfurt am Main: Suhrkamp, 77–102.

Simon, Joseph (2003). *Kant: Die fremde Vernunft und die Sprache der Philosophie*. Berlin: Walter de Gruyter.

Sluga, Hans (1993). *Heidegger's Crisis: Philosophy and Politics in Nazi Germany*. Cambridge: Harvard University Press.

Sorel, Georges Eugène ([1908] 1969). *The Illusions of Progress*. Trans. Charlotte and John Stanley. Berkeley: University of California Press.

Spengler, Oswald (1931). *Der Mensch und die Technik: Beitrag zu einer Philosophie des Lebens*. München: Beck.

Sternhell, Zeev, Sznajder, Mario, and Asheri, Maia (1995). *The Birth of Fascist Ideology*. Trans. David Meisel. Princeton, NJ: Princeton University Press.

Szakolczai, Arpad (2011). 'Franz Borkenau on World Image'. *Humana Mente*, 18: 105–22.

Tugendhat, Ernst (1967). *Über den Wahrheitsbegriff bei Husserl und Heidegger*. Berlin: De Gruyter.

Vico, Giambattista ([1710] 1988). *On the Most Ancient Wisdom of the Italians: Unearthed from the Origins of the Latin Language*. Trans. L. M. Palmer. Ithaca, NY: Cornell University Press.

Vico, Giambattista ([1708–9] 1965). *On the Study Methods of Our Time*. Trans. Elio Gianturco. Indianapolis, IN: Bobbs-Merill Company.

Voegelin, Eric ([1943] 2002). 'Letter to Alfred Schütz'. In *The Collected Works of Eric Voegelin*. Vol. 6. Ed. David Walsh. Trans. Gerhart Niemeyer and M. J. Hanak. Missouri: University of Missouri Press, 45–61 (https://voegelinview.com/letter-to-alfred-schuetz-on-husserl-pt-1/).

Wagner, Richard (1881). 'Heldenthum und Christenthum'. *Bayreuther Blätter*. Vierter Jahrgang, 249–58.

Wagner, Richard ([1878] 1911). 'Was ist Deutsch?'. *Sämtliche Schriften und Dichtungen*. Vol. 10. Leipzig: Breitkopf & Härtel, 36–53.

Williams, Bernard (2005). *Descartes: The Project of Pure Enquiry*. London: Routledge.

Wittgenstein, Ludwig (1969). *On Certainty*. Trans. Denis Paul and G. E. M. Anscombe. Oxford: Basil Blackwell.

Wundt, Max (1924). 'Was heißt völkisch?' *Friedrich Mann's Pädagogisches Magazin*. Heft 987, Langensalza, 5–33.

Index